**Harry McQuinn "King of the Midgets"**

Dirt Track, Sprint Car, and Midget Racer; Airplane Pilot; and Race Official

© 2017 Brad T Tinkle / Left Paw Press

All rights reserved. No part of this book shall be reproduced, stored in a retrieval system, or transmitted by any means, electronic, mechanical, photocopying, recording, or otherwise, without written permission from the publisher. No patent liability is assumed with respect to the use of information contained herein. Although every precaution has been taken in the preparation of this book, the publisher and author assume no responsibility for errors or omissions nor is any liability assumed for damages resulting from the use of the information contained herein.

International Standard Book Number: 978-1-943356-55-3

Library of Congress Control Number: 2017940702

Printed in the United States of America

First Printing August 2017

All terms mentioned in this book that are known to be trademarks or service marks have been appropriately capitalized. Left Paw Press cannot attest to the accuracy of this information. Use of a term in this book should not be regarded as affecting the validity of any trademark or service mark.

Every effort has been made to make this book as complete and as accurate as possible, but no warranty or fitness is implied. The information provided is on an "as is" basis. The author and the publisher shall have neither liability nor responsibility to any person or entity with respect to any loss or damages arising from the information contained in this book.

Cover design by Maria Charina Gomez.

Published by Left Paw Press.

For educational, corporate, or retail sales accounts, email: info@LeftPawPress.com. For information, address: Left Paw Press, c/o Lauren Originals, Inc. 8926 N Greenwood Avenue #293 Niles, IL 60714. www.leftpawpress.com.

# HARRY MCQUINN

*"King of the Midgets"*

**DIRT TRACK, SPRINT CAR, AND MIDGET RACER; AIRPLANE PILOT; AND RACE OFFICIAL**

## Dr Brad T Tinkle

### Foreword by Donald Davidson

# Contents

Foreword ............................................................................................ vii

Introduction ....................................................................................... xi

   1. Early Years .................................................................................. 1

   2. Dirt Track Racing ....................................................................... 5

   3. Big Car Driver ........................................................................... 35

   4. The Mighty Midgets .................................................................. 71

   5. Race Official ............................................................................ 249

   6. Airplane Pilot .......................................................................... 273

   7. Later Years .............................................................................. 287

Epilogue ......................................................................................... 293

Acknowledgements ....................................................................... 295

Appendix A McQuinn Career Highlights ..................................... 297

Appendix B Persona of the Era ...................................................... 301

Resources ....................................................................................... 311

About The Author .......................................................................... 313

# FOREWORD
# by Donald Davidson

Harry McQuinn is someone to whom I owe a HUGE deal of gratitude.

Friday, May 15, 1964 was the magic day I finally arrived at the Indianapolis Motor Speedway from England, after seven years of dreaming, planning and saving up.

I entered the ticket office located in the old single-story brick building on the corner of West 16th Street and Georgetown Road and asked for Miss Frances Derr, a wonderful lady who was the Director of Ticket Sales. I had been corresponding with her by mail for the previous several months, and upon acknowledging my purchase of a ticket some weeks earlier, she had informed me that as an overseas visitor, I would be furnished with a bronze badge which would allow me access to the hallowed Garage Area.

I could hardly believe my good fortune.

I had been blessed with the ability to memorize (and retain) miscellaneous facts and figures about the "500" (which hadn't worked for school studies!) and while over the previous half a dozen years I had memorized quite a bit about the drivers, the car owners and the chief mechanics, what I was NOT prepared for was just how friendly and engaging virtually all of them would be.

Armed with my bronze badge, I headed straight for the Garage Area and almost immediately, I started meeting participants, both past and present, and I was amazed at just how warmly I was received, and how genuinely interested everyone seemed to be over what I had done.

The following morning was Saturday, the first day of qualifications, and things were pretty quiet in the Garage Area, because the activity had generally moved out to the pit lane, where, unfortunately, my bronze badge would not allow me.

So, I strolled around the Garage Area, and as I turned a corner, walking straight towards me was someone I had been most anxious to meet, the famed anchor for the IMS Radio Network broadcast, Sid Collins.

Sid was extremely courteous and after a couple of minutes of conversation, and noting that I was "confined" to the Garage Area, he reached into his pocket, and to my amazement he handed me a card which was effectively a one-day guest pit pass. "Bring it back to me at the end of the day," he said.

It turns out I only needed it for a couple of hours.

It wasn't long after entering the pits that somebody introduced me to Harry McQuinn. Long since retired as a driver, he had later served for several years as the Chief Steward for the "500," and while that role was now being filled by another former driver, Harlan Fengler, Harry was still the Chief Steward for all of the other races which comprised the United States Auto Club National Championship series.

In addition to having memorized Harry's "500" record, I was well aware of his reputation as a no-nonsense, hard-nosed driver from the days of wheel-to-wheel midget car racing who glared down his opponents before a race and gave them little ground during it. I also knew that he had officiated in a similar fashion, and a few months later, I would have several opportunities to witness his very stern approach for myself from close quarters.

As with just about everybody else up to that point, he was both amused and a little incredulous at what I had done, laughing and then asking me questions about myself. Almost immediately, he began calling out to old colleagues as they passed by, saying, "Hey, come over and listen to this," whereupon I would pinch myself as I began to recite my interpretation of the career of yet another person I had been reading about for years. Harry would stand there, greatly amused at their reaction, which usually entailed them looking around for signs that this was all a put-on, with them the victim.

After a couple of hours of this, I recall walking along with him and saying, "Look, I really appreciate you doing all of this, but surely you must have other things to do, and I'm perfectly happy to find my own way around."

"Are you kidding?" was his rejoinder. "This is the most fun I've had in YEARS. I just love seeing the expression on their faces while you are telling them about themselves."

He then looked at my bronze badge, plus the card Sid had loaned me, and said, "Come with me. We'll get you something better."

We headed for the trackside United States Auto Club office, tucked under the grandstands just north of Gasoline Alley, and there we encountered Frankie Bain, a Chicago native who for years had served as the IMS registrar in charge of issuing credentials to the participants. He was not exactly the friendliest individual one could ever encounter, but in all fairness, he had been listening to sob story after sob story over the years and his job really needed someone who could evaluate a situation, stand their ground, and whenever appropriate, say "No."

"Donald here needs a better credential," growled Harry. "Give him a silver."

Not surprisingly, Frankie didn't appear particularly happy about the situation, but evidently Harry had plenty of clout and Frankie reluctantly obliged. I signed the necessary waivers and a couple of minutes later, was in possession of the finest credential anyone could ever hope for.

Minutes after that, I headed up to the Master Control Tower to find Sid Collins and return, a few hours early, the temporary pass he had so kindly loaned me.

Harry continued to be my unofficial chaperon pretty much for the remainder of my three-week stay, and when somebody introduced me to Harry's wife, Juanita, she exclaimed, "I don't know how many people have come up to me and told me I have a new son!"

Harry introduced me to Tony Hulman and Eddie Sachs and goodness knows who else, and he took me to function after function, including the inaugural meeting of the Autolite Pacemakers club, an exclusive organization for drivers who had led at least one lap of the Indianapolis 500. That is where I met Ray Harroun, Troy Ruttman, the infamous Kelly Petillo, and countless others, including a Henry Ford grandson, Benson Ford, the man who drove the Ford Mustang pace car that year.

During some down time on the second qualifying day, we were strolling past the pace car when Harry motioned me to climb in. Moments later, we were off on a rapid "track inspection" with Harlan Fengler at the wheel.

At some point, we made another visit to the trackside USAC office to see Frankie Bain, who also happened to be USAC's fulltime Business Manager.

"Donald will need to keep up on USAC when he is back in England," barked Harry, "So put him on the complimentary mailing list so he can get USAC News."

Frankie looked just about as thrilled as he had when "instructed" to issue me the silver badge, but once again he complied.

And so it went on.

Eleven months later, I was back at the track, this time on a one-way ticket and carrying a "green" card.

To cut a long story short, on Thursday morning, June 3, just three days after Jim Clark had won the 1965 Indianapolis 500, I landed a job with USAC. Another former driver, who had also become like an Uncle to me, was 1950 AAA National Champion Henry Banks, now USAC's Director of Competition. He ran the day to day operations, along with the Business Manager, who was my old friend Frankie Bain. Frankie must have thought he was never going to be rid of me.

I lived in a dream world working at USAC. Drivers would come in and out every day, and as Chief Steward of all the USAC National Championship races other than the "500," Harry was a frequent visitor.

I have to say I was totally unprepared for fall and winter, having just assumed, quite naively, that Indianapolis would be sunshine and occasional showers all year 'round. Just as I was coming to terms with the harsh reality that snow and bitter winds would probably soon be coming, to my rescue came Harry McQuinn!

"Bud Kerr and I are flying out for the Phoenix race in his plane," he told me one day in early November, "Wanna go with us?"

Indeed I did, and I thought I'd died and gone to Heaven. We left Indianapolis on a cold and frosty morning and a few hours later, I was basking in the sun in Phoenix, looking at blue sky, cactus plants, and people in brightly-colored short-sleeved shirts driving two-toned convertibles with the tops down.

There is so much more, but for now, I would just like to say, "Thank you, Harry McQuinn. Thank you for all of your kindnesses and for being like an Uncle to me from the time I showed up. You were a huge part of my life."

—*Donald Davidson*

# INTRODUCTION

Growing up I was fortunate enough to be often in the presence of my grandparents and my great grandparents. Harry and Juanita McQuinn were my maternal great grandparents and still active enough to take me fishing and boating on many occasions. As a youth, I didn't comprehend "Daddy Harry's" stories about racing and don't honestly think they were many as these were things in the past often not talked about. However, he showed their toll. His legs were terribly scared from fire and he had chronic back trouble (but you wouldn't know it) from a previous spine fracture. He had raced many cars across all parts of the US and had flown planes. He definitely was intelligent and I would say crafty. He was an avid learner of the latest technologies and had always wanted me to pursue computer technology.

Throughout the house was many trophies and memorabilia from racing, especially the Indianapolis 500. We never went to the track together. As a child, I did not appreciate the legacy he had. My uncle, Harry's grandson, carried on with involvement in the 500 but not as a racer and he had pass this down to his sons. I had little to remind me except the memories as they were too brief in my life.

Inexplicably, my son, Zachary Tinkle, got interested in karting. He was about 8 or 9 at the time and we had an outdoor track near our house. We went to see what it was all about and unfortunately, he was too young for rental carts. We were informed that we could have him on the track if we owned one. Money wasn't the only issue, I knew nothing about karting including the mechanics and strategy. Disappointed, we still occasionally went to a local race car track in Winchester, Indiana, a track with a lot of history that we only simply thought of it as a local country circuit.

A few years later, we moved to the Chicago area. We had seen signs for an indoor karting entertainment complex and thought we'd try it out. Zachary loved the karting and we saw the chance for him to go through a driving program and start in a junior league. It didn't start with "he's a natural" but after one season, he had picked up a lot and was still 'rough' but showed promise. We continued for another season and he was invited to join an outdoor team. We had gotten a driving coach who was teaching us all aspects of karting but this led shortly into the winter season. While in the off season, we attended an auto show at which we saw "mini cups"- half-sized NASCAR style cars. Zachary had been following with a passion, NASCAR (and not Indy car that was a part of his legacy too).

As parents, we thought these mini-cups were safer and made the switch. Let's say there was a large learning curve for him and us. But once vested, it became a neat family activity. On one occasion, one of the local tracks (Grundy County) had a "Hall of Fame Day". They had old racers exchanging stories and old photos on display. I hadn't seen many of Harry's old photos but had seen some but mostly from the Indy 500. I was looking through the hundreds of pictures and came across one of Harry McQuinn at the Grundy County Fairgrounds track. He was in one of the midgets which I had known little about but felt that weird connection, here we are racing on a track that my great grandfather had- not really since it had moved from Mazon to Morris but it did not negate the connection. I wondered what other tracks he had raced at.

I started to search for information. The internet was very useful but didn't have a lot of historical data. Time solved some of this with digitization of newspapers and persistence in looking in many areas for information. Many people have been wonderfully helpful in my quest. But, realize that his early racing career, much less his early years, started about 100 years ago. Many tracks had historians but even they had few and inconsistent records from this time-period. Thus, much presented here come from newspaper accounts with all too brief accounts of his life much less his racing.

The newspaper accounts were done at a time of typesetting and multiple errors. Inaccuracies were common including one account that listed Harry as having died "off the tracks" in the 1930's. The stories were also at times colorful. Harry was given many nicknames such as "Handsome Harry", "Leadfoot", "One-lap", and "King of the Midgets" among many.

Having gotten involved in the racing culture, I have a new respect for all that Harry had accomplished and that he survived when many of his fellow racers did not (fortunately safety has come a long way since). The following is more of a historical narrative and lacks details and stories, most long forgotten. This book is a chronicle of the information that remains in hopes to make it endure and tell the story of one who came before that helped blaze the path in auto racing.

# 1
# EARLY YEARS

NOT MUCH WAS KNOWN OF **Harry McQuinn's early years before his auto racing. He was born in Nineveh, Indiana on December 13, 1905. According to the 1910 Census, he was registered as a 4-year-old living in Franklin, Indiana with his father Everett, mother, and sister.**

In 1918 at the age of 13, he was a lieutenant of the thrift army of the Marion county schools (School No. 43) and lived at 4507 N. Illinois St in Indianapolis.

In 1919, he participated in the Indianapolis Boys' Bugle and Drum Corps in the fife section.

By the 1920 Census, the then 14-year-old Harry was living in Indianapolis with his family.

He attended Arsenal Tech High School. Like many young men of the era, he attended military training camp as a cadet. He was active in the Northwood Christian Church.

After graduation, Harry found himself looking for a direction. He was known as the manager of a band, the Princess Bell Hops. He became a tailor and owned his own shop with several employees by the age of 19.

In 1922, Harry found an illicit love of cars after some boyhood "joy-riding". He fortunately found his way with the love of a good woman, and married Juanita Wagner on April 21, 1923.

Harry settled down but continued his love affair with cars becoming a chauffeur and later a mechanic.

Harry on the far left of the Princess Bell Hops.
*McQuinn Family records.*

# Early Years

Harry on far left. *McQuinn Family records*.

# 2
# DIRT TRACK RACING

HARRY MCQUINN'S LOVE AFFAIR WITH cars started as a misguided youth. He and several other adolescents would go "joyriding" and then later abandon the cars. One night, tragedy struck, when one of the "gang" hit and killed a pedestrian. McQuinn turned himself into the authorities ending his mischievousness involvement. But he could not stay away from cars. Harry became gainfully employed as a mechanic in an auto garage and as a chauffeur. Even then, he was "heavy-footed" [*The Republic, page 4, June 3, 1924*].

In 1924, he noticed a friend building a Studebaker race car. He came upon the thought that he could build one too. He stripped down and souped up a Buick C-10 intending to race it at the Osgood Fair track. Not having a race trailer, he drove the car to the track. Feeling it's power and speed, he continued to push along the winding roads. With a sharp turn, he flipped the car, going into a culvert near North Vernon IN and tore off a wheel. It was said that he landed on his feet twenty feet away [*The Republic, page 4, July 5, 1924*]. He may be the only race car driver to join the "over-club" before he even started one race [*Gene Powlen, National Speed Sports News, April 11, 1951*].

Being determined, he went back that same night, replacing the radiator, bending out the frame and replacing some wiring—off to the track he still went. On July 4, 1924, having kept the car on the road and the track, he found that the C-10 had no "oomph" and had a very disappointing finish having driven 32 laps before retiring due to mechanical issues [*The Republic, page 4, July 5, 1924*]. McQuinn and fellow racer, Emmett Benefiel, decided to work on the Buick C-10 for an entry in the upcoming July 20th race at North Vernon.

It is not clear what happened or if or how much time elapsed but it is reported that a neighbor who had entered the races had a 'pretty good' car but it had been wrecked. The neighbor decided racing wasn't for him so Harry had convinced him to sell him the car. He brought the car home and stuck it in the basement to work on. This may have been the first "Basement Bessie" [*Gene Powlen, National Speed Sports News, April 11, 1951*].

Not much information was obtainable for 1925 and 1926 except for a few news reports of which many are incomplete. It is unclear if Harry was able to race throughout the season or had multiple setbacks. Comments from later stories suggested he had some bad luck but persevered.

## 1926

## Bloomington Speedway, Bloomington IN, June 5, 1926

Two Columbus IN drivers entered the Memorial Day (5/31/1926) races at Bloomington, Dillard Beatty and Harry McQuinn [*The Republic, page 6, May 28, 1926*]. Bloomington Speedway was a 5/8-mile dirt track located south of Bloomington. The event had three races planned that were 15, 25, and 40 miles. Beatty had a Chevrolet and McQuinn a Durant Special. While qualifications were held, the races were rained out.

Before the May 31, 1926 event, McQuinn had been asked to try out one of the six R. B. Specials owned by Ray Bucher. After McQuinn's qualification performance on May 31st, Bucher asked McQuinn to join his racing crew and he accepted [*The Republic, page 2, June 2, 1926*].

The speedway previously had creosote applied to the track. While driving for qualification, the creosote covered dust had gotten into McQuinn's eyes, causing considerable problems including total blindness, which put him out of racing for over three weeks [*The Republic, page 4, June 7, 1926*].

Having a less than spectacular start to his racing career, he joined the Hoagland Hippodrome Auto Polo Show for the 1926 and 1927 seasons. Hippodroming was often staged races at local fairgrounds. These races were often "close" to thrill the fans. However, some had auto polo shows similar to polo but having cars with a driver and "malletman". Cars were known to run into each other, overturn, and cause serious injury if not death in some cases.

At the beginning of the 1928 season, he leased a very fast "Fronty Ford" for the Osgood IN opening race. He won the feature prize of $380 and went to the bank plunking down his "wad of winnings" stating he'd be back weekly—which of course did not happen that way.

> "By the 1920's, there were many parts available for the Ford engines. These were made by Louis Chevrolet under the trade name of Frontenac. When W. C. Durant bought out the Chevrolet brothers in 1916, they were not allowed to use their name for cars or car parts. Louis' brother Arthur originally used the Frontenac name to make bicycles. These modified engines later became known as 'Fronty'". *The History of America's Speedways: Past & Present*, 3rd ed., by Alan E. Brown, 2003.

Details of this June 10th race in 1928
at Rochester IN were not available. This shows McQuinn after
the races having placed 2nd presumably in the main feature.
*McQuinn Family records.*

### 1928

## Wayne County Fairgrounds, Richmond IN, September 3, 1928

This was the first ever dirt track racing program at the fairgrounds which was a half-mile oval dirt track located near Centerville. It was being held on Labor Day. Freeman Huey lost control of the rear of the car and hit a post on the track being then thrown from his car onto the track. Unfortunately, he was run over by other cars and killed.

Bob Carey won the first ten-mile race with McQuinn second and Orville Emery third. Emery did not challenge Carey but had many brushes with McQuinn to provide some exciting racing. Wall won the second 10-mile event followed by Ed Maupin and Copeland. Carey won the 25-mile feature with Wall and Maupin following [*The Indianapolis Star, page 1, September 4, 1928*].

## Wayne County Fairgrounds, Richmond IN, October 7, 1928

The second event of this new venue, hosting again two 10-mile events and a 25-mile feature. Fortunately, no injuries at this event despite seven cars involved in accidents.

"Wild Bill" Chittum won one of the 10-mile events as well as the feature. In the other 10-mile event, Ed Maupin and McQuinn battled for the lead with Maupin having had a slight lead until he crashed on the south curve. McQuinn took over the lead and finished well-ahead of the remaining field by 100 yards with Korger second and Bohannon third. In the feature, Chittum quickly took over the lead from Billman and lapped the entire field except for Billman [*The Richmond Item, page 8, October 9, 1928*].

## Rushville Motor Speedway, Rushville IN, October 14, 1928

Harry McQuinn in his No. 4 car, c.1928.
*McQuinn Family records.*

Rushville Motor Speedway was a half-mile dirt oval. For the last race of the season, two 25-mile races were scheduled following a compromise between the promoters and Judge Will M. Sparks whereby this one was permitted if no others were conducted on Sunday. The crowd was not as large as in the past, held down probably by the report that the races would be stopped by Sheriff L. M. Coons on order of Judge Sparks [*Rushville Daily Republican, page 5, October 15, 1928*].

Due to a large number of qualifiers, the eight fastest were divided into the first race. The first race was won by Harry McQuinn driving car number four. McQuinn made the fastest time of any car in the qualification runs and won the first event easily. In the second race, Cy Marshall won after L. Updegraff went out with a blown tire. He finished well ahead of the field after Updegraff dropped out.

## 1929

*After the stock market crash of 1929, information of the 1929 and 1930 seasons was very sparse. McQuinn placed third in the 15-mile race to Bill Cummins at Rockville [The Indianapolis Star, page 14, May 20, 1929]; second in the first five-mile event to Mauri Rose but did not place "in the money" in the feature [Brazil Daily Times, page 2, August 12, 1929].*

## 1930

## Jungle Park Speedway, Rockville IN, July 27, 1930

Jungle Park was a half-mile dirt track located just south of Sugar Creek in a heavily wooded area just off of Indiana Highway 10. The field was composed of many hot drivers: Red Campbell, Ray Meyers, Howdy Wilcox, Harry McQuinn, Mark Billman, and Benny Benefiel. The temperature at the track was nearly 100 degrees. Ray Meyers lost control and ended up in the trees. He was fortunately thrown from the car before it was smashed up in the trees. The five-lap heat race was won by Red Campbell. During the 30-lap main feature, Red Campbell also had lost control and ended up in the trees and fortunately was spared grievous injury. That could not be said for Frank "Teenie"

Jenkinson of Lafayette who also lost control, hit a tree and died from his injuries. The race was won by Mark Billman [*"The Ghosts of Jungle Park", by Tom Williams*].

## 1931

## Walnut Gardens Speedway, Indianapolis IN, September 7, 1931

Walnut Gardens Speedway was a half-mile oval dirt track southwest of Indianapolis near Camby. Ira Hall wins one of the five-mile and the 20-mile feature. Other five-mile events were won by Vern Tresta and McQuinn [*The Indianapolis Star, page 14, September 8, 1931*].

## 1932

## Bartholomew County Fairgrounds, Columbus IN, August 19, 1932

The track was another half-mile dirt oval. The closing event of the county fair was a 50-mile feature. McQuinn captured the feature followed by Charles Crawford and then Jiggs Yeager [*The Republic, page 1, August 20, 1932*].

## Walnut Gardens Speedway, Indianapolis IN, August 21, 1932

The events consisted of three five-mile preliminary races, a three-car match race, and the 50-mile feature. As an added attraction, Speed Green and Harry McQuinn piloted two stock cars in a head-on collision. The three-car match race included Harold Shaw, Jimmy Garringer and McQuinn.

Jimmy Garringer won the match race as well as one of the five-lap elimination races. Charles Read and Charles Crawford each captured one of the other five-lap races. Garringer won the 50-mile feature followed by Les Duncan and G. Sowers [*Indianapolis Star, page 13, August 22, 1932*].

Harry McQuinn in his #M1 Morgan Garage Special, c.1932.
*McQuinn Family records.*

### Charlie Wiggins

Walnut Gardens Speedway was the scene of the Elks Gasoline Derby on August 21, 1933 with some twenty odd "Negro" drivers. The winner was placed in a special featured match race with Harry McQuinn, white dare devil who has issued a challenge to the winner. Another featured match race will be staged between Charles Wiggins and Les Adair another white pilot who has done a lot of speeding on local tracks [*The Indianapolis Recorder, page 2, August 19, 1933*].

Wiggins is also said to have fueled the racist passions of Louisville on at least one occasion. It was known that Wiggins liked to drive the cars he was working on to better appreciate any potential concerns. He is said to have done this for McQuinn in a practice run and was soon thereafter placed in custody [*Todd Gould, "For Gold and Glory: Charlie Wiggins and the African-American Racing Car Circuit", Indiana University Press, 2007*].

## Jungle Park Speedway, Rockville IN, August 28, 1932

Indianapolis Star, page 36, August 28, 1932.

The 50-mile (100-lap) feature was marred by the death of Edward Leeper. His car plunged off the track during warming up before the feature event. For some unknown reason, his car went into a skid and lost control. When the car left the track, Leeper was thrown out and against a tree.

McQuinn won the feature with Everett Saylor, Bill Richter and Joe Reed finishing in that order [*The Morning Star, page 8, August 29, 1932*].

## Jungle Park Speedway, Rockville IN, September 11, 1932

Harry McQuinn, driving the No. M-1 and who captured the last 50-mile grind at Jungle, was again considered the top contender. Special match race occurred between McQuinn and Everett Rice. The two tangled and Rice ended up with a broken nose. Both cars were repaired and the drivers continued for the evening but Rice had to withdraw later as the pain and swelling became too much. Charley Crawford went on to win the feature [*The Indianapolis News, page 19, September 8, 1932*; "The Ghosts of Jungle Park" by Tom Williams].

McQuinn Family records.

## Walnut Gardens Speedway, Indianapolis, October 2, 1932

Everett Rice won the 50-mile feature besting Bill Smith.

McQuinn won the five-lap match race against Ed Saylor and Charles Crawford [*The Indianapolis Star, page 11, October 3, 1932*].

## Frankfort Speedway, Frankfort IN, October 9, 1932

The Frankfort Speedway was a half-mile dirt oval at the Clinton County Fairgrounds. McQuinn won the first five-mile preliminary and Bill Smith won the second. Everett Saylor was victorious in the 20-mile headliner, followed across the finish line by Everett Rice and Les Duncan [*The Indianapolis Star, page 12, October 10, 1932*].

## Walnut Gardens Speedway, Indianapolis, October 16, 1932

The last event of the season at Walnut Gardens consisted of a special match race between Verne Tresler, Everett Saylor and Everett Rice in addition to three five-mile eliminations and a 20-mile feature event. Saylor won the six-lap challenge race. McQuinn, Saylor and Tresler each won one of the three elimination events. McQuinn took the 20-mile feature with a come-from-behind effort passing on the last lap to win [*Indianapolis Star, page 19, October 17, 1932*].

## Walnut Gardens Speedway, Indianapolis, October 30, 1932

There was a special match race between Harry McQuinn, Everett Saylor, and Charles Crawford in addition to two five-mile elimination races and a 20-mile feature. McQuinn won the five-lap match race in addition to one of the five-mile elimination races. The second elimination race was won by Les Duncan. McQuinn triumphed in the 20-mile feature with Les Adair and Les Duncan following [*Indianapolis Star, page 13, October 31, 1932*].

McQuinn is listed as the Walnut Grove track champion for 1932,

http://www.autoracingrecords.com/tracks.php?lid=20316

### 1933

*With the country struggling through the Great Depression, most auto racing events were canceled throughout the US. What remained of the 1933 season was operated under the American Automobile Association (AAA) observation banner.*

## Walnut Gardens Speedway, Indianapolis, April 23, 1933

Opening race of the season. A fifty-mile feature race and three shorter events comprised the program with a special match race between Harry McQuinn and Everett Saylor [*Indianapolis Star, page 19, April 16, 1923*]. Les Adair won the 50-mile feature followed by Everett Saylor and then Everett Rice [*Indianapolis Star, page 11, April 24, 1933*].

## Cincinnati-Hamilton Speedway, Hamilton OH, May 7, 1933

Al Jones, piloting a C-8 special, roared to victory in both the twenty- and six-mile events. Harry McQuinn was first in the ten-mile race. Jerry Berry was first in the eight-mile race. Jack Barnes was injured in the ten-mile race but was released from the hospital later with only cuts and bruises [*Indianapolis Star, page 18, May 5, 1933*].

## Bloomington Speedway, Bloomington IN, June 18, 1933

The event featured two five-mile races and a 20-mile main. McQuinn, considered one of the outstanding dirt track stars of the middle west, drove the entry of Morgan's Garage of Indianapolis which was a new model "B" double overhead cam 'job', considered very fast [*Republic, page 4, June 17, 1933*]. Harry McQuinn won the first automobile race of five miles but a three-car smashup in which none was injured stopped a scheduled second auto race [*The Indianapolis Star, page 7, June 19, 1933*].

Morgan's Garage Special with Harry McQuinn outside of Morgan's Garage in Indianapolis. *McQuinn Family records.*

## Cincinnati-Hamilton Speedway, Hamilton OH, June 24, 1933

A five-mile match race between "Wild Bill" Cummings and Mauri Rose who recently finished one-two in the Indianapolis 500 race was scheduled. They battled each other with Cummings leading and Rose catching up around the turns. However, Rose could not overtake Cummings. "Doc" McKenzie won one of the five-mile races as did Clay Weatherly with McQuinn placing third. McKenzie won the 15-mile feature [*The Indianapolis Star, page 13, June 25, 1933*].

## Walnut Gardens Speedway, Indianapolis, July 9, 1933

Three five-mile races and a 20-mile feature were scheduled. The first five-mile event was won by McQuinn, the second by Everett Rice, and the third by Louis Brown. The feature was won by McQuinn with Ray Thomas second and Everett Rice, third [*The Indianapolis Star, page 12, July 10, 1933*].

**McQUINN OUTSTANDING.**

## Jungle Park Speedway, Rockville IN, July 16, 1933

"Red" Campbell won a five-mile preliminary and the 25-mile feature race. McQuinn placed second in the feature [*Muncie Evening Press, page 7, July 17, 1933*].

## Frankfort Speedway, Frankfort IN, July 23, 1933

McQuinn won the 25-mile feature with Ted Salay second and W. M. Lewis, third. Hal Jennings and Ted Hartley won each of the five-mile elimination races. During the feature, George Faith collided with Lester Adair then proceeded to go over the north turn, fracturing his arm [*The Franklin Evening Star, page 5, July 24, 1933*].

*Harry McQuinn
Winner of Race*

## Walnut Gardens Speedway, Indianapolis, July 30, 1933

The event consisted of six races: a 15-mile race, three five-mile preliminaries, a five-mile consolation and a three-mile special helmet race. Johnny Rogers won the 15-mile feature with McQuinn placing second. Carl Beale won the five-mile race and McQuinn triumphed in the special helmet race of the three fastest qualifiers [*The Kokomo Tribune, page 6, July 31, 1933*].

## Bloomington Speedway, Bloomington IN, August 6, 1933

Indianapolis drivers dominated the automobile race card held at Bloomington, winning all three events. Harry McQuinn won the first race of two miles and the third event of ten miles. Lester Adair won the second race of five miles [*The Indianapolis Star, page 13, August 7, 1933*].

## Bartholomew County Fairgrounds, Columbus IN, August 11, 1933

The first 10-mile event at this half-mile dirt oval track saw Jimmy Brown starting from pole and continued to lead in front of McQuinn for all of the race. The second 10-mile race was a battle between Buzz Mendenhall and Lester Duncan. The two were yards within each other until the 11th lap when Duncan hit the fence. However, Duncan was able to get back on the track and trailed Mendenhall considerably but Mendenhall had engine trouble allowing Duncan to take the lead and win.

During the feature, Harry McQuinn quickly took the lead from Brown when Brown, having started from the pole position, skidded in the first turn. McQuinn, in his golden Morgan Special, was one-fifth of a lap in front of Jimmy Brown, in Ted Everroad's Rose Special, when the rain began on the 40th lap halting the race [*The Republic, page 1, August 12, 1933*].

## Frankfort Speedway, Frankfort IN, August 14, 1933

The Frankfort Speedway was another half-mile dirt oval track located at the Clinton County Fairgrounds. Harry McQuinn won three of four dirt track races including a two and one-half mile, a five-mile, and the 20 mile events. The other five-mile event was won by Les Adair. Buzz Mendenhall suffered a back injury when his speedster overturned during time trials [*The Indianapolis Star, page 12, August 14, 1933*].

## Kentucky State Fair, Louisville, September 16, 1933

McQuinn rolled his Morgan Blue Streak Special down the fence and over an embankment, coming out with a torn-up race car and his body covered with scratches and bruises [*The Franklin Evening Star, page 2, September 18, 1933*].

## Walnut Gardens Speedway, Indianapolis, September 17, 1933

Having wrecked his car in the preceding day at Louisville, McQuinn worked all night to repair it.

McQuinn triumphed in the 15-mile feature as well as two other races gaining 620 points in the Indiana dirt track championship. Jimmy Kneisley placed second in two events boosting his total to 1,035 points. McQuinn won the feature, a five-lap match race against Les Adair, and one of the five-mile races. Adair and Everett Saylor won each of the two remaining five-mile events [*The Franklin Evening Star, page 2, September 18, 1933*].

*McQuinn Triumphs At Gardens Track*

## Frankfort Speedway, Frankfort IN, September 24, 1933

The events included three five-mile races and a 12½-mile feature. Everett Rice and Doug Berry won one each of the five-mile races. McQuinn won the remaining five-mile race as well as the feature. Les Adair and Ray Telles were second and third, respectfully, in the feature [*The Indianapolis Star, page 11, September 25, 1933*].

## Walnut Gardens Speedway, Indianapolis, October 1, 1933

This was the final of three races for the Indiana Dirt Track Championship. Although Harry McQuinn was the favorite in the final race, he did not take part in the first program that made up the Championship. In the second race, McQuinn scored enough points to take second overall.

The event was composed of a fifteen-mile feature race, three five-mile events and a three-lap match race. The driver with the greatest number of points for the three days of competition was to receive a silver trophy emblematic of the Hoosier Dirt Track Championship [*The Indianapolis Star, page 21, October 1, 1933*].

Johnny Rogers won the feature and McQuinn won one of the five-mile heats. Jimmy Kniesley secured the Indiana dirt track championship with McQuinn second [*The Indianapolis Star, page 12, October 2, 1933*].

## Frankfort Speedway, Frankfort IN, October 8, 1933

During time trials, McQuinn broke the track record with a 27 second half-mile lap. The races were however, postponed due to rain [*Franklin Evening Star, page 2, October 9, 1933*].

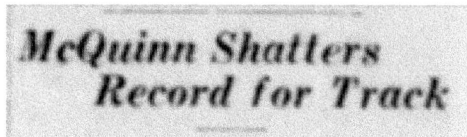

## Frankfort Speedway, Frankfort IN, October 15, 1933

The three dirt track racing champions of Indiana, Ohio, and Illinois as well as the runner-up in the Indiana title race met for the Tri-State Championship. Jimmy Kniesley, Indiana champion; Everett Saylor, the Ohio champion, and "Red" Marley, who won the Illinois title, in addition to Harry McQuinn, the runner-up to Kniesley, competed for the Tri-State title.

The championship event would top a 32½-mile program, sanctioned by the National Auto Racing Association. A 15-mile feature, two five-mile eliminations and a five-mile handicap race made up the card.

McQuinn and Kniesley won each of the two five-mile races. Rice triumphed in the handicap race. McQuinn was forced out of the 15-mile event after he had been leading with only one mile to go, with Everett Rice as the winner.

McQuinn won the 32½-mile feature and Tri-State championship. Red Farley was second and Kniesley third [*The Indianapolis Star, page 12, October 16, 1933*].

**HARRY McQUINN TAKES TRI-STATE DRIVING LAURELS**

*By the end of the 1933 season, McQuinn had experienced major mechanical issues or having wrecked in 11 of 45 races but scored 25 first place finishes along with eight seconds, and one third leading to his Tri-State championship at Frankfort. He had set multiple one-lap records at Shenandoah IA, Auburn NE, Frankfort IN and Bloomington IN tracks as well as all records from three to ten laps at the Walnut Gardens track in Indianapolis. McQuinn had proven himself to be "Indiana's leading dirt track driver and is considered by some of the 'railbirds' as the outstanding star of the middle west, due to his spectacular showing" [Paul Foss, Hoosier Sports Week, January 12, 1934] that year. It had been a long five years leading up to this as many had felt that he had a well-known jinx which had been following him everywhere he went.*

## 1934

### Jungle Park Speedway, Rockville IN, April 22, 1934

First race of the season and under the sponsorship of the AAA. Ira Hall won the first five-mile race over Kelly Pettillo. The second five-mile was won by Al Miller with Bill Chittum second and McQuinn, third. The third five-mile race was won by Emil Andres followed by Charles Nisel. The 15-mile feature was captured by Ira Hall, with Pettillo and McQuinn, second and third, respectively [*Motor Sport Magazine, page 372, June, 1934*].

### Greenville Motor Speedway, Greenville OH, May 13, 1934

Charles Engle won the feature followed by McQuinn, Mauri Rose and Al Thiesen. Ira Hall and Everett Saylor had separate accidents but were unhurt. Hall came back to win one of the three five-mile elimination contests with Bill Haskell winning the second [*Muncie Morning Star, page 5, May 14, 1934*].

### Cincinnati-Hamilton Speedway, Hamilton OH, May 20, 1934

Ira Hall won one of the preliminary races. He then announced his retirement stating he decided to be the oldest race driver alive. Al Theisen took over Hall's racer and won the 15-mile feature with McQuinn second and Weatherly third [*Palladium-Item, page 5, May 21, 1934*].

### Winchester Speedway, Winchester IN, May 27, 1934

Winchester, also known as Funk's Motor Speedway, was a half-mile high-banked oiled dirt track. James Patterson skidded on the last lap of one of the five-mile events. He locked wheels with another racer (Weatherly) then went over the north curve embankment. Patterson was killed when he struck a tree.

Al Theisen captured one of the five-mile races with Rex Mays second. Charles Engle won the second five-mile race with Ted Horn placing second. C. H. Haskell took the third five-mile contest with McQuinn second. The feature was an 18-mile race that was won by Theisen with Mays, Engle and Haskell following in that order [*The Star Press, page 9, May 28, 1934*].

"Troy Oil Company Sponsors Dirt Track Racing Cars.

Two of the top-notch dirt track racing creations on the Indiana circuit are shown in the above photograph taken at Troy Oil Company's service station at 820 Troy avenue. The Troy company sponsors the cars which are fueled by Tydol Ethyl gasoline and Veedol motor oil, which carried Louie Meyer to victory in the 500-mile race last year.

The car on the left is driven in racing by Mauri Rose, although Ted Everroade, its owner, is at the wheel in the picture. In the other car, owned by Morgan's Garage on the Bluff road is Harry McQuinn, driver.

The Troy company is distributor here for Tydol and Veedol and other products of the Tidewater Oil Company." *Indianapolis Star, page 47, April 29, 1934.*

## Fort Wayne Speedway, Fort Wayne IN, June 10, 1934

The Fort Wayne track was another high-banked track of 5/8 mile. Al Theisen won the 30-lap feature event of the opening race program of the season at the Fort Wayne Speedway. Mauri Rose took the lead at the start of the feature but Theisen got ahead after the third lap and remained so. Mauri Rose took second place and Doc McKenzie, third.

Three ten-lap elimination races were won by: Theisen, followed by Rose and McKenzie; Clay Corbitt, followed by Charles Engle and McQuinn; Harry Kearns, Emil Andres, Henry Zieglenthaler finished in order for the third [*The Indianapolis Star, page 14, June 11, 1934*].

## Hamilton OH, June 24, 1934

Wild Bill Cummings won over Mauri Rose in the feature which was the same as the Indianapolis 500 race a few weeks earlier. Clay Weatherly won one of the other races over H. Ziegenthaler, second, and McQuinn, third [*Journal and Courier, page 9, June 25, 1934*].

*While Harry did race again on dirt, he had just finished his first Indianapolis 500. While there were other circuits to have in the "big cars" it was the little ones that got his passion.*

*McQuinn Family records.*

McQuinn Family records.

McQuinn Family records.

*McQuinn Family records.*

*McQuinn Family records.*

*McQuinn Family records.*

*McQuinn Family records.*

*McQuinn Family records.*

Dirt Track Racing

*McQuinn Family records.*

*McQuinn Family records.*

*McQuinn Family records.*

29

*McQuinn Family records.*

*McQuinn Family records.*

*McQuinn Family records.*

*McQuinn Family records.*

# HARRY MCQUINN

Harry McQuinn - Walls D.O. Fronty - Sterling, IL - c1930

http://www.kansasracinghistory.com/sullivan.htm

McQuinn Family records.

*McQuinn Family records.*

*McQuinn Family records.*

# 3
# "BIG CAR" DRIVER

IN 1934, HARRY MCQUINN WENT from dirt to the bricks. He had gained a reputation after several years of experience. Growing up and living in the shadow of the Indianapolis Motor Speedway (IMS), it would eventually beckon him.

IMS was the first race track built in the US for automobile racing. This was the idea of Carl Fisher who had staged a race at the Indiana State Fairgrounds on the horse track. IMS was designed as a 2.5 mile oval and opened in 1909 with the first organized Indianapolis 500 in 1911.

AP Photo (5/28/34). IMS Photo.

In 1934, McQuinn was employed in a garage in Indianapolis, where he worked during the winter months when not behind the wheel of a racing car. Harry drove a car entered by a former Hupmobile salesman of Indianapolis. These 'big cars', which were used at IMS, are similar to the sprint cars of today.

*IMS Photo of Harry McQuinn and Ralph Keller, 1934.*

The 1934 Indy 500 saw the return of only 33 starters as the number of deadly events continued. Unfortunately, this year saw the deaths of Jimmy Kries and mechanic Bob Hahn after their car went over the railing. Harry qualified his No. 63 DeBaets Special at 111.067 mph average. He started 30th with riding mechanic Ralph Keller. He completed only 13 laps before retiring due to a busted connecting rod finishing 31st.

Harry McQuinn with Ralph Keller (mechanic) in the DeBaets Special, 1934. *IMS Photo.*

## 1935

1935 had a few changes at IMS including the introduction of the Offenhauser engine which would continue for the next three decades and crash helmets were required for the first time. Harry McQuinn qualified his No. 66 four-cylinder Miller averaging 111.111 mph. He started 18th but finished last running only four laps before having broken a connecting rod.

*IMS Photo of Harry McQuinn, 1935.*

*IMS Photo with Harry McQuinn and Clay Ballinger, 1935.*

Johnny Hannon, a rookie but famous dirt track driver, dies after an accident on his first practice lap. Veteran driver Stubby Stubblefield and his mechanic Leo Whittaker are also killed during a qualifying run. And Clay weatherly, is killed in the 9th lap of the race, in the same car that Hannon drove.

## 1936

McQuinn qualified for the 1936 500-mile Memorial Day race in Harry Hartz's No. 28 Sampson Radio Special at 114.118 mph. This qualified him for 27th position. The Sampson Special is a rear-drive four-cylinder, with an engine of 237 cubic-inch displacement. At 250 miles, Harry had climbed into 10th place and the final ten miles of the race found him in 8th place. Harry ran out of gas on the backstretch on the 196th lap, finishing 13th. Only 10 of the 33 cars finished that year.

## "Big Car" Driver

*IMS Photo with Harry McQuinn, 1936.*

Louis Meyer came from 28th place to eventually dominant late in the race to win. This was the first year of the famous Borg-Warner trophy.

"Every one seems to be unanimous that Harry McQuinn in 28 and Ray Pixley in 41, put on the best driver's dual of the lot. Both these boys were not over a hundred feet apart for 350 miles, first one would take the lead for abut ten laps then the other would zoom ahead, they were averaging about 110 M.P.H. [*National Auto Racing News, page 11, June 11, 1936*].

*McQuinn Family records.*

McQuinn (28) and Connors (38) fighting for position.
*Unknown newspaper clipping, McQuinn Family records.*

## 1937

In 1937, McQuinn drove the No. 47 Shorty Cantlon's four-cylinder Sullivan & O'Brien Special with James Chappell as mechanic. McQuinn set the time for the second fastest lap ever at Indy at 126.760 mph. He also set the record for the fastest six laps before blowing a tire with an average of 126.400 mph. During practice, he posted 127.880 mph.

## "Big Car" Driver

"Colonel Rickenbacker, Speedway president, looks over the rear-engine car with Harry McQuinn looking in." *Unknown newspaper clipping, McQuinn Family records.*

"This is what a tire looks like after making three laps around the Speedway at better than 125 miles an hour." *Unknown newspaper clipping, McQuinn Family records.*

McQuinn started 22nd and finished 29th after 47 laps due to a broken piston. He also was a relief driver for Lietz from laps 59 through 71. His earnings… $560.

*IMS Photo of Harry McQuinn and Jim Chappell, 1937.*

41

"Harry McQuinn thundering down the front stretch."
*Unknown newspaper clipping, McQuinn Family records.*

*IMS Photo Harry McQuinn and Jim Chappell, 1937.*

McQuinn Family records.

Harry McQuinn, in the #47 Sullivan-O'Brien car is captured in a rare snapshot photo by Howard Lee. *Unknown newspaper clipping, McQuinn Family Records.*

## 1938

The 1938 Indy 500 saw another innovative car design. The No. 45 car of McQuinn was a new Marchese "hand-built" chassis that was designed with streamlining in mind to improve aerodynamics and therefore speed. Before being built, Tudy and Carl Marchese took a model and experimented with it in a wind-tunnel in Chicago. McQuinn had run midgets for the Marchese brothers and they decided with that knowledge to build their own "big car".

Unknown newspaper clipping, McQuinn Family records.

Its unique design was a crowd attraction. Its hood came to a pencil point just above the front axle. Its undercarriage lay within a horizontal fin. Underneath, it had innovative double-elliptical springs which provided rigid front end support. It also had new lightweight drop center wheels and a tubular steel frame. The motor was 183 cubic inches and also unusual as the engine block was spilt as two separate four-cylinder blocks. It also had four small side radiators replacing the customary front cooling system. The car represented an approximate $12,000 investment [*Indianapolis Star, page 3, April 24, 1938*].

This year saw no riding mechanics. McQuinn qualified the car at 119.492 mph allowing him to start 25th. On the 48th lap, McQuinn's car skidded on the North turn, darting to the inside apron but he was able to hold on and continue in the race. He was running in 8th at the 400-mile mark but had advanced to 5th by 450 miles. Making only two pit stops the entire race, he wound up finishing 7th overall. His 7th place purse netted $2175.

Of note, Emil Andres hit the outside wall of turn 2 on lap 45 and rolls. A tire flew off the car, bouncing up into the stands killing a spectator. Floyd Roberts outlasts several competitors to win with Snyder and Householder burning up their superchargers.

*Unknown newspaper clipping, McQuinn Family records.*

*IMS Photo in the streamlined Marchese special, 1938.*

*McQuinn Family records.*

*IMS Photo of Harry McQuinn in the No. 45 Marchese in the garage area, 1938.*

*McQuinn Family records.*

*McQuinn Family records.*

*McQuinn Family records.*

"FIGHTING IT OUT
Joel Thorne, millionaire sportsman, and
Harry MacQuinn in his Marchese Miller, fight for position.
Harry finished in 7th; Joel 8th."
*Unknown newspaper clipping, McQuinn Family records.*

## 1939

The beginning of 1939 saw 'practically all of the leader drivers in America' form the United States Racing Association to negotiate directly with the sponsoring organization of each race. They became affiliated with the AAA vowing to make the events better. The drivers also wanted bigger purses and a reduction of the 500 qualifying distance from 25 miles to 10 [*The Palladium Item, page 6, January 13, 1939*].

McQuinn was again in the streamlined Marchese (No. 12) but a broken crankshaft ended that hope. McQuinn then switched to the No. 38 Elgin Piston Pin Special qualifying 32nd at the closing minutes with an average qualifying speed of 117.287 mph. The motor blew ending his race at 110 laps with a finish of 21st. He was able to relieve Tony Gulotta for laps 111-127.

*Unknown newspaper clipping, McQuinn Family records.*

Floyd Roberts hits another car that spun out of control and died with a broken neck. Chet Miller and Bob Swanson are also seriously hurt.

Shaw wins when Lou Meyer blows a tire on lap 192. Meyer re-entering the race, had his sights on Shaw and had more speed. However, on lap 198, he again spun out, hitting the inside fence and having been thrown out of the car. Later, Meyer states that while he is flying through the air, he was probably the first driver to quit in mid-air [*Indianapolis 500 Chronicles, page 67*].

*IMS Photo of Harry McQuinn in the No. 38
Elgin Piston Pin Special, 1939.*

October 15, 1939, saw the 'Race of Champions', a 100-mile, AAA sanctioned event on the dirt at the Illinois State Fairgrounds in Springfield IL. Bill White, race car owner, had purchased the champion Alfa Romeo that outclassed many European drivers in 1936 and was to be piloted by Harry McQuinn, making his first dirt 'big car' event since being injured at Racine WI [*Belvidere Daily Republican, page 6, October 14, 1939*].

Emil Andres had won the pole and did not have to look back leading all the way to the finish. Mauri Rose was second, Floyd Davis third, and Lew Webb in fourth. There were no accidents but the race for second was a thrilling spectacle. The hailed Alfa was said to have performed poorly on the dirt, forcing McQuinn to retire early in the race [*The Decatur Herald, page 5, October 16, 1939*].

## "Big Car" Driver

### 1940

In 1940, the Brickyard showed fewer bricks this year with the backstretch now paved with asphalt.

Bill White, owner of the newly rebuilt Alfa Romeo with 181 cubic-inch displacement and a supercharger, was looking for a new Indy driver for 1940. He scouted Harry McQuinn at his title match at the 124th Field Artillery Armory. Harry won the National Indoor Championship for the third consecutive year and continued to impress White despite the less than stellar finish in the Alfa last fall at Springfield. The Alfa placed 5th the previous year at Indy. When accepting the deal McQuinn promised "I'm going to finish up front or else."

"Or else what?" Bill White responded.

"Or else go back to midget racing," he replied [*The Indianapolis Star, page 54, May 30, 1940*].

McQuinn did qualify the No. 41 Pay Day Special for a 15th place starting position. The Pay Day Special was an eight-cylinder engine in the Alfa Romeo with an aluminum body. McQuinn was able to keep it in the top 10 for most of the race with his highest of 7th at 275 miles. The race was called on account of rain at 192 (480 miles) of the 200 laps. He appeared to have finished 10th but on appeal, Rene LeBegue was given 10th place and McQuinn, 11th.

George Bailey was the lone fatality this year during practice.

Wilbur Shaw won the Indy 500 that year. It was his third and he was the first to win the 500 in

*Unknown newspaper clipping, McQuinn Family records.*

*Unknown newspaper clipping, McQuinn Family records.*

51

consecutive years. The race ended on yellow for the final 100 miles due to a light rain. The first-row starters finished in the same order.

> "Rough, tough Harry McQuinn was White's driver in 1940. McQuinn was one of the most aggressive (and least liked) stars in midget racing but had never had a good ride at the Speedway. Although he lived in Indianapolis and drove a midget for a Milwaukee car owner, he was always associated with the "Chicago Gang" of the small car set. He had already tried one other car before White put him in the Alfa. If the face behind the wheel was new, so were several other things. The car was now silver and big letters alongside the cockpit identified it as a "Hollywood Payday Spl." The name referred to a candy bar manufactured in Illinois and had nothing to do with Friday at a movie studio. The pitman arm and drag link were outside the body instead of faired over. Slits in the bodywork flanking the cockpit now cooled the driver. McQuinn qualified at 122.486 (mph) and, if this was two and a half miles per hour off its 1939 time, the pole speed had dropped just as much. He started 15th.
>
> McQuinn was never a factor in the race. He got the car up to eighth at the halfway mark, then pit stops dropped him out of the top 10. At 375 miles, the yellow flag came out because of rain and the positions were frozen from there to the finish. McQuinn was flagged at 192 laps, stuck in 11th position.
>
> In 1941, it was painted blue and named the "Ziffrin Spl." Despite his uninspired performance in 1940, McQuinn got the nod again and responded with the car's best qualifying run to date — 125.449, good enough for the inside of the second row.
>
> By now the car was starting to look somewhat old-fashioned. The nose had been revamped and was now more vertical instead of sloped, perhaps to aid cooling. Nevertheless, McQuinn took off in fourth place, just behind the front row starters, was third at 150 miles and second at 200. Then it fell back. The

problem was less the car than McQuinn's stamina. Kelly Petillo, the 1935 winner, was finally put in the cockpit and had the car up to seventh place by the end of the race."

http://www.shorey.net/newsletters/Alfa%20Owner/1980/Alfa%20Owner%201980-09.pdf

This is likely the Marks Special #21 that Duke Nalon raced in the 1940 Indy 500 but with McQuinn sitting in the cockpit. He would often test drive cars. A Wilson Photo. *McQuinn Family records.*

*McQuinn Family records.*

*IMS Photo of Harry McQuinn.*

*McQuinn Family records.*

*McQuinn Family records.*

*McQuinn Family records.*

McQuinn ran several more AAA 'big car' events in 1940. In August, he raced the Boyle Racing Headquarters car at the Illinois State Fairgrounds starting 9th but did not finish getting 13th place. Rex Mays finished first, followed by Al Miller, and Duke Nalon.

The season finished in a 100-mile event in Syracuse on a 1-mile oval dirt track. Rex Mays won the event with George Robson finishing second in the race. The race was marred by the fatality of Lou Webb who went out of control on the 17th lap striking the car of Kelly Petillo. A second caution came out when McQuinn's Boyle Racing Headquarters' car hit the fence on lap 91 [*The Courier-News, page 15, 3 September 1940*]. McQuinn started 9th in his 1936 M. J. Boyle Hartz/Offenhauser but finished 12th.

Rex Mays' victory clinched the National Racing Drivers championship for 1940.

Overall, McQuinn finished 5th in the AAA Midwestern Circuit Big Car Championship. Emil Andres was the overall winner that year.

# 1941

The 1941 Indianapolis 500 event saw any early morning garage fire destroying three cars and the electrical system at the track. It took workers a few hours to fix the issues with the timing system and the race was on with 31 starters.

McQuinn was faster in his eight-cylinder No. 15 Bill White's Zifrin Special, the re-painted and re-bodied Alfa from last year, with his top speed being 126.339 mph in his first lap and his average for the four 125.449. McQuinn started in fourth and maintained this position through 100 miles advancing to third at 150 and second at 200 miles. Thereafter, he fell out of the top 10. Kelly Petillo went in as relief advancing to 8th position at the 350-mile mark. He advanced to 7th at 400 miles and maintained that through the finish.

Shaw vying to be the first four-time winner of the 500 was leading at 380 miles when he lost a wheel and slammed into the wall. Mauri Rose won that year but in another car. He started on pole but his car had a mechanical failure on lap 60. He took over his teammate's (Floyd Davis) car moving steadily through the field to capture the checkered flag.

"Big Chief Chitwood Goes on Race Path
Joie (Big Chief) Chitwood (left), Cherokee Indian from Topeka, Kas., gets a few pointers on the 500-mile race from his new boss, Bill White (right) of Hollywood, Cal. White has just signed Joie and Harry McQuinn (center), Indianapolis driver, to pilot his cars in the gasoline classic May 30. Big Chief is a former Haskell University athlete, 26 years old and smashed 20 dirt track records during the past season. This will be his first attempt for 500-mile glory."
*Unknown newspaper clipping, McQuinn Family records.*

## "Big Car" Driver

### 'Whose Move Is It, Boys?'

"A few oranges from the Speedway lunch stand, the checkered flag from the A. A. A. office, and drivers Billy DeVore (left) and Harry McQuinn could pass away the time in Gasoline Alley during yesterday's cold snap. Better weather will find DeVore driving the four-cylinder Surber Special and McQuinn in the seat of Bill White's eight-cylinder Alfa Romeo, seen here in the backgrounds. Whose move is it, boys?"
*Unknown newspaper clipping, McQuinn Family*

"Fireman, Fireman, Save That Chill
It was too hot anything but gags and soft drinks out at the Speedway's Gasoline Alley yesterday. And as Harry McQuinn complained loudly of the heat Fireman Herbert Marsh put on Harry's helmet, gave the driver his hat, and sprayed the pilot who came equipped for the shower. By the way, McQuinn turned down a fireman's hat with an unlucky number."
*Unknown newspaper clipping, McQuinn Family records.*

*McQuinn Family records.*

*IMS Photo of Harry McQuinn in the Ziffrin Special.*

Soon after the 1941 Indianapolis 500, several drivers put on two races of 15 and 25 miles for the Murat Temple Shriners' at the Indianapolis Motor Speedway. The winner of the 15-mile sprint was Harry McQuinn in the Bill White's Zifrin Special. Chet Miller was second and Russ Snowberger was third. The 25-mile feature required all drivers to make one pit stop for a tire change. Miller won the feature with McQuinn second and Connors third.

"THIS IS McQUINN receiving the checkered flag while 10,000 Shriners and their wives cheered."
*Indianapolis Star, page 13, June 10, 1941.*

In July, five Indy drivers put on another spectacle for the Union Printers. It also consisted of two events, one 15-mile and the other a 10-mile event. McQuinn was last in the 10-mile event with Chet Miller winning. The 15-mile event required a single pit stop to change a tire. Despite having the longest pit stop, McQuinn won the 15-mile feature [*Franklin Evening Star, page 2, July 30, 1941*].

*George Connor, Cliff Bergere, Harry McQuinn, Russell Snowberger and Chet Miller (left to right.)*
*Indianapolis Star, page 16, July 30, 1941.*

*INTERLUDE...*

*World War II broke out later that year. Racing came to a standstill by federal mandate in 1942. IMS was offered to the federal government but it declined. The speedway was severely neglected.*

## 1946

At the beginning of 1946, the track was in massive disarray having been neglected during the war. It was bought by Tony Hulman, Terre Haute business man, from Eddie Rickenbacker. Wilbur Shaw became president of the IMS. Many were concerned that there was a general loss of interest in the 500.

```
 "Harry McQuinn's Aeronca trainer is shown as he
  circled the Speedway race track yesterday just before
 making the first landing on the oval. At the right, McQuinn
  hands his entry blank for the 500-mile classic, May 30,
         to Wilbur Shaw, Speedway president."
       Indianapolis Star, page 21, February 8, 1946.
```

McQuinn was going to run in another Maserati. He ran the six-cylinder T.E.C. Special in which Ted Horn had placed third in 1941 and the late Jimmy Snyder set the one lap and four lap (qualification) speed records. McQuinn qualified though in the No. 14 Mobilgas Special owned by Bob Flavell with a speed of 124.499 mph. He started 18th and had been running third until a valve problem occurred at 345 miles ending his day resulting in a 13th place finish.

# HARRY MCQUINN

McQuinn with Wilbur Shaw after McQuinn landed the plane on the brickyard in 1946 to hand in his application for the upcoming race. *IMS Photo.*

Four look on as the track and the cars are readied for the speedway. From left to right is the new IMS President Wilbur Shaw; Rex Mays; Billy De Vore; Harry McQuinn. *Unknown newspaper clipping, McQuinn Family records.*

McQuinn, Wally Mitchell, Joie Chitwood,
and model, 1946. *IMS Photo.*

Mobile Gas Special No. 14 driven by
Harry McQuinn, 1946. *IMS Photo.*

*Post card from the Craft Greeting Card Co., Indianapolis IN.*

*McQuinn Family records.*

## 1947

The running of the 1947 Indianapolis 500 was in jeopardy of losing several talented drivers. The American Society of Professional Auto Racing (ASPAR) representing the drivers and the teams were holdouts. ASPAR wanted to have an increase in payouts from the IMS. That year saw many such protests as the teams stated that the costs of building and re-building cars had gotten more expensive since the war. Many of the tracks agreed to the payout totaling 40% of the track's receipts and others who did not, went bankrupt. Drivers in ASPAR included Ralph Hepburn and Tony Bettenhausen among others. Finally, a compromise was made between ASPAR and IMS President Wilbur Shaw.

*The Indianapolis Star.*

Many 'insiders' gave considerable credit to Harry McQuinn who was not part of ASPAR. "The Speedway race is bigger than any group of drivers or the Speedway management," he said. Many of these holdouts had little time to prepare their cars for the rigors of IMS resulting in fewer qualifying that year to have only a field of 30. Harry himself tried to get into action, but his Maserati speedster developed serious types of mechanical difficulties during qualifications and was not able to qualify [*Indianapolis Star, page 3, June 29, 1947*].

Bill Holland, in his first 500, had a huge advantage entering into 180 laps. He was told to slow down. Unfortunately, his teammate, Mauri Rose, in second, place did not and passed him with 7 laps remaining. Holland did finish second. Shorty Cantlon trying to avoid Holland who had spun in a turn on lap 41 hit the outside wall and was killed.

## 1948

McQuinn started in the 1948 Indy 500 in the No. 65 Lynch Motors Special in 26th position. After one lap, the supercharge failed resulting in a last place finish earning him another nickname- "One Lap Harry".

Mechanical problems forced 21 of the 33 starters out of the race attributed to the blistering pace set by the leaders. Rex Mays started on pole for a record fourth time. Mauri Rose and Bill Holland finished again one-two with Duke Nalon in a Novi supercharged V8, third. When Rose crossed the finish line, only 11 cars were still on the track.

*IMS Press Photo of Harry McQuinn in the No. 65 Frank Lynch Special, 1948.*

Frank Brisko and his son Gerald prepare the Maserati 3030 engine for Harry McQuinn for the 1948 Indianapolis 500. *From the Ludvigsen Library Series.*

## 1949

For the 1949 Indianapolis 500, McQuinn was unable to secure a ride for the race and marked his retirement as a driver.

*The Indianapolis Star, page 70, May 1, 1949.*

As part of the Indianapolis' Sesquicentennial Celebration, a two-lap race using antique race car was held. McQuinn drove the 1907 Itala winning the race against five other antique racers. A 1909 Fiat driven in the "antique" race by 1941 winner Floyd Davis grabbed second place in a photo-finish scramble down the straightaway with McQuinn [*The Indianapolis Star, page 1, October 11, 1971*].

*The Indianapolis Star, page 1, October 11, 1971.*

# 4
# THE "MIGHTY" MIDGETS

AUTOMOBILE RACING HAS BEEN AROUND since there have been automobiles. Probably the first midget race was conducted in the Hughes Stadium in Sacramento CA on June 4, 1933. Although this is a point of argument amongst historians, small cars the size of the midgets were raced before in California, Michigan and Wisconsin. However, the midgets that were raced in 1933 were by professional race car drivers and thus the era began. Due to their unique size, these diminutive cars were able to race on small tracks common to fairgrounds and athletic fields. This started a craze for midgets at locations closer to many spreading this across the nation at local venues.

The first track for midget racing was Gilmore Stadium in Los Angeles built in 1934. The oldest active midget track in the nation is Angell Park Speedway in Sun Prairie WI and is the site of the National Midget Hall of Fame. By 1937, midget racing was one of America's fastest growing recreational activities.

Midget cars were miniaturized versions of the larger AAA Championship cars. They weighed about 750 pounds, had wheelbases ranging from 66 to 72 inches, and were as low as 4 inches off the ground. These lighter-weight cars ran at speeds upward of 70-80 mph. These midgets were difficult to turn in the corners at speeds of 40 to 50 mph. These cars and drivers became known as "diminutive dynamite."

Midget race cars were more economical than the champ cars. In addition, they ran on smaller dirt or cinder tracks often less than one-half mile. Such tracks sprung up on high school athletic fields and fairgrounds. Over time, these midgets were raced on tracks as big as a mile and on indoor as small as one-seventh of a mile.

Mike Popp put on the first midget exhibition program in the Chicagoland area on October 28, 1934. The race was held at the Calumet Speed Bowl near Lansing, IL just southwest of the current intersection of 170th street and Torrence Ave.

The new rage of midget auto racing moved indoors that winter to the 124th Field Artillery Armory, located at 52nd and Cottage Grove Ave in Chicago. Harold Shaw won the first indoor midget race in the US in November 18, 1934.

Many drivers would gain fame in the Midwestern midget auto racing. Drivers such as Harry "Leadfoot" McQuinn, Ray "The Highland Park Flyer" Richards, Myron "The Milwaukee Blitzkrieg" Fohr, Teddy "The Flying Rail" Duncan, Pete "The Flying Serb" Romcevich, Frank "Candy Man" Burany, Bob "Bombshell" Muhlke, Joie "Chief Wahoo" Chitwood, and Mike "The Flying Irishman" O'Halloran were often seen on these tracks and gained national attention. A smaller group of well-recognized drivers came from the Chicago area and were collectively known as the "Chicago Gang." Such drivers were Wally "The Human Cyclone" Zale, Tony "Tinley Park Express" Bettenhausen, Dennis "Iron Duke" Nolan, Cletus "Cowboy" O'Rourke, Jimmy "South Side Speed King" Snyder, Emil Andres and Paul Russo.

> "Holding forth at the Armory was a rough group of journeyman race drivers still referred to as the "Chicago Gang." This famous or infamous (depending on whether you were watching them or running against them) aggregation included names guaranteed to strike terror into the more faint-hearted competitors: Jimmy Snyder, Duke Nalon, Paul Russo, Wally Zale, Bob Muhlke, Shorty Sorenson, Emil Andres and the fun-loving, popular Cletus "Cowboy" O'Rourke. Harry McQuinn ran with this group and was perhaps the roughest of them all but he was an Indianapolis product. After his stormy career as a driver was over, McQuinn's knowledge of the rules of racing (undoubtedly he had broken most of them) earned him an appointment as chief steward

> of the Indianapolis 500 as well as boss of the AAA and USAC Championship divisions. He ruled with an iron hand enclosed in a glove of pure steel."
> *"The Mighty Midgets" by Jack C. Fox.*

## 1934

1934 saw Harry McQuinn introduction to the Indianapolis Motor Speedway. But out West, the mighty midgets were racing and introduced to the Midwest the same year. McQuinn who was over six-foot in height and weighing nearly 200 pounds, squeezed into a Morgan Outboard for the "Winter Indoor Circuit". Little information was found about his endeavor for that year.

## 1935

In 1935, McQuinn switched to a new creation of Pop Dreyer and started "his winning ways". McQuinn would run at St. Louis, Indianapolis, Milwaukee, and Chicago's Riverview in a midwestern circuit.

One of the most enduring indoor arenas for midget racing was the 124th Field Artillery Armory located at 52nd Street and Cottage Grove Avenue in Chicago.

> March 20, 1935 was the first midget race at the Indiana State Fairgrounds, an indoor 1/6-mile dirt track.
>
> "The floor was dirt, and when drivers named Harry McQuinn, Jimmy Snyder, Ronnie Householder, Tony Willman, Marshall Lewis, Ted Hartley and Wally Zale demonstrated the fine art of broadsliding the spectators couldn't believe it.
>
> One of the most winning drivers in the midgets was McQuinn who later became the chief steward at the 500-Mile Race.
>
> "I was the first guy who ever drove the Speedway before I drove a midget," Harry said last week. "I drove the Speedway in '34 and then went to the midgets that fall.

> "I drove a Harley powered a job in the first race, but it wasn't any good. We went from here to Chicago where I drove a midget built for Snyder. After that I drove for the Marcheses who built a car that had half a Miller engine.
>
> "I think it was the first double overhead cam engine ever in a midget. They turned it around and took the drive off the front for reverse torque. It was virtually unbeatable and we won races all over the country with it."
>
> *"Speaking of Speed: Coliseum Race Has Great Past" by George Moore, March 3, 1974.*

## 124th Field Artillery Armory, Chicago, March 21, 1935

McQuinn was driving the Bernard-Lee racer owned by Ralph Morgan of Indianapolis but in its first showing, had motor issues. The 25-lap feature was won by Tony Willman followed by Frank Brisko [*National Auto Racing News, page 2, April 11, 1935*].

## Indiana State Fairgrounds Coliseum, Indianapolis, March 27, 1935

Ronney Householder won the 25-lap feature against a close race with Tony Willman. Pat Warren and Johnny Sawyer finished third and fourth, respectively. A special event, the Hoosier Special, for Indiana drivers only was held. Louis Schneider won the event with Harold Shaw, second and McQuinn finishing third. Shaw had been injured earlier that night being pinned between two cars but bandaged up, and continued to race [*The Indianapolis Star, page 14, March 28, 1935*].

## Indiana State Fairgrounds Coliseum, Indianapolis, April 3, 1935

The first event saw McQuinn and Wally Mitchell tangled together causing both to go out of the race. Marshall Lewis won the first heat, who also won the 10-lap handicap followed by Ronney Householder. Marshall Lewis won the feature [*National Auto Racing News, page 3, April 11, 1935*].

## 124th Field Artillery Armory, Chicago, April 7, 1935

Marshall Lewis took three events and set a new 15-lap track record. Lewis won the first heat over Ronney Householder. Ted Hartley won the second heat; Tony Willman, third; Chuck Neisel, fourth; McQuinn, fifth. In the feature, Lewis, Willman and Householder were battling it out but Willman blew a tire on the 8th lap. Lewis was able to secure the lead and went on to finish. McQuinn clipped Jimmy Snyder and had to pull off on the 13th lap [*National Auto Racing News, page 3, April 18, 1935*].

## Arena Park Speedway, St. Louis, April 9, 1935

Marshall Lewis won the Commodore Edwin C. Koenig cup race in front of 8,600 fans in St. Louis. Ronney Householder, Tudy Marchese, Tony Willman and McQuinn gave little competition during the main event. Lewis had won four of the five races placing only second in a 25-lap class A final to Tony Willman only after his engine started to miss allowing Willman to take over the lead.

One of the more spectacular events, Schneider tried to overtake Marchese on the inside which was too narrow. The car drove up and onto Marchese's and rolled over twice, landing upright. Schneider continued the night after a brief interlude and won the Class A Consolation race. Lou Snyder had been in two accidents and his brother Jimmy a third, overturning after crashing into a bale of hay. Jimmy went on to drive in two additional thrilling races, winning the Class B semi-final and final races [*The St. Louis Star and Times, page 16, April 10, 1935*].

## Indiana State Fairgrounds Coliseum, Indianapolis, April 10, 1935

Marshall Lewis, driving a new midget, won the main feature of 30 laps which was dedicated to Mayor John Kern of Indianapolis. Tony Willman was second, Ronney Household, third, with McQuinn fourth. Lewis also won one of the other 10-lap sprints. McQuinn won two preliminary events and set a new eight-lap track record of 1 minute and 27.4 seconds [*The Indianapolis Star, page 25, April 11, 1935; National Auto Racing News, page 3, April 18, 1935*].

*Harry would often spend much of May in Indianapolis for the 500-mile race. However, during the height of the midget racing, he often continued his five-city tour racing weekly racing in Chicago (Sundays), St. Louis' Arena Park/Walsh Stadium (Tuesdays), Indianapolis State Fairgrounds/Butler Bowl (Wednesdays), Cleveland and Detroit in that order [The Franklin Evening News, page 2, April 16, 1935].*

## 124th Field Artillery Armory, Chicago, April 14, 1935

Frank Brisko grabbed the main feature. Householder won the first heat, Brisko the third, and Cuck Neisel the fourth. Tudy Marchese won the fifth event followed by McQuinn. Art Foley won the sixth. In the first semi-final, Brisko took over the lead from Ronney Householder when he slid wide and kept it until the finish. Ernie Carlson won the second preliminary, the second semi-final and helmet dash. The 25-lap feature had Brisko for the win, Householder second, and McQuinn fifth. In the final race, a 10-lap Borneo, Householder won after starting in last place. McQuinn finished second with his car afire [*National Auto Racing News, page 3, April 25, 1940*].

## Indiana State Fairgrounds Coliseum, Indianapolis, April 17, 1935

The night was marred by mechanical failures and crackups. Ronney Householder and Tudy Marchese each won three of the events. Householder won the 30-lap main event winning over Marchese by a car length. Marshall Lewis placed third, Johnny Sawyer fourth and McQuinn, fifth. Tony Willman won an eight-lap dash, after his car broke down but allowing him to coast past the finish line, still in the lead. McQuinn flipped his car, changed plugs, and re-entered still placing in third. McQuinn did win one of the other eight-lap races [*The Indianapolis Star, page 14, April 17, 1935; National Auto Racing News, page 2, May 9, 1935*].

## Indiana State Fairgrounds Coliseum, Indianapolis, April 24, 1935

Ronney Householder and McQuinn started in back in heat one and came forward placing in that order. Marshall Lewis won the second and Johnny Rogers the third. Tony Willman captured the fourth heat. The 10-lap handicap went to Holmes with McQuinn placing second. Householder won the six-lap match race against Holmes, McQuinn and Balus. The 30-lap feature was captured by Willman with Marshall Lewis second and Jimmy Snyder third. Householder and McQuinn were eliminated when they collided and went into the wall [*National Auto Racing News, page 2, May 9, 1935*].

## 124th Field Artillery Armory, Chicago, April 28, 1935

Emil Andres and Ted Tetterton collided sending both cars tumbling over several times. Andres suffered a fractured shoulder. Jimmy Snyder won the main feature and Ronney Householder took one of the elimination heats and the semi-final. McQuinn was third in the first heat and the semi-final. In the feature, McQuinn, Snyder and Householder lapped the field by 10 laps but McQuinn developed motor trouble on the 11th. Householder took the lead but was slowed by another car allowing Snyder to take the lead on the 17th lap [*National Auto Racing News, page 2, May 9, 1935*].

## Arena Park Speedway, St. Louis, April 30, 1935

In the main event, on the ninth lap, Tony Willman hit and then climbed the back of Al Pavacal's midget. Ronney Householder then hit Willman's car tipping it over. Willman was pinned underneath but remained uninjured. McQuinn led the event until the 13th lap after spinning out in the north turn. Jimmy Snyder then overtook the lead and won. Willman went on to race in the final event, a 10-lap handicap against Marshall Lewis. Willman eventually took the lead from Lewis on the fifth lap and went on to win.

The 15-lap semi-final was won by Householder but was under protest. "McQuinn, who had the pole position, contended that he was not leading when the starter dropped the flag. He pulled up at the starting line while the other drivers continued in the race and completed the 15 laps before they were flagged down. McQuinn's contention was overruled and the judges awarded the race to Householder with Willman second, Snyder third, and Carlson fourth." McQuinn did win the 10-lap heat one and the Australian pursuit of 15 laps [*St. Louis Post Dispatch, page 16, May 1, 1935*].

## Indiana State Fairgrounds Coliseum, Indianapolis, May 1, 1935

Jimmy Snyder won the 30-lap feature leading by one second over Ronney Householder. Tony Willman was third and Harry McQuinn, fourth. Householder won two of the ten dashes finishing second in another two. McQuinn, Lewis, Shorty Sorenson, Jimmy Rogers, Ernie Carlson, and Ted Hartley also won events [*The Star Press, page 12, May 2, 1935*].

## Michigan State Fairgrounds Coliseum, Detroit, May 4, 1935

McQuinn took the 20-lap main feature and a 10-lap elimination. Jimmy Snyder was second and Tony Willman third in the feature [*National Auto Racing News, page 3, May 9, 1935*].

## 124th Field Artillery Armory, Chicago, May 5, 1935

Jimmy Snyder captured the evening winning the first preliminary, the 15-lap semi-final and the 30-lap feature. McQuinn, Marshall Lewis and Tudy Marchese were in hot pursuit of Snyder in the feature but he drove an error-free race. In the semi-final, McQuinn and Snyder were battling it out. Snyder slid wide on the 9th lap and McQuinn took the lead. However, on the next lap, McQuinn blew a tire. Snyder was able to regain the lead and pull into final victory. McQuinn started in 8th position in the feature and "burned up the track" and his engine, going out after eight laps while in second place. The feature final order was Snyder, Lewis, and Tony Willman [*National Auto Racing News, page 2, May 16, 1935*].

## Arena Park Speedway, St. Louis, May 7, 1935

The main event saw McQuinn leading the first 13 laps but spun in the north turn losing all places. Jimmy Snyder then overtook first and went on to victory followed by Ernie Carlson and Jimmy Rogers.

The first heat was won by McQuinn; second, Tony Willman; third, Marshall Lewis; fourth, Rogers. The 15-lap Australian pursuit race was won by McQuinn. The night saw Willman hit the car driven by A. Pavasil. Then, Ronney Householder plowed into the two overturning Willman's car but he was uninjured. [*National Auto Racing News, page 3, May 9, 1935*].

## 124th Field Artillery Armory, Chicago, May 12, 1935

Marshall Lewis won the 30-lap feature race beating Tony Willman with Tudy Marchese finishing third. The semi-final heat of 15 laps was won by Snyder, who beat Harry McQuinn in the closest finish of the meet right at the finish line.

"Harry McQuinn qualified for the Soldiers' Field races during the evening, finishing in the money several times. Others to qualify were Marchese, Johnny Sawyer, Gale

Lower, Art Foley, Snyder, and Willman" [*Chicago Daily Tribune, page 18, May 13, 1935*].

## Kentucky State Fair Pavilion, Louisville, May 17, 1935

This was the inaugural event of this 1/10 mile concrete indoor track. Harry "Leadfoot" McQuinn in the Morgan Elto 'super-midget' swept five events. The first elimination event was won by McQuinn, the second by Marshall Lewis, and the third by Harry Lewis. A special match race was won by McQuinn over Tony Willman. Another match race of the four fastest cars was also won by McQuinn over Lewis and Snyder. McQuinn won the 25-lap feature with Lewis second and Snyder third. The last event of the evening was a 10-lap Borneo which McQuinn also captured [*National Auto Racing News, page 5, May 30, 1935*].

## Soldiers' Field, Chicago, May 19, 1935

This was the first outdoor race of the season for the Midwest Auto Racing association. Marshall Lewis gained the lead on the fifth lap going on to lapping the field. Snyder finished second with Marchese third. Willman suffered a broken rod and had to pull out of the race [*Chicago Tribune, page 21, May 20, 1935*]. "Harry McQuinn, a late starter in the indoor meets, will have to come from far back, but he is expected to be in the contention before the race is over" [*Chicago Daily Tribune, page 32, May 19, 1935*]. However, McQuinn is never mentioned in the money so it is unclear if he entered.

## Butler University Bowl, Indianapolis, May 22, 1935

This dirt track was located at the university football field. Jimmy Snyder, won the feature event. The track record was set by Harry McQuinn on the fifth-mile track at 16.43 seconds [*Franklin Evening Star, page 2, May 27, 1935*].

## League Park, Fort Wayne IN, May 25, 1935

This was the inaugural event of this new midget auto race track that was a 1/5 mile dirt oval. Pat Warren won the first event and Curly Mills the second. Jimmy Rogers won the third, Tony Willman the fourth and Ralph McDaniel for the fifth. Curly Mills won the 25-lap feature with Harold Shaw second. McQuinn was second in the fourth event but did not place in the feature [*National Auto Racing News, page 4, June 6, 1935*].

## Walsh Memorial Stadium, St. Louis, May 31, 1935

Tony Willman, having dominated the indoor Arena, won handily in the inaugural outdoor race events at Walsh Stadium taking three events including the main and missing a fourth when the right rear wheel came off. McQuinn ran time trials but was never mentioned in any race results so it is unknown if he had mechanical failure or simply 'a bad night' [*St. Louis Post-Dispatch, page 10, June 1, 1935*].

## League Park, Fort Wayne IN, June 1, 1935

McQuinn was fastest in time trials. He was leading in the feature until the 15th lap when a tie rod snapped. Being helpless in the middle of the track, Art Foley collided forcing both cars into the fence and turning over McQuinn's. McQuinn suffered a broken rib. McQuinn won the first event but lost the match race with Jimmy Snyder. Snyder took the 25-lap feature with Marshall Lewis second and Harold Shaw, third [*National Auto Racing News, page 3, June 20, 1935*].

## Walsh Memorial Stadium, St. Louis, June 4, 1935

Tudy Marchese won the 20-lap main feature. Tony Willman and Marshall Lewis, previous winners, were not in contention. The rain fell making the track wet. McQuinn was second in two of the eight-lap heats but was 'not in the money' for the main [*The St. Louis Star and Times, page 20, June 5, 1935*].

## League Park, Fort Wayne IN, June 8, 1935

Art Foley and Harry McQuinn were involved in a two-car wreck that was "one of the most spectacular accidents ever witnessed on a midget track." Both were seriously bruised but recovered in short order [*The Times, page 60, June 13, 1935*].

## Butler University Bowl, Indianapolis, June 12, 1935

Jimmy Snyder took the top honors, including the Sportsman's trophy, victorious in the 25-lap Butler Handicap. McQuinn was second and Marshall Lewis, third. Tony Willman was forced out late in the main feature. McQuinn beat out Snyder, Willman and Lewis in a four-lap dash featuring the four fastest cars. Snyder, Willman, Henry Myers and Harold Shaw also won events [*The Indianapolis Star, page 20, June 13, 1935*].

## Mt. Lawn Speedway, Newcastle IN, June 13, 1935

"Jimmy Snyder, of Chicago, and Harry McQuinn, of Indianapolis, carried off the lion's share of prize money at the Mt. Lawn track in the opening card last week" [*The Star Press, page 8, June 18, 1935*].

## Northside Ballpark Speedway, Cincinnati, June 20, 1935

A light drizzle fell on the 1/5-mile dirt track making it slippery. The events were still held with the main being taken by Pat Warren who also took two other events. Jimmy Rogers overturned his car and fractured his shoulder. McQuinn won one of the eight-lap heats as did Warren and Marshall Lewis [*The Cincinnati Enquirer, page 20, June 21, 1935*].

## Wolf Lake Midget Speedway, Hammond IN, June 22, 1935

Tony Willman, 1934-35 indoor midget champion, skidded on the treacherous south turn and turned over in the fifth event fracturing his right shoulder. Tony was driving Jimmy Rogers' car after he had snapped a crankshaft earlier in the night.

Tudy Marchese won the feature event, with Harry McQuinn in second and Wally Mitchell in third. Marchese won two other events. McQuinn and Mitchell each won an event and had two second place finishes.

## Northside Ballpark Speedway, Cincinnati, June 27, 1935

McQuinn took several firsts including the first elimination heat, a match race against Jimmy Snyder, and the 30-lap main feature. Jimmy Snyder placed second in the feature followed by Tudy Marchese [*National Auto Racing News, page 3, July 4, 1935*].

**M'QUINN COPS AT CINCINNATI**

*National Auto Racing News, page 3, July 4, 1935.*

## Walsh Memorial Stadium, St. Louis, July 2, 1935

Marshall Lewis won the main event. Jimmy Snyder and Art Foley vied for the lead and got caught up together. This allowed Lewis to pass with only a few laps to go. On the last lap, Lewis had blown a tire and coasted across the finish line. McQuinn won the third 8-lap preliminary and the 16-lap handicap [*The St. Louis Star and Times, page 15, July 3, 1935*].

## Butler University Bowl, Indianapolis, July 3, 1935

A special match race between Marshall Lewis and Harry McQuinn led off the card but the track remained wet and the American Racing Association postponed the event [*The Indianapolis Star*, page 12, July 4, 1935].

## Northside Ballpark Speedway, Cincinnati, July 11, 1935

"Tony Willman, Tudy Marchese and 'Handsome Harry' McQuinn each won two races, while the feature handicap of 20 laps went to Pat Warren" [*The Cincinnati Enquirer*, page 19, July 12, 1935]. It was later reported that McQuinn fractured two ribs [*St. Louis Post-Dispatch*, page 16, July 15, 1935].

## Neil Park Speedway, Columbus OH, July 12, 1935

Neil Park was a 1/5 mile dirt track located within the Columbus Red Birds' coliseum. McQuinn ran over the axle of Shorty Enslow, throwing him out and he was dragged for 50 feet underneath the car. He suffered five broken ribs and many bruises [*National Auto Racing News*, page 3, August 15, 1935].

**HARRY M'QUINN HURT IN RACE CAR CRACKUP**

The Indianapolis Star, page 12, July 13, 1935.

## Walsh Memorial Stadium, St. Louis, July 25, 1935

McQuinn 6th in time trials but never placed 'in the money' in any event [*St. Louis Post-Dispatch*, page 16, July 26, 1935].

## Neil Park Speedway, Columbus OH, August 2, 1935

McQuinn won the 25-lap main event jumping into an early lead. Jimmy Snyder, signaling for a stop, was hit by Harold Shaw throwing Snyder out and turning the car over and over. Snyder was pinned underneath but suffered only from cuts; Harold Shaw was hospitalized after an accident [*National Auto Racing News, page 3, August 8, 1935; National Auto Racing News, page 3, August 15, 1935*].

## Walsh Memorial Stadium, St. Louis, August 6, 1935

Paul Russo won the 25-lap feature followed by Tudy Marchese, Jimmy Snyder, Lou Schneider, and Duke Nalon. McQuinn was last in time trials and lost his grudge match to Schneider [*St. Louis Post-Dispatch, August 7, 1935*].

## Chicago Midget Speedway, Evanston IL, August 7, 1935

In the first race of the evening, an 8-lap helmet dash, Wally Zale and McQuinn started the thrills with a thrilling finish with Zale outdistancing McQuinn by less than a car length. McQuinn eventually retired for the night with a broken axle in the first heat which was won by Ronney Householder. The feature was won by Carlson in record time over Householder after lapping the entire field [*National Auto Racing News, page 3, August 15, 1935*].

## Walsh Memorial Stadium, St. Louis, August 20, 1935

Duke Nalon won the 50-lap Welcome Inn Sweepstakes with Ronney Householder second. Householder was in the lead on the thirty-eighth lap when he developed engine trouble allowing Nalon to take the lead; he, however, was able to hold on to second place. The 50-lap (10 mile) feature was the longest held to date at Walsh Stadium. McQuinn won two of the eight-lap preliminaries [*St. Louis Post-Dispatch, page 17, August 21, 1935*].

## Walsh Memorial Stadium, St. Louis, August 27, 1935

The close of the outdoor season for the Walsh Stadium featured a 15-mile (75 lap) main event. Wally Zale took the main by a lap over the second-place finisher, Duke Nalon. Jimmy Snyder took third and Lou Schneider fourth. Zale took home a purse of $375.

McQuinn driving the new, streamlined Catfish Special, replacing Harold Shaw as driver. McQuinn did not feel it lived up to expectations and relinquished the car to Emil Andres. Andres did win a match race with it against Les Adair. McQuinn won a 3-lap grudge race against Schneider [*The St. Louis Star and Times, page 21, August 28, 1935*].

## Roby Speedway, Hammond IN, September 15, 1935

Babe Stapp won the Roby 50-mile derby with Jimmy Snyder, second. Wild Bill Cummings and Wilbur Shaw, finished third and fourth. McQuinn lost control of his midget racer on the 20th lap and hit the fence. "Despite the searing flames, McQuinn held his car under control until he could bring it to a stop without endangering the lives of any of the 15,000 spectators" [*Hammond Times, page 10, September 16, 1935*]. He jumped free of the burning wreck but not before his arms and legs were burned [*Chicago Tribune, page 18, September 16, 1935*], reportedly 'near death' the following day [*The Franklin Evening Star, page 2, September 16, 1935*].

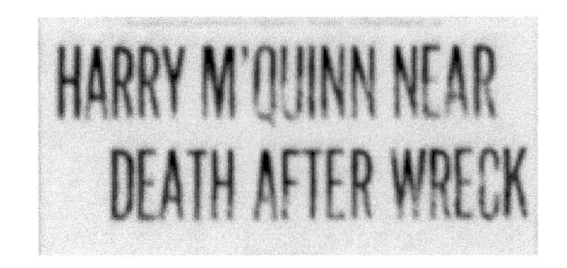

**HARRY M'QUINN NEAR DEATH AFTER WRECK**

> "THANKS
>
> Harry McQuinn, seriously burned at Roby on Sept. 15, and now recovering at St. Margaret's Hospital in Hammond, Ind., wishes to express his appreciation to all his friends and fans who have visited him during his confinement there."
> *National Auto Racing News, page 6, September 26, 1935.*

```
"Harry (Lead-Foot) McQuinn, seated in the Bud's Auto Parts
Catfish, in which he will endeavor to establish a world's
   straightaway record for midgets on the Salt Beds near
Salt Lake City, Utah, in the near future. This car is owned
by Jimmy Triplett, of Chicago. McDowell built the 85 h. p.
motor and Dreyer the chassis and body. It is expected that
   this midget will attain a speed of 130 miles per hour.
 Ronny Householder was first selected to drive, but due to
            certain contracts was forced to withdraw."
      National Auto Racing News, page 1, September 26, 1935.
```

## Michigan State Fairgrounds Coliseum, Detroit, November 6, 1935

Paul Russo and his teammate, Harry McQuinn, finished first and second in the feature event [*Detroit Free Press, page 20, November 9, 1935*].

## 124th Field Artillery Armory, Chicago, November 10, 1935

Jimmy Snyder and Ronney Householder, who started in the first row, lapped the entire field by the 34th lap in the 50-lap main feature. On the 35th lap, Snyder spun and lost two laps before recovering. Householder went on to win by 1½-lap over the next contender, Wally Zale.

McQuinn showed up at the track minus his Bridges Special "doodle bug." On the way to the track, the trailer hitch snapped which they were unaware of and they spent the entire night before the races in search of the car. McQuinn had borrowed a car and placed fourth in the first heat. McQuinn led out the field in the handicap but fell off on the 9th lap with ignition troubles [*National Auto Racing News, page 2, November 21, 1935*].

## 124th Field Artillery Armory, Chicago, November 17, 1935

Householder again captured the 50-lap main followed by Zale. Jimmy Snyder, Paul Russo, and Harold Shaw won the 15-lap heats. Snyder also won the 12-lap match race. McQuinn placed fourth in the first heat [*Chicago Tribune, page 23, November 18, 1935*].

## 124th Field Artillery Armory, Chicago, November 24, 1935

Jimmy Snyder and Ronney Householder again left the field behind in the 50-lap feature with Householder in the lead which did not change for the entire race. McQuinn had trouble at the start and retired from the field.

In the first heat, Jimmy Snyder and Wally Zale were in a hub-rubbing duel following Householder. Curly Mills dropped out on the 9th lap with ignition issues and McQuinn in the Bridges Special tangled with Ray Richards on the same lap. McQuinn was able to get restarted but did not place. In the second heat, Curly Mills led off pole but fell out with motor troubles on the 4th lap. Duke Nalon hit a rut on the south turn and rolled over but Nalon was uninjured. The third heat went to McQuinn after another restart gave him the advantage. The 12-lap handicap was won by Zale. Zale took the early lead from Lou Schneider on the second and by the third, McQuinn and Snyder had passed Schneider as well. Snyder was able to overtake Zale on 7$^{th}$ lap but this quickly went back to Zale who kept it to the end [*National Auto Racing News, page 2, November 28, 1935*].

## 124th Field Artillery Armory, Chicago, December 1, 1935

Jimmy Snyder triumphed over Ronney Householder to win the 50-lap main event after taking the lead from Householder on the third lap. McQuinn placed second in the fifth race [*Chicago Tribune, page 24, December 2, 1935*].

**McQuinn to Compete.**

Harry McQuinn, whose handling of racing cars has won fame in both dirt track and midget ranks, will be among the pilots who will compete in Promoter Earl Reflow's speed program next Tuesday night at the Arena. The event will be in the nature of a comeback for McQuinn, who has submitted to a series of skin grafts recently during his stay in an Indiana hospital.

St. Louis Post-Dispatch, page 19, November 26, 1935.

## Arena Park Speedway, St. Louis, December 3, 1935

This was an unusual event as it started with the wedding of Marshall Lewis. Sorenson won the 30-lap feature over McQuinn, Ronney Householder, and Wally Zale in that order. Third elimination race won by McQuinn [*St. Louis Post-Dispatch, page 15, December 4, 1935*].

### 124th Field Artillery Armory, December 8, 1935

In one of the most thrilling indoor auto races ever run in Chicago, Curly Mills beat Ronney Householder to win the 50-lap main event. McQuinn placed third in the second race; won the 12-lap handicap race; and placed third in the 50-lap feature behind Curly Mills and Ronney Householder [*Chicago Daily Tribune; December 9, 1935; page 23*].

### Wisconsin State Fair Park Coliseum, December 12, 1935

Harry McQuinn, broke three records in winning as many events at the State Fair Park midget races. He won the 25-lap feature, a 10-lap race and the five-lap event for the fastest qualifiers. Curly Mills was second and Tony Willman, third in all three races. Willman was absent for three weeks because the Marchese brothers withdrew their Miller after several lean weeks. He reappeared driving the car in which Harry Jastroch was killed previously at the Wisconsin State Fairgrounds [*Milwaukee Journal, page 18, December 13, 1935*].

### Michigan State Fairgrounds Coliseum, Detroit, December 14, 1935

Curly Mills won the 30-lap main for the fourth consecutive week. He was followed by Jimmy Snyder with McQuinn placing fifth. Ronney Householder won the first event, Mills the second, Chuck Neisel, third, and McQuinn, fourth [*National Auto Racing News, page 2, December 19, 1935*].

### 124th Field Artillery Armory, Chicago, December 15, 1935

The 50-lap 'mid-season championship' main feature was won by Tony Willman with Jimmy Snyder and Emil Andres finishing second and third, respectively. A 40-lap race was won by Curly Mills. McQuinn won the second 12 lap race [*Chicago Tribune, page 22, December 16, 1935*].

## Wisconsin State Fair Park Coliseum, Milwaukee, December 19, 1935

Curly Mills, recently dominating Midwest tracks, led the field in the 40-lap feature. On lap 12 though, Mills had spun allowing McQuinn to overtake him and capture the feature. The night started with spectacular crashes. Ronney Householder lost control and went into a skid stalling in the turn which caused Pat Warren to broadside him. Frank Burany, went high to avoid the two but did not clear Warren's car, clipped the rear wheel then went into the wall [*National Auto Racing News, page 2, December 26, 1935*].

## Michigan State Fairgrounds Coliseum, Detroit, December 21, 1935

Ronney Householder set a new one-lap track record in qualifying. However, this did not keep Curly Mills from capturing his fifth straight Armory feature win. Householder collided with Doc Shanebrook taking Householder out of the feature. McQuinn placed third behind Chuck Neisel.

Mills won the first heat, Shanebrook took the second, Neisel the third and McQuinn the fourth heat [*National Auto Racing News, page 3, December 26, 1935*].

## 124th Field Artillery Armory, Chicago, December 22, 1935

Curly Mills won the 40-lap feature having lapped the entire field. McQuinn was second in the first race and in the fifth race but went out in the feature with motor troubles [*Chicago Daily Tribune, page 25, December 23, 1935; National Auto Racing News, page 3, December 26, 1935*].

## Michigan State Fairgrounds Coliseum, Detroit, December 28, 1935

Curly Mills won the 35-lap feature even after snapping a rod. Pat Warren was second, Chuck Neisel, third and McQuinn fourth [*National Auto Racing News, page 3, January 2, 1936*].

### 124th Field Artillery Armory, Chicago, December 29, 1935

Pat Warren defeated Paul Russo to win the 40-lap feature. Tony Willman took the lead early but Warren had taken over after the third lap. Ray Richards and McQuinn started in 6th and 7th. Richards made his way through the field with McQuinn literally pushing his car forward. McQuinn also placed third in the third race; he won the eighth race ("free for all"); he placed fourth in the main event [*National Auto Racing News, page 2, January 2, 1936*].

## 1936

### Wisconsin State Fair Park Coliseum, Milwaukee, January 9, 1936

McQuinn won the 25-lap feature. Ted Tetterton overturned his racer in the feature warm-ups and sustained several fractures and severe cuts and abrasions [*Green Bay Press-Gazette, page 16, January 10, 1936*].

### Michigan State Fairgrounds Coliseum, Detroit, January 11, 1936

Jimmy Snyder added an extra set of wheels for additional traction allowing him to defeat Curly Mills for the main feature of 30-laps. McQuinn placed third and won one of the earlier heats [*Detroit Free Press, page 40, January 12, 1936*].

### 124th Field Artillery Armory, Chicago, January 12, 1936

Jimmy Snyder won the 40-lap feature over Curly Mills. Mills and Pat Warren bumped causing Warren to be held back and allowing McQuinn to take over third. McQuinn won one of the 12-lap races as well as the handicap [*Chicago Daily Tribune, page 22, January 13, 1936*].

## Wisconsin State Fair Park Coliseum, Milwaukee, January 16, 1936

Wally Zale won two of three feature races. McQuinn charged that Steve Milton deliberately "bumped" his car on several occasions and a fist fight ensued [*Green Bay Press-Gazette, page 17, January 17, 1936*].

## 124th Field Artillery Armory, Chicago, January 19, 1936

Ronney Householder won feature. Harry Lewis involved in a crash and suffered concussion and dislocated shoulder. McQuinn won the fourth race of 12 laps and the pursuit race of 15 laps [*Chicago Daily Tribune, page 19, January 20, 1936*].

## 124th Field Artillery Armory, Chicago, January 26, 1936

Pat Warren won the 30-lap feature. McQuinn won the 12-lap third and sixth races [*Chicago Daily Tribune, page 16, January 27, 1936*].

## Arena Park Speedway, St. Louis, February 11, 1936

Ronney Householder won the six-mile feature leading from pole to finish with Curly Mills, Jimmy Snyder, Pat Warren, and McQuinn following. McQuinn was second in the second heat and won the third [*St Louis Dispatch, page 18, February 12, 1936*].

## Chicago Riding Club, Chicago, February 12, 1936

This track was an 1/8-mile indoor venue. Tony Willman won the 30-lap feature with McQuinn second, Shorty Sorenson third and Frank Brisco fourth. McQuinn won the eight-lap heat and the Australian pursuit [*Chicago Daily Tribune, page 24, February 13, 1936*].

### 124th Field Artillery Armory, Chicago, February 23, 1936

Ronney Householder won the 100-lap grind after grabbing the lead from Pat Warren who had led for more than half the distance. Harry McQuinn moved up from tenth-place to finish third in a spectacular spurt [*Southtown Economist, page 11, February 27, 1936*].

### Wisconsin State Fair Park Coliseum, Milwaukee, February 27, 1936

"Six weeks of cold weather and impassable roads prevented holding races at the Wisconsin State Fair Park Coliseum. This nine-race event included a 25-lap main and a 15-lap handicap. Among those expected to compete are Harry McQuinn of Indianapolis, who holds the five, 10 and 25 lap records here, and Curly Mills and Pat Warren, California stars; Wally Zale, Chuck Neisel, Ray Richards, and Pip Hansen, Chicago; Tony Willman, Cy Drew, Johnny Sawyer, Frank Burany and Steve Milton, Milwaukee" [*Milwaukee Journal, page 11, February 27, 1936*].

The feature was won by Zale followed by Warren. Warren had slid wide letting Zale overtake him for the lead and win [*National Auto Racing News, page 2, March 5, 1936*].

### Michigan State Fairgrounds Coliseum, Detroit, February 28, 1936

Ronney Householder won the main feature. McQuinn placed second [*Detroit Free Press, page 43, March 1, 1936*].

### 124th Field Artillery Armory, Chicago, March 1, 1936

Thirty-lap main feature was captured by Ronney Householder over Pat Warren. McQuinn placed fourth [*Chicago Daily Tribune, page 23, March 2, 1936*].

## Michigan State Fairgrounds Coliseum, Detroit, March 7, 1936

Ronney Householder won the main feature again, dominating this venue. McQuinn came in second place [*Detroit Free Press, page 50, March 8, 1936*].

## 124th Field Artillery Armory, Chicago, March 8, 1936

Householder again won the feature with Jimmy Snyder second. McQuinn, in a new racer, continued to have trouble with it. In the final feature, McQuinn and Paul Russo mixed it up on the third lap with both losing position. On the sixth, McQuinn and Curly Mills entangled in the same spot. However, they were not done for the evening again getting entangled on the 10th lap [*National Auto Racing News, page 3, March 12, 1936*].

## Michigan State Fairgrounds Coliseum, Detroit, March 14, 1936

McQuinn captured the 30-lap feature ahead of Ronney Householder by a good margin. McQuinn forced the advantage and captured first [*National Auto Racing News, March 19, 1936*]. Bill Warner's car slid in the wall and became pinned underneath resulting in a shoulder dislocation [*Detroit Free Press, page 46, March 15, 1936*].

## 124th Field Artillery Armory, Chicago, March 15, 1936

Jimmy Snyder snapped Ronney Householder's streak capturing the main feature of 70-laps. Curly Mills placed third; Duke Nalon, fourth; Pat Warren, fifth. McQuinn, up in front early in the feature, went wide to avoid a spun car and hit a hay bale hard enough to break his axle. McQuinn placed third in the 10-lap Sweepstakes [*Chicago Daily Tribune, page 21, March 16, 1936; National Auto Racing News, page 2, March 19, 1936*].

## Michigan State Fairgrounds Coliseum, Detroit, March 21, 1936

Jimmy Snyder lead the entire 30-laps to capture the feature. McQuinn continued to have motor issues throughout the night and never placed "in the money" [*National Auto Racing News, page 3, March 26, 1939*].

## 124th Field Artillery Armory, Chicago, March 22, 1936

Jimmy Snyder won the 40-lap feature beating out McQuinn. McQuinn won the 5th race; 2nd in the 6th [*Chicago Daily Tribune, page 21, March 23, 1936*]. "Harry McQuinn stole the show. Just give this boy a few more days and he's going to cop the feature just as sure as Mackenzie wears his whiskers at the Indianapolis "500". McQuinn tied Householder for the pole position, then got a hand from the crowd when he beat Ronney in a match race, to say nothing of the thrilling fast five laps of the 20-lap feature, which he ran on a rear tire nearly flat, causing the entire crowd to have near nervous prostration, and losing only five positions after trailing Snyder for 15 laps. Spills and hair-raising stunts were more prevalent than ever" [*National Auto Racing News, page 3, March 26, 1936*].

## Wisconsin State Fair Park Coliseum, Milwaukee, March 26, 1936

Wally Zale dominated the night with three wins including the 25-lap feature. McQuinn and Tony Willman locked wheels spinning McQuinn out and bouncing off one of the walls. This twisted his steering gear and took him out of competition for the evening [*National Auto Racing News, page 3, April 2, 1936*].

## Michigan State Fair Grounds Coliseum, Detroit, March 28, 1936

Wally Zale took the feature of thirty laps. McQuinn placed fifth in the feature and won one of the preliminary heats [*National Auto Racing News, page 3, April 2, 1936*].

## 124th Field Artillery Armory, Chicago, March 29, 1936

The last event of the evening was the 40-lap feature. Jimmy Snyder set a new track record in winning this event hotly pursued by McQuinn who finished second [*National Auto Racing News, page 2, April 2, 1936*].

## Michigan State Fairgrounds Coliseum, Detroit, April 4, 1936

Curly Mills took the main feature followed by Wally Zale. McQuinn finished fourth. Although Householder had not been doing well due to mechanical issues of late, he still retained the lead in the point standings with 105; McQuinn was second with 65 and Mills was gaining, now in third with 57 [*National Auto Racing News, page 2, April 9, 1936*].

"HARRY McQUINN in his latest Dreyer-built midget. This job carries the same motor as the old chassis, but approximately 200 pounds in weight was eliminated in the construction of the new Chassis. Harry keeps the crowd on its toes."
*National Auto Racing News, April 16, 1936.*

## 124th Field Artillery Armory, Chicago, April 5, 1936

McQuinn broke a crankshaft in the time trials. He switched to another Dreyer of Harold Shaw's and qualified second but this was disallowed as Shaw had already qualified this car. The car did not perform well with Harry. Duke Nalon took the 40-lap main feature [*National Auto Racing News, page 3, April 9, 1936*].

## Michigan State Fairgrounds Coliseum, Detroit, April 11, 1936

Pat Warren led the field out for the feature and kept the lead through three laps. Warren went wide allowing McQuinn to undercut him followed by Wally Zale. Both McQuinn and Zale had won earlier events and were the ones to watch. Zale went wide on the 15th lap allowing Warren to take back second but McQuinn held on to win. McQuinn kept second in the overall points standings but gained substantially on Householder and distanced him from Curly Mills, still in third [*National Auto Racing News, page 2, April 16, 1936*].

## 124th Field Artillery Armory, Chicago, April 12, 1936

Jimmy Snyder won the feature event and Duke Nalon second. However, the excitement was the fist fight on the track during the feature in an earlier event. McQuinn and Nalon had collided sending Nalon spinning. Nalon quickly got underway and slowed down in front of McQuinn and they collided again. Coming to a stop, Nalon quickly got out of his car. McQuinn, still recovering from earlier injuries, was slow to get out, but fists flew while both were still on the track with 10 'doodle bugs' flying by. The race was stopped due to the risk of the drivers and it took six military personnel to separate the two. It was settled by a special grudge match race that McQuinn won [*National Auto Racing News, April 16, 1936*].

## Michigan State Fairgrounds Coliseum, Detroit, April 18, 1936

McQuinn led the 30-lap feature through 29 laps, but was overtaken by Wally Zale who went on to finish first. Zale also won a 'special' 30-lap race and Pat Warren, the Australian pursuit [*Detroit Free Press, page 49, April 19, 1936*].

## 124th Field Artillery Armory, Chicago, April 19, 1936

A special challenge match headlined the events. A challenge was issued by Duke Nalon to McQuinn as a result of the altercation at last week's Armory races with each blaming the other for the accident. The matched race was heated with both races inches apart until McQuinn finally gained the upperhand.

The battle for the championship had Jimmy Snyder in the lead but with many others in close contention. Snyder extended his lead by taking the 50-lap feature with Curly Mills, Paul Russo, and McQuinn in second, third, and fourth, respectfully [*Chicago Tribune, page 21, April 20, 1936*].

## Michigan State Fairgrounds Coliseum, Detroit, April 25, 1936

Wally Zale won the main feature and the track championship. McQuinn finished sixth in the feature but won one of the 10-lap heats [*National Auto Racing News, page 2, April 30, 1936*].

## 124th Field Artillery Armory, Chicago, April 26, 1936

Duke Nalon captured the main over a close finish by Jimmy Snyder. Pat Warren and Snyder had dueled for the last five laps giving Nalon the lead. Snyder having re-asserted himself gained quickly on Nalon and finishing second by three quarters of car length. McQuinn finished fourth. McQuinn won the Special Match race against Duke Nalon, Pat Warren, and Jimmy Snyder [*Chicago Tribune, page 21, April 27, 1936*].

## 124th Field Artillery Armory, Chicago, May 3, 1936

Duke Nalon won the 50-lap feature and his second consecutive win over Tony Willman and Curly Mills. McQuinn placed third in the first elimination race but did not place in the money [*Chicago Tribune, page 21, May 4, 1936*].

## 124th Field Artillery Armory, Chicago, May 10, 1936

Wally Zale won the 40-lap main race. The lead exchanged several times with McQuinn taking the lead from the start but yielded to Pat Warren on lap 20. Nalon overtook Warren on the 30th lap but Zale took the race at the finish. The first elimination race was won by McQuinn. Jimmy Snyder was crowned Midwest Indoor Auto Driver Champion over Pat Warren [*Chicago Tribune, page 22, May 11, 1936*].

## Walsh Memorial Stadium, St. Louis, May 12, 1936

Wally Zale "squeezed out" a win over Duke Nalon in the 25-lap feature. Zale started on pole and Nalon took second over from McQuinn for second place on the fifth lap. McQuinn dropped out allowing Curly Mills to place third and Cowboy O'Rourke, fourth [*St. Louis Post-Dispatch, page 21, May 13, 1936*].

*Carthage Fair Grounds, Cincinnati, May 14, 1936*

## Carthage Fair Grounds, Cincinnati, May 14, 1936

This was the inaugural event at Carthage meant to become one the most spectacular shows in the Midwest. The events were staged by the Ohio Valley Midget Racing Association. McQuinn won the 15-lap main feature but the most exciting race was the match race with McQuinn and Marshall Lewis. Lewis and McQuinn nearly finished even at the finish line but Lewis was the victor. McQuinn also won the first race of ten laps followed by Curly Mills and Marshall Lewis [*Cincinnati Enquirer, page 8, May 15, 1936*].

## Walsh Memorial Stadium, St. Louis, May 19, 1936

The 25-lap feature had Duke Nalon, Wally Zale, and Harry McQuinn finishing in that order. McQuinn won the first 10-lap heat with Pat Warren, Art Hartsfeld, and Marshall Lewis winning their heats [*St. Louis Post-Dispatch, page 19, May 20, 1936*].

## Carthage Fair Grounds, Cincinnati, May 21, 1936

"Handsome Harry McQuinn, daring race driver from Indianapolis, pushed his Tennes Special to victory last night at Carthage Fair Grounds over Bobby Swanson, Pacific Coast champion, in a finish that left 3,500 fans gasping for breath" [*Cincinnati Enquirer, page 8, May 22, 1936*]. McQuinn won the first race of eight laps over Emil Andres and Jimmy Snyder. McQuinn won the handicap against Johnny Sawyer and Bobby Swanson.

**AUTOMOBILE RACES.**

Handsome Harry McQuinn, daring race driver from Indianapolis, pushed his Tennessee Special to victory last night at Carthage Fair Grounds over Bobby Swanson, Pacific Coast champion, in a finish that left 3,500 fans gasping for breath.

## Walsh Memorial Stadium, St. Louis, May 26, 1936

"In the fourth elimination race on the north turn on the last lap, Buddy Door's car burst into flames. He stuck with the car, standing up in the seat and driving with one hand while beating the flames off with the other until his car came to the pits, when he jumped out and rolled in the dirt. This act of bravery on Buddy's part possibly prevented a serious crash with other cars.

Harry McQuinn, seeing the accident from the other side of the track, came roaring down the track and spun into the pits, grabbed a can of oil and gave Buddy first aid. The ambulance driver tried to cut across the track several times, but had to wait some time. And is this guy McQuinn tough! Just ask the two park guards, Harry knew what pain Buddy was suffering better than anyone else, after his experience last year when his own car burst into flames" [*National Auto Racing News, page 6, June 4, 1946*].

McQuinn won the 25-lap feature with Pat Warren, second, and Marshall Lewis, third [*The St. Louis Star and Times, page 26, May 27, 1936*].

## Carthage Fair Grounds, Cincinnati, May 28, 1936

Pat Warren took the main feature from Jack Schultz and Bob Swanson. McQuinn was absent due to obligations at the Indianapolis 500 [*Cincinnati Enquirer, page 15, May 29, 1936*].

## Carthage Fair Grounds, Cincinnati, June 4, 1936

Pat Warren again took the feature, his second win of the season at Carthage for the Vogelsang Diamond Trophy. McQuinn was again absent [*Cincinnati Enquirer, page 22, June 5, 1936*].

## Riverview Speedway, Chicago, June 7, 1936

McQuinn dominated the night setting three track records. McQuinn led from the start to finish of the 30-lap main event, though he was challenged repeatedly by Carl Peterson, Jimmy Snyder and Marshall Lewis. Lewis took second money and Snyder third. McQuinn also won the first race of eight laps, and the fifth race of eight laps [*Chicago Daily Tribune, page 23, June 8, 1936*].

**M'QUINN BREAKS AUTO RECORDS AT RIVERVIEW**

## Walsh Memorial Stadium, St. Louis, June 9, 1936

Wally Zale took the honors in the feature 30-lap midget auto race. He was able to control his car after it had contacted Harry McQuinn's car that was trying to block Zale for the lead on the twenty-second lap. McQuinn's car ran into the infield fence, but Zale controlled his and finished ahead of Jimmy Snyder and Marshall Lewis. Zale also won the 10-lap race, defeating McQuinn and Marshall Lewis [*St. Louis Post-Dispatch, page 18, June 10, 1936*].

## Riverview Speedway, Chicago, June 14, 1936

Riverview was a 1/5-mile dirt oval located next to the Riverview Amusement Park. Harry McQuinn defeated Pat Warren in the 35-lap feature midget auto race the new Riverview speedway. Art Hartsfeld nosed out Marshall Lewis for third place [*The Republic, page 3, June 15, 1936*].

## Carthage Fair Grounds, Cincinnati, June 18, 1936

Pat Warren won the main feature. However, the night was marred by several accidents. Paul Shough and Shorty Inloes collided in the first turn just after the start of the race.

Shough's car overturned three times and resulted in skull fracture as well as multiple other bones [*Cincinnati Enquirer, page 16, June 19, 1936*]. The Carthage track would close shortly thereafter due to unsustained financial losses.

## Riverview Speedway, Chicago, July 1, 1936

The night's events were called off early due to rain, canceling the main feature. The 10-lap handicap saw Pat Warren and McQuinn in a close duel with Warren nosing out McQuinn at the end [*The Los Angeles Times, page 33, July 2, 1936*].

## Walsh Memorial Stadium, St. Louis, July 7, 1936

The 50-lap main feature was the longest of the midwest season. Duke Nalon and Wally Zale were tied for the Southwestern Championship with McQuinn a close second. The first race of 10 laps had Zale triumphing over Pat Warren and Harry McQuinn. McQuinn won the second race. The feature was won by Zale with McQuinn trailing by half a lap in second and Cowboy O'Rourke third. McQuinn set a new track record for a single lap of 15.46 seconds besting the old record of 15.70 [*St. Louis Dispatch, page 14, July 7, 1936; St. Louis Post-Dispatch, page 14, July 8, 1936*].

## Riverview Speedway, Chicago, July 8, 1936

McQuinn won the 40-lap feature beating Ted Tetterton by half of a lap. Jimmy Snyder was third and Wally Zale, fourth [*Chicago Tribune, page 24, July 9, 1939*].

## Wisconsin State Fair Park, Milwaukee, July 9, 1936

"Harry McQuinn of Indianapolis, who ran out of gas while in sixth place after 499 miles in the 1936 Indianapolis race, had better luck before 3,900 midget auto racing fans at State Fair park Thursday night when he won all four feature events. Grabbing pole position in all the races. McQuinn was unbeatable despite the fact that the field was the best assembled here in two years. Wally Zale placed second in three of

McQuinn's victories, while Art Hartsfeld finished third twice in fast races. In winning the feature, McQuinn set a track record, beating Zale's 25-lap time of 7:33. McQuinn toured the track in 7:23.6 [*Milwaukee Journal, page 16, July 10, 1936*].

## Harry McQuinn Steals Show at Midget Races

### Riverview Speedway, Chicago, July 12, 1936

Pat Warren won the 30-lap feature over McQuinn [*Salt Lake Tribune, July 13, 1936*].

> "M'QUINN LEADS TROUP INTO S. E.
>
> Harry "Leadfoot" McQuinn holder of four track records and possibly a world's record, namely: Ft. Wayne, Milwaukee, Riverview and the recent St. Louis :15.46 for a fifth-mile, is leading a troupe of a dozen of the best midget racers who have been showing around Chicago, into virgin territory. Pat Warren, Chuck Neisel, Johnny Sawyer, Marshall Lewis, Jimmy Thompson, Al Wainwright, Bill Klein, were all scheduled to leave Sunday nite, July 12th, for Virginia Beach, Va., where a series of midget races will be introduced for the first time under the promotion of Mr. James Brink, connected with a well-known Eastern amusement service.
>
> Meets will be run there every Wednesday and Sunday nites.
>
> Art Hartsfeld, former Toledo motorcycle champ, and of late kingbee with his super-midget 6, is also slated to make his appearance at the Southern track, but a last minute accident to his car will necessitate his delay in starting until his car has been repaired. H. A. Fosdick (father of the electric eye), has supplied the crew with one of his latest timing devices to be used at the meets."
> *National Auto Racing News, page 4, July 16, 1936.*

## Walsh Memorial Stadium, St. Louis, August 4, 1936

Curly Mills set a world speed record in capturing the 20-lap feature in his Black Comet. McQuinn jumped out in the lead early and fought off multiple challenges. Mills was in third and fought his way to the front with five laps to go. Ronney Householder finished second and McQuinn, third [*The Philadelphia Inquirer, page 15, August 5, 1936*].

## Walsh Memorial Stadium, St. Louis, August 11, 1936

McQuinn bested Curly Mills in two 'thrilling' finishes in earlier events. Mills jumped into the lead in the first turn and out distanced his competitors. McQuinn developed engine trouble and dropped out on the fourth lap [*The Philadelphia Inquirer, page 20, August 12, 1936*].

## Walsh Memorial Stadium, St. Louis, September 1, 1936

Bob Swanson started late in the night due to motor troubles. However, when he got underway, Swanson set two records beating the current 20-lap record of 7 minutes and 4.7 seconds by more than 12 seconds. McQuinn won the first event of the night but did not place in the main feature. The night opened in silent tribute to Ray Pixley, midget driver who was recently killed and Curly Mills that was seriously hurt in New York, having re-gained consciousness after several days [*The Philadelphia Inquirer, page 22, September 2, 1936*].

### Harry McQuinn Undaunted by Many Crackups—Stands High In Midwest Racing Association

"Harry McQuinn Undaunted by Many Crackups—Stands High In Midwest Racing Association

Continuing Adding Laurels in Midget Racing "Game"

Undismayed by his many crackups, Harry McQuinn of Indianapolis, formerly of this city, is continually adding to his reputation as a well-known midget race driver.

The son of Mr. and Mrs. Everett McQuinn, of Indianapolis, where he virtually grew up in the shadow of the speedway.

He has been driving for ten years, making his debut at Osgood. It was not until he embarked as a midget driver, however, did "Handsome Harry," as he is affectionately known to his friends come into his own.

He made his third appearance as a driver at the Indianapolis Motor Speedway this year. He has been the victim of a number of accidents, the most serious having occurred at Roby Speedway last year when his car caught fire and he escaped with his life after having been badly burned.

He suffered three other crack-ups in his career, one at Columbus, Ohio, last July when he was dragged 75 feet beneath a car and broke five ribs. He previously had smashed up at Richmond, Indiana, and Louisville. His success as a midget driver is attested by his high point standing in the Midwest Auto Racing Association. He is a tailor, married and has a boy 12 years old.

Included among his achievements is the fact that he holds the lap record at the Cavalier Kennel Club at Virginia Beach, Norfolk, Virginia." *The Franklin Evening Star, page 2, August 10, 1936.*

# NEWS FLASH!

## A SPEED DEMON

**New York, N. Y.** – This picture was taken just before the midget car races were held at Madison Square Garden Bowl, Long Island City, N. Y. The most recent edition in the competition for the championship of the world's midget car racers, is Harry MacQuinn. He has shown the same degree of success as marked his career with big cars. At Indianapolis last year, in the 500 mile race, he ran out of gas within a few hundred feet of the finish line, which would have assured him of at least fifth place in that gruelling contest.

*Unknown newspaper clipping, September 5, 1936.*

## Riverview Speedway, Chicago, September 6, 1936

Shorty Sorenson won the main feature being pushed all the way by Wally Zale. McQuinn returned to the Midwest following his eastern stent. But his No. 4 Elto continued to have motor troubles [*National Auto Racing News, page 5, September 17, 1936*].

## Riverview Speedway, Chicago, September 9, 1936

Marshall Lewis captured the mid-week feature. Jimmy Snyder finished second and McQuinn third [*National Auto Racing News, page 4, September 24, 1936*].

## Terre Haute, September 14, 1936

Harry McQuinn won both the 15-lap and the 25-lap Memorial Sweepstakes. McQuinn started on the pole [*National Auto Racing News, page 2, September 24, 1936*].

## Riverview Speedway, Chicago, September 23, 1936

Art Hartsfeld won the main. Marshall Lewis was able to secure second place. McQuinn continued to have motor troubles and placed in the middle of the pack for most events [*National Auto Racing News, page 8, October 1, 1936*].

## Indiana State Fairgrounds Coliseum, Indianapolis, October 7, 1936

McQuinn winner of the 25-lap main feature [*The Indianapolis Star, page 16, October 8, 1936*].

## Indiana State Fairgrounds Coliseum, Indianapolis, October 14, 1936

Marshall Lewis won the 25-lap feature and sat a new track record, leading all the way. Wally Zale spun while chasing Lewis clipping him but this did not alter his course.

McQuinn hit a straw bale and carried it halfway round the track until it stalled his motor [*National Auto Racing News, page 2, October 22, 1936*].

## Indiana State Fairgrounds Coliseum, Indianapolis, October 21, 1936

Art Hartsfeld won four events including the first preliminary, fourth handicap, the five-lap match race, and the 25-lap main feature. McQuinn won the third race and finished fourth in the main driving James Mannix's mount as his collided with Wally Mitchell and had a bent axle [*The Indianapolis Star, page 18, October 22, 1936; The Indianapolis Star, page 40, October 25, 1936*].

## Indiana State Fairgrounds Coliseum, Indianapolis, October 28, 1936

Art Hartsfeld won the 25-lap feature and a 10-lap preliminary. During the main, McQuinn overturned his car after leading twelve laps but was uninjured. McQuinn did win a preliminary event [*St. Louis Post-Dispatch, page 19, October 28, 1936; The Indianapolis Star, page 16, October 29, 1936*].

## Arena Park Speedway, St. Louis, October 1936 [exact date unknown]

Art Hartsfeld won the main feature. McQuinn during the qualifications suddenly lost control and rolled the car ending up pinned underneath [*National Auto Racing News, page 2, November 5, 1936*].

## 124th Field Artillery Armory, Chicago, November 15, 1936

In the 30-lap main race, Shorty Sorenson, Jimmy Snyder, and Tony Willman placed first, second, and third. McQuinn went out on the 18th lap after hitting a track marker [*Chicago Tribune, page 21, November 16, 1936*].

## Indiana State Fairgrounds Coliseum, Indianapolis, November 18, 1936

"McQuinn, a nationally prominent driver and winner of a twenty-five-lap race at the Coliseum a few weeks ago, will promote future midget events here and consequently will relinquish his mount to another pilot Wednesday" [*Indianapolis Star, page 15, November 16, 1936*].

## 124th Field Artillery Armory, Chicago, November 29, 1936

In a very close finish, Duke Nalon won over McQuinn in the 30-lap main event. Tony Willman was third and Chick Havelin fourth. McQuinn won the second elimination race and a special match race with Jimmy Snyder [*Chicago Tribune, page 18, November 30, 1936*].

## 124th Field Artillery Armory, Chicago, December 6, 1936

Duke Nalon won his third successive 30-lap feature event and went into the lead for the indoor midget auto racing championship. Jimmy Snyder, current indoor champion, was second after passing McQuinn in the 25th lap. McQuinn won the second race and the handicap event by coming from last place. He also won the match race against Jimmy Snyder [*Chicago Tribune, page 24, December 7, 1936*].

## 124th Field Artillery Armory, Chicago, December 13, 1936

Duke Nalon took his fourth straight main feature. Shorty Sorenson came in second then Jimmy Snyder and McQuinn [*National Auto Racing News, page 3, December 17, 1936*].

## 124th Field Artillery Armory, Chicago, December 20, 1936

Shorty Sorenson and McQuinn riding in new Marchese Millers took first and second place in the main feature. Jimmy Snyder was third and Duke Nalon, fourth. McQuinn won the 15-lap handicap and clipped eight seconds from the record for the distance. He also won the first elimination race [*Chicago Tribune, page 23, December 21, 1936*].

## 124th Field Artillery Armory, Chicago, December 27, 1936

"The team of (Shorty) Sorenson and McQuinn got off to a good start. Snyder came up from behind and challenged McQuinn on the 24th lap. The two bumped and locked down the backstretch. Snyder spun but McQuinn was able to hold on. However, Snyder came back challenging Sorenson for the lead. He had crowded Sorenson in a corner thus allowing McQuinn to pass for the lead on the last lap. To most it appeared that McQuinn had won but the official results listed Sorenson as the winner.

After the race, Snyder entered McQuinn's pit and the "fists were flying". Duke Nalon got a monkey wrench to the head while trying to be peacemaker. The Armory's National Guard unit had to intercede as the fights turned into a riot. Snyder was barred from further competition at the Armory until apologies were made." *"The Iron Duke" by George Peters, Bar Jean Enterprises, 2005.*

It was Sorensen's second straight victory in the feature event pushing him into first place in the point standing for the indoor championship. McQuinn won the 15-lap handicap, setting a new record for the distance, clipping five seconds off his own record the previous week.

The racers and the 5,000 spectators stood as "Taps" were played for Curly Mills, who died Tuesday as the result of injuries sustained in a race last August in New York [*Chicago Tribune, page 21, December 28, 1936*].

Harry McQuinn and his Ray Tennes Special, c.1936.
*McQuinn Family records.*

## 1937

### 124th Field Artillery Armory, Chicago, January 3, 1937

McQuinn, Jimmy Snyder, and Art Hartsfeld raced hard for the lead but McQuinn took it in the 5th lap and never gave it up. Snyder finished second and Hartsfeld third in the 30-lap feature. Shorty Sorenson finished fourth. McQuinn placed second to Hartsfeld in the first 12-lap elimination race. McQuinn won the six-lap special match race against Hartsfeld [*Chicago Tribune, page 25, January 4, 1937*].

### 124th Field Artillery Armory, Chicago, January 10, 1937

The feature found McQuinn in the lead at the start. McQuinn had trouble early with a wheel locking but the Marchese Miller gave a sudden jerk that sent the car of Harry Lewis over but landing back on all four tires. He was stunned but otherwise uninjured. Art Hartsfeld stole the lead on the 24th lap and went on to victory. Shorty Sorenson was out of the feature due to a broken rear end, Ted Tetterton froze a piston, and Jimmy Snyder broke a radius rod. McQuinn had also broke a rod in the feature but held on until the 23rd lap when the universal snapped.

McQuinn won the first heat after a terrific battle with Hartsfeld. Tony Willman won the second over Snyder. Paul Russo in Zale's No. 5 Elto won the third heat. McQuinn won the 15-lap handicap as well [*National Auto Racing News, page 2, January 14, 1937*].

### 124th Field Artillery Armory, Chicago, January 17, 1937

The Marchese Twins were at it again. Shorty Sorenson and McQuinn each took a heat race, McQuinn won the handicap, and Sorenson and McQuinn placed one-two in the feature. Sorenson was never challenged for the lead but McQuinn and Jimmy Snyder battled it out for second [*National Auto Racing News, page 3, January 21, 1937*].

## 124th Field Artillery Armory, Chicago, January 24, 1937

A large purse of $1000 in a 100-lap (20 miles) main feature attracted 50 cars to compete for the Central States Auto Racing Championship. Tony Willman took the lead on the 60th lap and never gave it back. The Marchese 'twins' finished 2-3 with Shorty Sorenson in second and McQuinn, third. Marshall Lewis finished fourth and Duke Nalon followed [*Chicago Tribune, page 20, January 25, 1937*].

## 124th Field Artillery Armory, Chicago, January 31, 1937

Art Hartsfeld won the 40-lap feature. Marshall Lewis was second; McQuinn, third; Ray Richards, fourth; Shorty Sorenson; fifth. Driving in a special five car race, Duke Nalon was seriously injured when Hartsfeld crashed into his car during a turn. McQuinn won the third 12-lap elimination race and the 15-lap handicap. He placed second in the Special 10-lap race which was won by Jimmy Snyder [*Chicago Tribune, page 23, February 1, 1937*].

## 124th Field Artillery Armory, Chicago, February 7, 1937

Shorty Sorenson won the 60-lap feature. Art Hartsfeld was second, Paul Russo was third, and McQuinn finished fourth [*Chicago Tribune, page 22, February 8, 1937*].

## 124th Field Artillery Armory, Chicago, February 14, 1937

The 80-lap main event is the third of the series in the progressive competition for the title of Midwest Indoor Champion, the final of which was set for next week. Going into the race, Shorty Sorenson was leading in points.

Jimmy Snyder dominated the field having lapped everyone else. Tony Willman placed second with Paul Russo, Art Hartsfeld, and Emil Andres following in that order [*Chicago Tribune, page 20, February 15, 1937*].

## 124th Field Artillery Armory, Chicago, February 21, 1937

In the first heat, Art Hartsfeld was in the lead from the start and Jimmy Snyder following. Tony Willman went out on the third lap with a malfunctioning gear box. Snyder passed Hartsfeld on the fifth lap when Hartsfeld spun and McQuinn, unable to avoid him, piled into him. Shorty Sorenson couldn't get his No. 5 Marchese Miller to perform and retired for the evening. The second heat saw Ted Tetterton and Wally Zale out to the lead with McQuinn and Hartsfeld following. McQuinn clipped a hay bale spinning out and bending a wheel rim. Tetterton won with Zale second. The third heat saw McQuinn, Hartsfeld, Ray Richards and Emil Andres four abreast fighting for the lead. As it sorted out, Hartsfeld finished first and McQuinn, second.

The 100-lap feature, Marshall Lewis took the lead initially followed by Snyder. Snyder was able to break through taking the lead on the fourth lap. McQuinn was tight on the inside and passed several cars until Zale had blocked his way forward. McQuinn hit a hay bale on the 13th lap and collected Willman causing both to be delayed by a half of a lap. On the 35th lap, Andres and Duke Nalon mixed it up failing back one lap. Snyder and Lewis lapped the field before finishing in this order: Snyder, Lewis, Zale, Hartsfeld, Tetterton, McQuinn, Andres, O'Rourke [*National Auto Racing News, page 3, February 25, 1937*].

## 124th Field Artillery Armory, Chicago, February 28, 1937

Extending his streak to three, Jimmy Snyder again took main feature followed by Tony Willman and McQuinn. Hartsfeld led for the first five laps until McQuinn took over. McQuinn and Snyder collided in the 25th lap allowing Snyder to take the lead and causing McQuinn to fall to third [*Chicago Tribune, page 24, March 1, 1937*].

## 124th Field Artillery Armory, Chicago, March 7, 1937

Shorty Sorenson re-took the championship lead by winning the 30-lap main feature. McQuinn was a close second and Hartsfeld, third [*Chicago Tribune, page 19, March 8, 1937*].

## 124th Field Artillery Armory, Chicago, March 14, 1937

Wally Zale copped the 30-lap feature with Duke Nalon driving Jimmy Snyder's Elto chomping at his heels. This was Zale's second successive win. McQuinn finished third in the feature.

The first heat was won by Zale. The second heat was taken by Paul Russo in Zale's No. 5 with McQuinn second. O'Rourke took the third heat [*Chicago Tribune, page 23, March 15, 1937; National Auto Racing News, page 3, March 18, 1937*].

## 124th Field Artillery Armory, Chicago, March 21, 1937

Wally Zale captured his second in a row. Paul Russo finished second and McQuinn was third. McQuinn won the 15-lap handicap race against Emil Andres and Paul Russo [*Chicago Tribune, page 21, March 22, 1937*].

## 124th Field Artillery Armory, Chicago, March 28, 1937

Another 100-lap feature culminating in the Western Indoor Midget Auto Racing Championship. McQuinn took the lead from the start but was hotly pursued by Jimmy Snyder. Snyder's engine failed on the 65th lap dropping him out. Shorty Sorenson was second, Art Hartsfeld third and Duke Nalon fourth [*Chicago Tribune, page 21, March 29, 1937*].

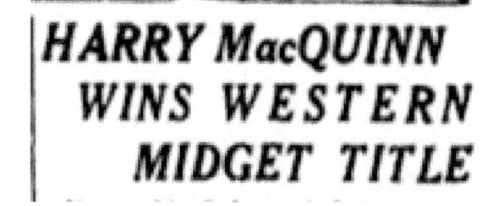

**HARRY MacQUINN WINS WESTERN MIDGET TITLE**

## Indiana State Fairgrounds Coliseum, Indianapolis, March 31, 1937

This was the last program of midget auto races to decide the championship for the winter season to be held at the Indiana Fairgrounds Coliseum. Coming into the race, Harry McQuinn was first in the standings with Shorty Sorenson second.

Wally Zale took the lead early and set the pace easily. However, his car suffered mechanical troubles and he dropped out. Snyder finished closely behind McQuinn and Art Hartsfeld took third. McQuinn was crowned the Indiana Fairgrounds Coliseum Track Champion [*The Indianapolis Star, page 19, April 1, 1937*].

## 124th Field Artillery Armory, Chicago, April 4, 1937

Shorty Sorenson outpaced McQuinn by two car lengths to win the first of series of 50 lap preliminary events for the National Indoor Midget Auto Racing Championship. Paul Russo was third with fourth occupied by Tony Willman and fifth place went to Duke Nalon. Wally Zale, Jimmy Snyder, McQuinn and Harold Shaw won each of their 12 lap elimination events. McQuinn also won the 15-lap handicap [*Chicago Tribune, page 22, April 5, 1937*].

## 124th Field Artillery Armory, Chicago, April 11, 1937

Snyder won in a spectacular finish over Ted Tetterton. Duke Nalon, Paul Russo, Wally Zale, and McQuinn finished in third, fourth, fifth, and sixth respectively [*Chicago Tribune, page 21, April 12, 1967*].

## 124th Field Artillery Armory, Chicago, April 18, 1937

McQuinn led from the start and took the 50-lap feature over Shorty Sorenson. McQuinn set a new one-lap track record during the feature. McQuinn won the first elimination race [*Chicago Tribune, page 22, April 19, 1937*].

## 124th Field Artillery Armory, Chicago, April 25, 1937

Duke Nalon won the fourth of the 50-lap races that lead to the crowning of the indoor title. Jimmy Snyder was second and McQuinn, third [*Chicago Tribune, page 20, April 26, 1937*].

## 124th Field Artillery Armory, Chicago, May 2, 1937

"For the final evening of the indoor track season, the track was coated and rolled in clay. This was said to have elongated the track an additional 120 feet but it was considerably faster. Harry McQuinn established a new track record of 13.8 seconds. After qualifying, soft spots developed in the clay which were rolled out again. Well into the feature, huge holes opened up. The outlying straw bales were moved inwards to cover the holes. This occurred several times and shortened the track considerably such that laps were completed in 9 seconds." *From: "The Iron Duke: The Illustrious Racing Career of Duke Nalon, 1934-1954" by George Peters; Bar Jean Enterprises; 2005.*

The 1936-1937 season finale consisted of a 100-lap feature. Despite McQuinn's track record being disallowed due to moving of the hay bales, he remained the fastest of the night winning the feature. McQuinn won the first elimination race as well. For the season, Shorty Sorenson won the overall season title [*Chicago Tribune, page 18, May 3, 1937*].

**MacQUINN WINS NATIONAL INDOOR AUTO RACE TITLE**

> "Shorty Sorenson was one of the famed and feared Marchese Miller Team drivers along with Harry McQuinn. "Shorty Sorenson finally bulled his way to the Chicago Armory championship beating his Marchese Miller teammate, Harry McQuinn. Sorenson, as broad as he was tall, was rough and ruthless and although he didn't possess the finesse of McQuinn he did drive to win and to survive. Sorenson and McQuinn with their little white cars were feared from coast to coast." *The Mighty Midgets* by Jack C. Fox, Carl Hungness Publishing, Speedway IN, 1985.

## Highland Park Stadium, Minneapolis, June 9, 1937

Opening night of the midget races at Highland Park which was a 1/5-mile dirt oval located in Minneapolis. Wally Zale won the 20-lap feature with Ronney Householder, second, and McQuinn, third. Zale and Perry Grimm won the elimination events. McQuinn won the novelty event against Householder [*The Minneapolis Star, page 21, June 10, 1937*].

## Wisconsin State Fair Park, Milwaukee, June 10, 1937

Sorenson won and McQuinn second in the feature event [*Green Bay Press-Gazette, page 19, June 11, 1937*].

## Highland Park Stadium, Minneapolis, June 17, 1937

Shorty Sorenson set a new one-lap track record and took the 30-lap main feature. McQuinn took second place. In the first elimination race, McQuinn bested his teammate Sorenson. Sorenson won the fourth race [*Star Tribune, page 26, June 18, 1937*].

## Highland Park Stadium, Minneapolis, June 23, 1937

Several drivers had mechanical trouble but this did not plague McQuinn. McQuinn won the feature in a "spectacular feature race" passing Art Hartsfeld after a jarring leap had 'upset' his motor. Shorty Sorenson took second [*Star Tribune, page 19, June 24, 1937*].

## Riverview Speedway, Chicago, June 27, 1937

Wally Zale, central states champion, won the 40-lap final leading his nearest competitor, Ted Tetterton, by half a lap. Harry McQuinn won the second 12-lap elimination race. McQuinn placed second in the 15-lap handicap and third in 40-lap feature [*Chicago Tribune, page 17, June 28, 1937*].

## Highland Park Stadium, Minneapolis, June 30, 1937

McQuinn took three first place finishes including the main feature in which he also broke the track record by several seconds [*The Minneapolis Star, page 20, July 1, 1937*].

## Wisconsin State Fair Park, Milwaukee, July 1, 1937

Sorenson won the 30-lap feature with McQuinn a close second [*Green Bay Press-Gazette, page 16, July 2, 1937*].

## Highland Park Stadium, Minneapolis, July 7, 1937

Wally Zale dominated the evening with four first-place finishes including a six-lap match race with McQuinn [*Star Tribune, page 17, July 8, 1937*].

## Wisconsin State Fair Park, Milwaukee, July 15, 1937

McQuinn won one of the 10-lap elimination races and the 30-lap final [*Green Bay Press-Gazette, page 19, July 16, 1937*].

### Lake Front Speedway, Milwaukee, July 18, 1937

This is a 1/5-mile dirt oval near downtown Milwaukee. McQuinn won three events including the 15-lap feature [*Green Bay Press-Gazette, page 13, July 19, 1937*].

### Highland Park Stadium, Minneapolis, July 21, 1937

Wally Zale won the 30-lap feature. McQuinn won a special match race with Zale following the feature [*The Minneapolis Star, page 17, July 22, 1937*].

### Wisconsin State Fair Park, Milwaukee, September 1937

The "Marchese Twins" of Shorty Sorenson and McQuinn were dominant at this event. Shorty won the first heat, the pursuit race and the 25-lap feature. McQuinn placed second to Shorty in the first event and the feature [*National Auto Racing News, page 2, September 9, 1937*].

### Grundy County Fairgrounds, Mazon IL, September 5, 1937

Shorty Sorenson, McQuinn and Wally Zale continued their hub-rubbing duels. Sorenson was able to be the victor [*National Auto Racing News, page 12, August 29, 1940*].

# The "Mighty" Midgets

"Midget Cars Thrill Fair Crowds

The boys won all of the races in the county fair and have been turning in record time in appearances coast to coast. From left to right in the top picture are driver Shorty Sorenson of Evanston, Ill., Tudy Marchese of Milwaukee, Wis., Carl Marchese and driver Harry McQuinn of Indianapolis *(picture not available)*.

The history of the midget racers the Marchese brothers had at the fair is an interesting story of how to make a business of public thrills. Carl Marchese, one of the brothers owning the two midgets, drove the Miller motor which was divided in half for the small cars, in the 500 mile Indianapolis classic in 1929 and finished fourth. The motor was then a straight eight in two four cylinder units and cost $4500. This motor, after rebuilding, made the power units for both the cars driven here and the Marchese brothers made the transformation. The cars are valued more by the money they make than by actual mechanical worth. There is quite an expense to racing. Motors are kept in best condition, tires, gas, oil, and traveling expenses all count up. Both Marchese racers are under midget specifications. They have only 85 cubic inches of piston displacement, the limit is 100 cubic inches. The motors have a 2½ inch piston with a stroke of 3½ inches and they sure can go.

Both Marchese cars were built for indoor racing but as the drive shaft runs down the outside of the chassis, the gears are changed for outside tracks. Number 5 car holds the midwestern indoor championship with Shorty Sorenson driving. Car number 4 (Harry McQuinn) holds the national indoor championship for 1937 won at Chicago. Championship standings are arrived at by car point standings in competition. Number 4 car is chain driven from the motor to the drive shaft but number 5 is gear driven—both cars have bevel gears on the rear axle. Number 4 car qualified on opening day of fair with time of 16.34 seconds – plenty fast for any human." *Sioux County Capital, page 7, September 2, 1937.*

## Grundy County Fairgrounds, Mazon IL, September 6, 1937

Shorty Soren and McQuinn, the "Marchese duo" battled Wally Zale the entire distance but Zale was able to capture the feature [*National Auto Racing News, page 12, August 29, 1940*].

## Gilmore Stadium, Los Angeles, September 30, 1937

Shorty Sorenson and Harry McQuinn, the Marchese 'twins', driving the Marchese brothers' cars that housed Miller engines suddenly appeared at the Gilmore track. These two midwestern midgeteers were a mighty team and banned from several tracks due to their team tactics. The 'twins' were not prepared for the first race having to make several mechanical adjustments to fit the track. Despite this, Sorenson did place third in the feature. Ronney Householder, the east champion and odds on favorite blew an engine while leading and Sam Hanks also went out due mechanical failure [*Los Angeles Times, page 36, October 7, 1937*].

> "Race Drivers Make Debut
>
> Two Indianapolis race drivers who have never appeared on the western speedways make their debut at Gilmore Stadium Thursday night. This was revealed yesterday with the announcement that Shorty Sorenson and Harry McQuinn, a midwestern team of rough and ready aces, are present to challenge the supremacy of mighty midget row.
>
> Sorenson and McQuinn have been barred at a number of eastern speedways for their racing tactics. These two boys race as a team. They attack the field in a united pair and suck one driver after another into the rear. A great hue and cry has gone up wherever they have raced, and the Coast racing veterans want to see what the speedy Miller Specials can do against their first cousin, the Offenhauser-powered bugs.

> The Marchese team will find a pair of teams in the local night speedway field which may get together in a grand high-speed team battle. Bob Swanson and Mel Hansen drive a pair of fast Tommy Lee cars and Gordon Cleveland and Louie Foy work for the Arnold brothers, who are looking forward to locking hubcaps with the Marchese clan." *The Los Angeles Times, page 20, October 3, 1937.*

## Gilmore Stadium, Los Angeles, October 7, 1937

Ronney Householder, the favored at the local track, told the Marchese 'twins' of Shorty Sorenson and Harry McQuinn that he would not race stating "I came to the Coast to get away from you fellows."

## Atlantic Boulevard Stadium, Los Angeles, October 19, 1937

Fog-shortened race won by Karl Young with McQuinn second [*The Los Angeles Times, page 35, October 20, 1937*].

> "MIDGET RACING FEUD CONTINUES THURSDAY
>
> LOS ANGELES — Resuming a bitter speed feud which started on the eastern and midwestern tracks, Ronney Householder, the eastern champion, lays his plans to make "chumps" out of Shorty Sorenson and Harry McQuinn this Thursday night in the midget racing picture at Gilmore Stadium. These three hot shots, right from the east, have blossomed into the Pacific Coast limelight shoving Karl Young, Bob Swanson, Sam Hanks, et al into the shadows.
>
> Householder told friends after his reappearance at Gilmore last week's program that he came to the coast first to get rid of the team tactics of Sorenson and McQuinn, drivers of the two Marchese Millers.

> Reports followed him that the three tangled many times and that ill feeling developed so far as to bar the Marchese "twins" off several midwestern nightways. They were charged with rough team tactics on the short track.
>
> However, Householder, by coming west, has just increased his competition. He not only has 13 Offenhauser powered mighty midgets to meet in this week's 50 lap main event, but he has Sorenson and McQuinn to face once again." *Corona Daily Independent, October 4, 1937.*

## Gilmore Stadium, Los Angeles, October 21, 1937

Third week featuring a 75-lap main event consisting of 12 cars and carries the largest point value for the Pacific Coast Championship. Most were powered by Offenhauser engines. But, Shorty Sorenson and Harry McQuinn driving 4-cylinder Miller motors. These motors are twin halves of an 8-cylinder Miller that raced at Indianapolis. The Marchese 'twins' were going up against Ronney Householder whom they raced against in the Midwest and Sam Hanks [*Van Nuys News, page 8, October 21, 1937*].

Qualifications were held and McQuinn was three hundredths faster than the rest of the field and was to take the pole. A fog rolled in and canceled the races for the following week.

## Houston Speed Bowl, Houston, November, 1937

"National Auto Racing News (NARN) reported that 'the first midget ever to run in the state of Texas' was held at Houston Speedway. The speedway would be part of a southwestern midget circuit. The November 18th issue of the NARN stated that 'The Houston Speedway continues to be the eighth wonder of the world, with the populace going gaga over the miniatures and packing the stands at the twice-a-week races.' Frankie Beeder and Harry McQuinn won the 20-lap features that week." http://www.texasopenwheel.com/index.php?showtopic=179

## Houston Speed Bowl, Houston, November 28, 1937

"In the 25-lap feature, fast qualifier Harry McQuinn led all the way around followed by Sorenson and Morrissey. Wally Zale and Frankie Beeder "staged the greatest knock'em down and drag'em out contest ever seen on a midget track" until the 13th lap when Zale put Beeder out of commission." http://www.texasopenwheel.com/index.php?showtopic=179

## 124th Field Artillery Armory, Chicago, December 12, 1937

The first 100-lap feature of the season at the Armory was won by Jimmy Snyder in a close finish beating out McQuinn. Marshall Lewis was third with Shorty Sorenson, fourth and Tony Willman, fifth.

"Snyder drove what many regarded as the most sensational race in armory history. He passed the leader, Lewis, on the 68th lap and then regained the lead from McQuinn on the 87th lap after McQuinn went ahead on the 86th circuit. Several cars burned up during the race, but the drivers escaped injury" [*Southtown Economist, page 17, December 16, 1937*].

## 124th Field Artillery Armory, Chicago, December 19, 1937

Harry McQuinn winner of the 30-lap feature leading start to finish. Art Hartsfeld and Jimmy Snyder finished second and third. Duke Nalon was shaken up when he was pinned underneath his car during one of the elimination races [*Chicago Tribune, page 19, December 20, 1937*].

## 124th Field Artillery Armory, Chicago, December 26, 1937

McQuinn won the 100-lap feature in his No. 4 Marchese Miller by a lap and a half in front of the nearest driver. Shorty Sorenson got out to an early lead followed by McQuinn and Duke Nalon. Sorenson spun out on the 24th lap putting McQuinn in the lead. Jimmy Snyder went out early due to a broken axle. At 50 laps, McQuinn had lapped the field followed by Nalon second. The positions remained the same afterwards except that Sorenson had been burning up the track himself and captured fourth.

The first heat was won by McQuinn followed by his teammate, Sorenson; Paul Russo was third. Duke Nalon hit a bale of hay and was delayed. Tony Willman clipped another bale on the 5th lap and Marshall Lewis went over Willman in the process. The second heat found Nalon the winner. The third heat was won by Lewis but Wally Zale went out by motor trouble. The 15-lap handicap showed the greatest battle. Myron Fohr and Wally Zale were started up front and Sorenson and McQuinn were in the back row. Snyder shot out to third from the middle of the pack in the first lap and by the third lap, was trying to take the lead from Zale. McQuinn had made its way up third on Snyder's tail. On the fifth lap, McQuinn and Snyder tangled and spun losing ground. The finishing order was Snyder, Sorenson and Zale [*National Auto Racing News, page 2, January 6, 1938*].

Harry McQuinn at Gilmore Stadium, c.1937.
*From Bruce R. Craig Photograph Collection, reprinted with permission from Revs Institute.*

Shorty Sorenson and Harry McQuinn walking the Gilmore Track, Los Angeles. *From Bruce R. Craig Photograph Collection, reprinted with permission from Revs Institute.*

The Marchese 'twins' of Shorty Sorenson (left) and Harry McQuinn (right) in Los Angeles, 1937. *McQuinn Family records.*

# HARRY MCQUINN

Harry McQuinn on the outside and Marshall Lewis.
*From Bruce R. Craig Photograph Collection, reprinted with permission from Revs Institute.*

Harry McQuinn ready for the start, c.1937.
*From Bruce R. Craig Photograph Collection, reprinted with permission from Revs Institute.*

Harry McQuinn (standing) talking with Shorty Sorenson in Los Angeles. *From Bruce R. Craig Photograph Collection, reprinted with permission from Revs Institute.*

Harry McQuinn on the outside first row at the start of a race at the Gilmore track, c.1937. *Available from the Indiana Memory Digital Library.* http://indiamond6.ulib.iupui.edu/cdm/ref/collection/IMS/id/12642

Publicity photos taken at Gilmore Stadium, Los Angeles, demonstrating broadsliding. *McQuinn is in the No. 4 with his teammate Shorty Sorenson in the No. 5. November, 1937. McQuinn Family records.*

Sam Hanks, Shorty Sorenson, and Harry McQuinn at Gilmore Stadium, c.1937. *From Bruce R. Craig Photograph Collection, reprinted with permission from Revs Institute.*

Shorty Sorenson and Harry McQuinn, Gilmore Stadium, c.1937. *From Bruce R. Craig Photograph Collection, reprinted with permission from Revs Institute.*

Shorty Sorenson (left) and Harry McQuinn (right) in St. Paul, MN, c.1937. *McQuinn Family records.*

Demonstration of 'broadsliding' at Gilmore Stadium in Los Angeles, c.1937. *McQuinn Family records.*

Harry McQuinn out in Los Angeles, perhaps at the
Gilmore Stadium, Los Angeles, c.1937.
*From Bruce R. Craig Photograph Collection, reprinted
with permission from Revs Institute.*

## 1938

## 124th Field Artillery Armory, Chicago, January 2, 1938

Cowboy O'Rourke won the 50-lap main event. O'Rourke started in third tailing McQuinn until the 6th lap and moved up to second behind Shorty Sorenson. On the 15th lap, O'Rourke got the upper hand and took the lead and was never headed. They finished in that order: O'Rourke, Sorenson, and McQuinn.

In the first elimination heat, Sorenson and Jimmy Snyder led the field out. The two tangled in the first turn sending Snyder into the wall. Snyder had suffered a broken upper jaw and lost several teeth. McQuinn went on to win the first heat; Duke Nalon won the second; Bill Shindler, third; Ted Duncan, fourth [*National Auto Racing News, page 2, January 6, 1938*].

## 124th Field Artillery Armory, Chicago, January 9, 1938

Art Hartsfeld won the 40-lap main race driving his No. 6 Elto. Shorty Sorenson started on pole with Hartsfeld on the outside of the first row. Hartsfeld, the "Toledo flash", dove into the inside on the first lap and stole the lead from Shorty and held it to the finish. McQuinn's No. 4 Marchese Miller was not up to snuff for the evening and he drove the No. 7 Finkel Special, the car usually driven by Jimmy Snyder, out from the previous week.

The first heat was taken by Sorenson. Johnny Ritter captured the second heat; Cowboy O'Rourke the third [*National Auto Racing News, page 2, January 13, 1938*].

## 124th Field Artillery Armory, Chicago, January 16, 1938

Duke Nalon trailing Art Hartsfeld for 79 laps, overtook the lead and went on to the win. McQuinn came in third. The first heat was won by Hartsfeld; the second by Shorty Sorenson; the third by Emil Andres; and Myron Fohr for the fourth [*National Auto Racing News, page 2, January 20, 1938*].

## 124th Field Artillery Armory, Chicago, January 23, 1938

Art Hartsfeld won the 25-lap main event and the first feature, setting a new track record. In a special match race, Cowboy O'Rourke won against Duke Nalon, crossing the finish line upside down and in so doing, set a new track record. The first heat was won by Hartsfeld followed by Shorty Sorenson and McQuinn. Nalon captured the second heat and O'Rourke the third. McQuinn placed fourth in the feature moving him into second place in the overall standings [*Chicago Tribune, page 20, January 24, 1938; National Auto Racing News, page 3, January 27, 1938*].

## 124th Field Artillery Armory, Chicago, January 30, 1938

Harry Lewis and Duke Nalon started on the first row of the feature. Lewis jumped out into the lead over Nalon but the two raced elbow to elbow but Lewis had the lead and the win. The Marchese twins, Shorty Sorenson and McQuinn, were not racing as the cars were stuck in Milwaukee and could not make it in time to Chicago due to impassable roads [*National Auto Racing News, page 3, February 3, 1938*].

## 124th Field Artillery Armory, Chicago, February 6, 1938

Art Hartsfeld again captured the Armory 25-lap main. Shorty Sorenson and Cowboy O'Rourke were in a ragged dog-fight for second but Sorenson was "top dog". McQuinn and Duke Nalon tangled and eliminated each other.

The first heat was won by Hartsfeld, Tetterton second, and McQuinn, back in the No. 4 Marchese, took the third heat. Ray Richards won the fourth [*National Auto Racing News, page 2, February 10, 1938*].

## 124th Field Artillery Armory, Chicago, February 13, 1938

Duke Nalon followed the Marchese twins of Shorty Sorenson and McQuinn. McQuinn having the lead, collided with Sorenson on the 90th lap and were effectively eliminated.

Nalon himself was the victim of a harrowing accident earlier but was uninjured and took several crew to put the car in functioning order. It worked well enough to take over the lead in the feature and carry Nalon to victory.

The first event was carried off by McQuinn. The Cowboy O'Rourke won the second. Myron Fohr won the third [*National Auto Racing News, page 2, February 17, 1938*].

## 124th Field Artillery Armory, Chicago, February 20, 1938

Wally Zale, still driving the No. 7 Elto of Jimmy Snyder, won the 25-lap feature. Zale took the lead on the 15th lap and held on from there. The order was: Zale; Emil Andres; Shorty Sorenson; Marshall Lewis; McQuinn. McQuinn won the "popularity race" involving Zale, Nalon and O'Rourke [*National Auto Racing News, page 2, March 3, 1938*].

## 124th Field Artillery Armory, Chicago, February 27, 1938

Wally Zale won the second main feature in a row. Zale led the field in the feature followed by Shorty Sorenson and Art Hartsfeld. The second lap had a pile up in the turn involving McQuinn, Duke Nalon, Marshall Lewis, Emil Andres, Ted Duncan, and Tony Willman. McQuinn continued on but had difficulty controlling the car and pulled off at the 18th lap with faulty steering.

Zale also won the first feature with McQuinn, Lewis Marshall, and O'Rourke also heat winners [*National Auto Racing News, page 2, March 3, 1938*].

## 124th Field Artillery Armory, Chicago, March 6, 1938

"Leadfoot" McQuinn started in 3rd for the 100-lap feature. He secured second on the 2nd lap and chased Art Hartsfeld riding in first. Hartsfeld had to retire on the 49th lap due to a clutch problem. McQuinn took over the lead followed by Duke Nalon. The Duke started to gain ground on McQuinn and was on his tail by the 88th lap. Nalon's pursuit helped drive McQuinn to set a new track record besting his old mark by half of a minute [*National Auto Racing News, page 2, March 10, 1938*].

## 124th Field Artillery Armory, Chicago, March 20, 1938

Another 100-lap feature at the Armory but "no less than 20 doodles crashed." Art Hartsfeld and McQuinn led off the others for the feature. Hartsfeld took the lead and stretched the distance. Shorty Sorenson, Wally Zale and Duke Nalon mixed it up on the 10th lap losing ground. Sorenson made up the distance so that by 50 laps, Sorenson was third behind the leader Hartsfeld and McQuinn. The leaders passed Ted Tetterton but Sorenson and Tetterton entangled and pursued to reconcile their differences with fisticuffs. This distracted much of the crowd while Art Hartsfeld crossed the finish line followed by McQuinn.

In the first event, Ted Duncan led the field. In the 4th lap, Myron Fohr stalled in the turn and Wally Zale following closely braked hard but McQuinn did not react quickly enough and plowed into Zale. Both drivers and cars were okay. In the second heat, Tony Bettenhausen started off followed by Emil Andres. Duke Nalon, Ted Tetterton and McQuinn were fighting it out mid pack and when Andres hit a hay bale, all three smacked into Andres. Hartsfeld and Zale managed to avoid the entangled mess and Hartsfeld caught up to and passed Bettenhausen for the heat win. The third heat, Marshall Lewis shot out in the lead with Ray Richards hot on his tail. McQuinn, Nalon, Tetterton, and Andres ended up in another pile on the 5th lap. The fourth heat was uneventful with McQuinn winning [*National Auto Racing News, page 2, March 24, 1938*].

## 124th Field Artillery Armory, Chicago, April 3, 1938

McQuinn in his No. 4 Marchese Miller won the 100-lap feature at the Armory lapping the entire field except Marshall Lewis. Jimmy Snyder returned recovered from his injuries. McQuinn, Snyder and Marshall Lewis were tight for 13 laps when Snyder lost ground and eventually had to pull out on the 26th lap due to ignition issues [*National Auto Racing News, page 2, April 7, 1938*].

## 124th Field Artillery Armory, Chicago, April 10, 1938

McQuinn led the point standings for the Midwest Indoor Automobile Racing Championship with Marshall Lewis only able to challenge him [*Chicago Tribune, page 4, April 10, 1938*].

## 124th Field Artillery Armory, Chicago, April 17, 1938

McQuinn won the second consecutive 100-lap feature and secured the lead in the points standing by about 200 points. McQuinn took the lead followed by Ted Duncan. McQuinn led all laps. Marshall Lewis finished in second.

In the first heat, Emil Andres grabbed the lead from the start but was passed by Lewis on the 9th lap. McQuinn and Andres then traded positions back and forth jockeying for second place. After the race, McQuinn came over to Andres and said something and walked away. However, this was taken as inflammatory by the observing pit crews and the two pit crews got into it. The fight was broken up then broke out again. It was reported that McQuinn and Andres walked away arm in arm laughing [*National Auto Racing News, page 3, April 21, 1938*].

## 124th Field Artillery Armory, Chicago, May 1, 1938

McQuinn won his third consecutive 100-lap feature and secured the 1937-'38 Midwest Indoor Auto Racing Championship. Marshall Lewis was runner up to McQuinn for the season title. The next three places went to Duke Nalon, Art Hartsfeld, and Shorty Sorenson, in that order. Sorenson had won the title last year [*Chicago Tribune, page 22, May 2, 1938*].

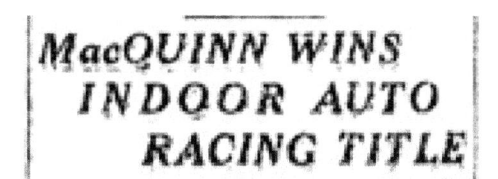

> MacQUINN WINS
> INDOOR AUTO
> RACING TITLE

> "The Midget era started at Ord in 1938 and ran off and on at Ord through 1956. That first year of Midget racing saw both day races dominated by Nineveh, Ind., native Harry McQuinn. McQuinn defeated a strong field of drivers including Carl Forberg, Danny Oakes, Eddie Kracek and others. Of course, 1938 just happened to be the year McQuinn scored an amazing 61 features wins in a Midget." http://www.midwestracingarchives.com/2011_12_01_archive.html

## Walsh Memorial Stadium, St. Louis, May 10, 1938

Walsh Stadium resumed after two years and was widened from 27 feet to 35. McQuinn started on pole and was able to fend off all contenders winning the 30-lap main event. Neilson and Saegesser collided during the second elimination race sending Neilson bounding over and over eventually pinning him underneath [*The St. Louis Star and Times, page 19, May 10, 1938*].

## Riverview Speedway, Chicago, June 5, 1938

McQuinn, driving for Marchese Brothers of Milwaukee, won the 40-lap feature. Ray Richards was second; Ted Tetterton, third. McQuinn also won the first handicap and the third qualifying races [*The Milwaukee Journal, page 10, June 6, 1938*].

## Riverview Speedway, Chicago, June 8, 1938

McQuinn won his second 40-lap feature at Riverview. Ted Duncan was second by two car lengths. Ted Tetterton was third [*Chicago Tribune, page 24, June 9, 1938*].

## Walsh Memorial Stadium, St. Louis, June 14, 1938

McQuinn won the 30-lap feature and one of the preliminaries. Shorty Sorenson came in second place and Jimmy Snyder finished in third place [*St. Louis Post-Dispatch, page 14, June 15, 1938*].

### Wisconsin State Fair Park, Milwaukee, June 15, 1938

Wally Zale capture the 40-lap main feature. McQuinn was second, and Ted Duncan, third [*Oshkosh Daily Northwestern, page 13, July 16, 1938*].

### Riverview Speedway, Chicago, June 19, 1938

Wally Zale and McQuinn battled for the lead ultimately pushing Zale to set a new track record in his win of the 40-lap main feature [*National Auto Racing News, page 3, June 23, 1938*].

### Walsh Memorial Stadium, St. Louis, June 21, 1938

Winning his fourth race of the season, McQuinn took the 40-lap feature. He had also set another one-lap track record [*St. Louis Star and Times, page 22, June 22, 1938*].

### Wisconsin State Fair Park, Milwaukee, June 24, 1938

McQuinn won the 50-lap feature and set a new track record. McQuinn led the entire way in the feature. McQuinn also won a special match event against Jimmy Snyder but Snyder won against McQuinn in another [*National Auto Racing News, June 30, 1938*].

### Riverview Speedway, Chicago, June 26, 1938

Jimmy Snyder won the 40-lap feature defeating McQuinn by a narrow margin. Snyder also defeated McQuinn narrowly in the first elimination race but lost to McQuinn in the eight-lap handicap [*Chicago Tribune, page 19, June 27, 1938*].

## Walsh Memorial Stadium, St. Louis, June 28, 1938

McQuinn won his fifth victory in seven scoring another 30-lap feature of the weekly midget races at the Walsh Stadium. Jimmy Snyder, second; Ted Duncan, third; Marshall Lewis, fourth [*St. Louis Post-Dispatch, page 16, June 29, 1938*].

## Riverview Speedway, Chicago, July 3, 1938

Jimmy Snyder secured the first heat and the main event. The finish had Ted Duncan and McQuinn mere inches behind as Snyder passed the finishline. The second heat was taken by McQuinn [*National Auto Racing News, page 2, July 7, 1938*].

## Walsh Memorial Stadium, St. Louis, July 5, 1938

McQuinn had tire trouble in the feature and Snyder had an easy victory [*National Auto Racing News, page 5, July 14, 1938*].

## Wisconsin State Fair Park, Milwaukee, July 8, 1938

McQuinn was able to win the 50-lap feature for the second consecutive week with Ted Duncan following all the way. Tony Willman won the first heat and three match races and was the driver to beat but the motor quit causing him to retire for the night [*National Auto Racing News, page 5, July 14, 1938*].

## Riverview Speedway, Chicago, July 10, 1938

Tony Willman chased McQuinn in the main feature pushing him to the win. Willman did get off to the lead but McQuinn squeezed through on the second lap. Willman won the first heat over McQuinn. Duke Nalon won the second heat. McQuinn won the 8-lap handicap [*National Auto Racing News, page 3, July 14, 1938*].

## Walsh Memorial Stadium, St. Louis, July 12, 1938

McQuinn won the 50-lap feature event when Tony Willman was injured after setting a fast pace early in the race. Willman was injured in the eleventh lap. The car of Clint Rose struck the east wall bounding back onto the track, and into the way of Willman's car, which in turn hit against the wall and then rolled over three times. Willman suffered numerous cuts and bruises and a broken rib. Ted Duncan was second in the with Marshall Lewis, third [*St. Louis Dispatch, page 14, July 13, 1938*].

## Riverview Speedway, Chicago, July 17, 1938

In his 19th feature win of the season, McQuinn takes the feature. Wally Zale and Myron Fohr gave the crowd a thrill battling for second. The first heat was won by McQuinn, the second by Bob Muhlke, third by Pete Romcevich, and the fourth by Ted Tetterton [*National Auto Racing News, page 2, July 21, 1938*].

## Wisconsin State Fair Park, Milwaukee, July 15, 1938

Zale won the 40-lap feature with McQuinn and Ted Duncan trailing [*Green Bay Press-Gazette, page 15, July 16, 1938*].

## Walsh Memorial Stadium, St. Louis, July 19, 1938

McQuinn of Indianapolis scored his seventh win with his winning of the 40-lap main event. Ted Duncan was second, and Johnny Rogan, third. McQuinn also won a preliminary of 10 laps in which 21 drivers competed. Tony Willman took the first 10-lap preliminary but motor trouble forced him out of the feature [*St. Louis Dispatch, page 12, July 20, 1938*].

## Wisconsin State Fair Park, Milwaukee, July 21, 1938

The 40-lap feature was won by Wally Zale. Tony Willman was on pole with Zale on the outside. Willman's car jumped out of gear allowing Zale to surpass him. McQuinn moved up to second but could not overtake Zale for the win [*National Auto Racing News, page 5, July 21, 1938*].

## Riverview Speedway, Chicago, July 24, 1938

McQuinn wins his third feature in a row. He crossed the finish line two lengths ahead of Ray Richards [*Chicago Tribune, page 16, July 25, 1938*].

## Walsh Memorial Stadium, St. Louis, July 26, 1938

McQuinn extended his winning ways with victory in the 50-lap feature; Paul Russo, second; Marshall Lewis, third. Mack McCoy and Ben Chesney, local drivers, gave the crowd most of its thrills when their wheels locked and McCoy's car turned over several times. McCoy suffered head, shoulder and back bruises in the accident [*St. Louis Post-Dispatch, page 15, July 27, 1938*].

## Riverview Speedway, Chicago, July 31, 1938

Ted Duncan broke McQuinn's winning streak at this track. Duncan leading all the way finished a half-lap ahead of the nearest competitor. McQuinn's No. 4 Marchese Miller suffered a broken rod necessitating McQuinn take over the Podzernik Miller. In the second heat, in inverted order, saw McQuinn, Marshall Lewis and Ray Richards battling it out to the delight of the crowd. However, Marshall Lewis prevailed with Richards second and McQuinn third [*National Auto Racing News, page 2, August 4, 1938*].

## Walsh Memorial Stadium, St. Louis, August 2, 1938

With eight feature wins at Walsh Stadium, McQuinn was favored to win. McQuinn's No. 4 Marchese Miller was in for repairs so he was driving Jimmy Snyder's 7-Up Elto Special. He led nearly 60 laps but was then passed by Ted Duncan driving in a new Miller. Wally Zale then overtook McQuinn and later Duncan to secure the win [*National Auto Racing News, page 2, August 11, 1938*].

## Riverview Speedway, Chicago, August 7, 1938

Wally Zale and Ted Duncan gave the crowd a thrill battling like gladiators for second as McQuinn dominated the 40-lap feature. The second heat of the night saw McQuinn and Myron Fohr within a few feet of each other throughout the race but Fohr had the inside and never gave up the lead [*National Auto Racing News, page 2, August 11, 1938*].

## Walsh Memorial Stadium, St. Louis, August 9, 1938

McQuinn won his ninth feature at Walsh out of 13 runnings for the season. McQuinn was the fastest in qualifications and therefore sat on pole for the feature [*National Auto Racing News, page 2, August 18, 1938*].

## Cahokia (IL) Midget Speedway, August 10, 1938

Cahokia was a former dog track turned into a banked quarter-mile track. This was the inaugural race. McQuinn won the 30-lap feature followed by Ted Duncan and Duke Nalon [*The St. Louis Star and Times, page 20, August 11, 1938; St. Louis Post-Dispatch, page 10, August 14, 1938*].

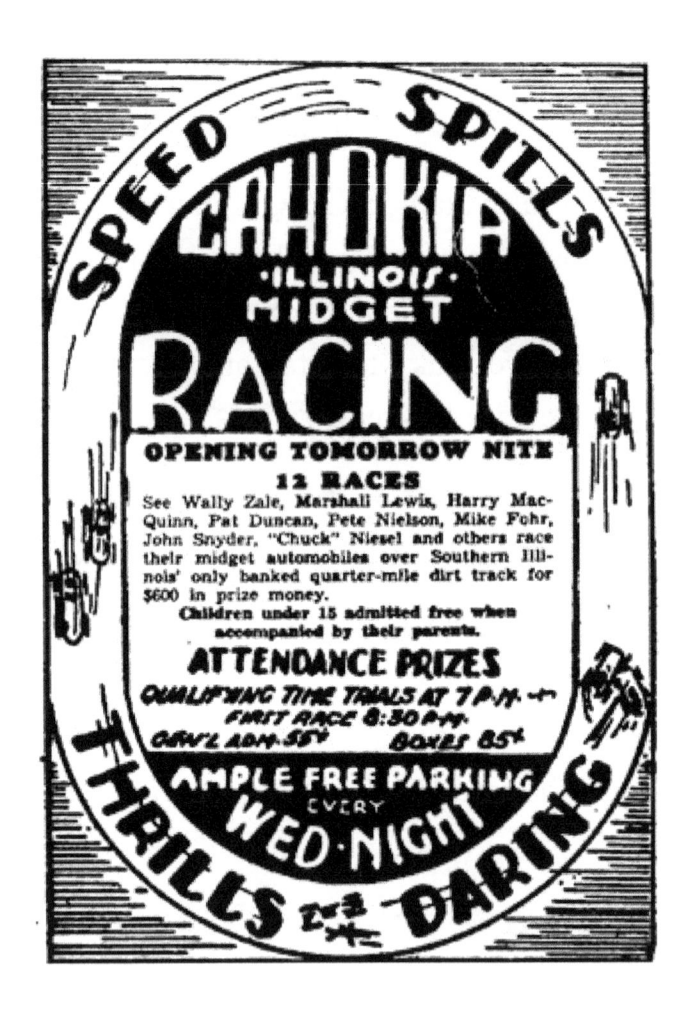

*The Edwardsville Intelligencer, page 8, August 9, 1938.*

## Wisconsin State Fair Park, Milwaukee, August 12, 1938

McQuinn, Ted Duncan, and Wally Zale battled it out for the feature. Duncan had taken the early lead followed by Zale and McQuinn. McQuinn finally passed Zale on the 31st lap and made up distance closing on Duncan. However, Duncan ran one of his best races keeping McQuinn at bay to finish first in this 40-lap feature [*National Auto Racing Arby, page 4, August 25, 1938*].

### Riverview Speedway, Chicago, August 14, 1938

McQuinn won the 40-lap main event with Ted Duncan coming into second [*Chicago Tribune, page 19, August 15, 1938*].

### Walsh Memorial Stadium, St. Louis, August 16, 1938

McQuinn stacked up the wins with the 60-lap feature, 25-lap Gold Cup race, the first heat, and two separate match races. The Gold Cup series is a set of three races with this night's race being the first of three.

Having secured an incredible lead in St. Louis as well as Milwaukee and Chicago, McQuinn was crowned the Mid-West Auto Racing Circuit Champion despite having done little racing in Detroit [*National Auto Racing News, page 3, August 25, 1938*].

### Walsh Memorial Stadium, St. Louis, August 23, 1938

McQuinn scored his eleventh victory of the season when he won the 60-lap main feature and the second Gold Cup race of 50 laps. Jimmy Snyder and Ted Duncan finished second and third [*St. Louis Dispatch, page 16, August 24, 1938*].

### Farmer City (IL) Fairgrounds, August 25, 1938

Farmer City Fairgrounds was a half-mile dirt oval. Harry McQuinn won the first feature of the season [*The Decatur Herald, page 2, August 31, 1938*].

### Riverview Speedway, Chicago, August 28, 1938

McQuinn won his 10th feature of the season at Riverview. He was the fastest qualifier setting a new track record and then set on pole for the feature. Once in the lead, he was never headed [*National Auto Racing News, page 2, September 1, 1938*].

## Walsh Memorial Stadium, St. Louis, August 30, 1938

This was the third in the series of Gold Cup races culminating in the final 100-lap event for the trophy emblematic of the Midwest Auto Racing distance championship as well as the last race of the season. McQuinn won the previous 25 and 50-lap cup events. McQuinn had recently took the sectional allround title by winning a series of races here, in Chicago, Detroit and Milwaukee. He will be honored for this tomorrow night [*St. Louis Post-Dispatch, page 11, August 29, 1938*]. However, McQuinn did not take part in the events due to busting his driveshaft in time trials. Tony Willman won the feature with Myron Fohr, second and third place went to Jimmy Snyder. Had Snyder won, he would have been awarded the "Gold Cup" but as McQuinn did not take place in the actual races, the officials and drivers voted giving McQuinn the cup [*The St. Louis Star and Times, page 24, September 1, 1938*].

## Wisconsin State Fair Park, Milwaukee, September 2, 1938

McQuinn continued his winning ways at Milwaukee "taking everything except the rubber tires used for markers". He won the main event, the first heat, and the pursuit race. McQuinn started on pole and Ted Duncan hotly pursued him for 15 laps but could not keep apace of the No. 4 Marchese Miller [*National Auto Racing News, September 8, 1938*].

## Grundy County Fairgrounds, Mazon IL, September 4, 1938

Ted Duncan was fastest in time trials. Duncan finished second in the first heat which saw Marshall Lewis dropping out with motor troubles. McQuinn finished second to Ray Richards in the second heat. Bob Muhlke won the third heat and later the 10-lap handicap.

The 30-lap feature had Duncan on pole with McQuinn on the outside. McQuinn took the lead on the backstretch on the first lap. Wally Zale, Myron Fohr and Ted Johnson were three abreast for 10 laps giving the fans a thrill. Zale's car developed issues and he had to pull off at 20 laps. McQuinn captured the win by ten lengths over Duncan followed by Muhlke [*National Auto Racing News, page 15, September 15, 1938*].

## Riverview Speedway, Chicago, September 4, 1938

McQuinn was fastest in time trials setting a new track record (breaking his own) and started in the rear of the first elimination heat. McQuinn made his way through the field to win the 8-lap elimination race where the two slowest cars were eliminated from the feature. The second heat was won by Pete Neisel followed by Ted Duncan in a close finish. The third heat was captured by Carl Peterson, the fourth by Marshall Lewis, the fifth by Pete Romcevich, and the last by Myron Fohr.

The 40-lap feature saw McQuinn on pole and out to the lead early. McQuinn was able to extend his lead from the field and was never challenged. Duncan placed second and Wally Zale, third [*National Auto Racing News, page 2, September 15, 1938*].

## Grundy County Fairgrounds, Mazon IL, September 5, 1938

McQuinn was the fastest qualifier. McQuinn and Johnny Zale came from the back in the first heat to finish first and second. In a similar fashion, Wally Zale started from the last row in the typical invert to win the second heat. The 10-lap handicap, Al York and Mike O'Halloran led the field to the start but McQuinn went wide and passed them readily. The remainder of the field had to work its way through leaving McQuinn out front to win.

By the end of two days of racing, the track was pretty torn up. This provided additional challenges but no driver wanted to compromise on speed. McQuinn on pole and jumped out to the lead. Wally Zale made his way up to challenge McQuinn on the fourth lap. Ted Duncan, Johnny Zale and Bob Muhlke were fighting for third. The race delivered plenty of excitement with thrills and spills but McQuinn dominated and Wally Zale finished second [*National Auto Racing News, page 15, September 15, 1938*].

The midgets at Mazon. *Courtesy of Grundy County Hall of Fame Archives, c.1938.*

*Gold Cup Trophy, won by Harry McQuinn, Sept. 5, 1938*

## Riverview Speedway, Chicago, September 5, 1938

McQuinn again was fastest in time trials and was able to secure the first elimination heat. Myron Fohr won over Wally Zale in the second heat. Zale and Ted Duncan were fighting it out for the lead when Fohr was able to get past the two for the win. Ted Johnson won the third heat with Johnny Zale close behind.

In the 40-lap feature, McQuinn and Wally Zale were battling for the lead during the first 10 laps with each trading off the lead. McQuinn was able to get into the lead and hold it by five lengths to win. Wally Zale went on to finish second, Duncan third and Johnny Zale, fourth [*National Auto Racing News*, page 2, September 15, 1938].

## Riverview Speedway, Chicago, September 11, 1938

Riverview saw a returning champion capture the feature as McQuinn and his "Marchese twin", Shorty Sorenson, had set off to the West. Ted Duncan captured the feature win when Marshall Lewis had to pull off on the 27th lap [*National Auto Racing News, page 2, September 15, 1938*].

## Goldman Stadium, Kansas City MO, September 16, 1938

This was the inaugural event at this 1/5-mile dirt oval speedway. McQuinn won the first heat and the 50-lap feature [*National Auto Racing News, page 4, September 22, 1938*].

## Olympic Field, Kansas City MO, September 18, 1938

This was a benefit race for Joe Anello who was killed at this track on Sept 11. McQuinn, "the world's fastest" midget driver, was the fastest in qualifying by eight-tenths of a second. McQuinn won the 50-lap feature [*National Auto Racing News, page 4, September 22, 1938*].

### Harry McQuinn Wins 4 Feature Races in 2 Days

"Harry McQuinn Wins 4 Features in 2 Days

Chicago.—Harry McQuinn, piloting the Marchese Miller and competing against America's best, won about all the honors that could be bestowed upon a driver by cleaning house both days at the Grundy County Fair at Mazon, Ill., and Riverview Speedway, Chicago where the Gold Cup mid-season championship was at stake.

A new record for attendance was established at Mazon when a crowd of 26,460 paid admissions filed thru the turnstiles—almost unbelievable to an outsider unless he actually witnessed the spectacle. Every available spot was taken by some thrill-seeking soul, the stands being sold out two hours before the first race started. At Riverview both evenings the stands were filled to capacity, and on both occasions the boys gave the customers all that was in them. Dog-fights, crashes, spins and spectacular hub to hub driving with all they had expected to see.

Much credit must be given to Wayne Carter, Wm. Meisner and Mr. Martin, Grundy county fair committee, for their untiring efforts to present one of the finest midget shows ever witnessed.

Likewise Bob Lundgreen and Harry Zorin, promoters of Riverview. Both worked unceasingly on publicity and track and were rewarded by a sell-out house and a track as slick as a billiard ball.

Cooperation between the officials of the two tracks made it possible for the drivers to compete at both places, and having the schedule run off promptly on the minute.

Sixty-three doodle-bugs of all shapes, colors and sizes turned out for Mazon; 33 of these were out of Chicago district—where the others came from no one seemed to know, they just popped up from the brush, in fact one came in towed behind a watermelon wagon." *National Auto Racing News, page 2, September 15, 1938.*

## Cahokia (IL) Midget Speedway, September 21, 1938

Harry McQuinn won the 35-lap feature race, while Ben Chesney won a match race from Clyde Dillon. McQuinn, Ted Duncan and Pete Mocco won the other events [*St. Louis Dispatch, page 19, September 22, 1938*].

## Raceway Park, Blue Island IL, September 24, 1938

This was the opening of this ¼-mile dirt track. McQuinn set the track record in qualifying and won the first heat. Ted Tetterton had a very promising night in winning the second, fourth and fifth heats of the evening in two separate cars. Marshall Lewis slipped into the lead of the main feature holding it for six laps until "Handsome Harry" took it. Ted Tetterton would have likely challenged McQuinn for the lead if it weren't for Lewis and him battling it out for second for almost 30 laps. Johnson lost a wheel and to avoid hitting him, McQuinn had to race through the infield. McQuinn went on to victory with Tetterton second [*National Auto Racing News, page 14, September 29, 1938*].

McQuinn and Wally Zale were reported to head East to compete at various venues including the Nutley Velodrome [*National Auto Racing News, page 14, September 29, 1938*].

## Raceway Park, Blue Island IL, October 1, 1938

This the second race of this new midget speedway and it was McQuinn's second straight feature victory and his 59th of the outdoor season. McQuinn was again fastest in time trials, setting a new mark. McQuinn won the inverted first heat with Myron Fohr battling it from the beginning. Ted Duncan dominated the second heat as did Pete Romcevich in the third. Wally Zale won the fourth heat and the 10-lap handicap.

McQuinn and Mike O'Halloran started up front in the first row for the feature. McQuinn held the early lead with O'Halloran on his tail but had to drop off on the fourth lap. Myron Fohr running second hit a bad rut launching himself and the car on top of the rub rail. No one else was able to challenge McQuinn for the win [*National Auto Racing News, page 2, October 6, 1938*].

**M'QUINN WINS HIS 59TH FEATURE OF OUTDOOR SEASON**

National Auto Racing News, page 2, October 6, 1938.

## Wisconsin State Fair Park, Milwaukee, October 2, 1938

Forty-five cars competed for honor of running the 75-lap feature. Ted Duncan was the quickest of the evening and won his elimination heat. Ted Tetterton took the lead in the second heat but was overcome by Wally Zale by the third lap. McQuinn came from last place challenged Zale but Zale held on "in one of the closest finishes" ever seen. McQuinn accumulated enough points for this season's track championship [*National Auto Racing News, page 2, October 6, 1938; National Auto Racing News, page 3, October 13, 1938*].

## Goldman Stadium, Kansas City MO, October 6, 1938

Buzz Bussard and McQuinn tied for the fastest in the time trials. Wally Zale took the lead in the first heat. McQuinn, starting from the rear of the field, was able to secure second behind Zale for the finish. In the second heat, Buzz Bussard had the lead until McQuinn, again coming from the back of the order, was able to overtake him for the victory. In the 50-lap feature, Zale had to drop out on the 30th lap with motor issues. McQuinn went on to victory [*National Auto Racing News, page 2, October 13, 1938*].

## Olympic Field, Kansas City MO, October 9, 1938

Harry McQuinn in his Marchese Miller broke the track record in qualifications. Wally Zale secured the first heat with McQuinn a close second. In the 50-lap feature, McQuinn had the early lead but was overtaken by Wally Zale after a few laps and held it onto the finish having lapped the entire field except for McQuinn [*National Auto Racing News, page 2, October 13, 1938*].

*The historians have a variable count as to the number of feature wins for McQuinn. Most have 61 or 62. However, these are of the outdoor season. This does not include the indoor feature wins which was at least five by the documented records.*

## American Royal, Kansas City, October 30, 1938

The season opener of this indoor track. McQuinn won the feature with Wally Zale second.

http://autoracingmemories.com/forums/album.php?albumid=293&pictureid=2299

## 124th Field Artillery Armory, Chicago, November 13, 1938

The season opened as the 'World's First Indoor Board Track'. The first race was plagued by many incidents, with only three drivers, McQuinn, Paul Russo and Duke Nalon, that were able to complete a lap under 10 seconds. Paul Russo won the 25-lap main event with Tony Willman, second, and Jimmy Snyder, third. McQuinn finished fifth in the feature [*Chicago Tribune, page 21, November 4, 1938*].

# HARRY MCQUINN

"While the new board track at the armory was a very popular affair, the armory closed the track the following week. The administration had felt that dismantling and re-assembling the track for each weekly event was too much." "The Iron Duke" by George Peters, Bar Jean Enterprises, 2005.

"Behind the Wheel

Today he is probably the hottest driver in the Midwest, but before he got the racing itch he made a swell living as—a tailor!

Harry McQuinn of Chicago was born in Franklin, Indiana, on the 13th day of December, 1905. After his school years he became a tailor and soon went into business for himself. When he became interested in auto racing, Harry had his own shop in Indianapolis and had several men working for him.

One fateful day in 1925, Harry saw an auto race and decided then and there that he couldn't be bothered with tailoring when there was auto racing to be done.

Nobody would give him a car to drive, so Harry bought himself a Chevy and took it to Osgood, Ind., where he discovered how little he really knew about racing. Later that year he drove the late Ray Butcher's Buick, but his record was miserable.

Goes To Town in Morgan Miller

He didn't win a race until 1926 and that, oddly enough, occurred at Osgood. In 1927 and 1928, Harry didn't do any racing at all, but worked with a Hippodrome troupe, touring the country and playing auto polo which, Harry says, is just

# The "Mighty" Midgets

as tough as it sounds. In 1929, he bought a Fronty and raced at Fort Wayne and most of the Midwestern big car tracks.

It wasn't until 1933, however, that he really went to town in the big cars. Ralph Morgan bought him the first Dreyer-motored car and Harry drove it to 33 feature victories, cleaning up whatever championship that were available. The Morgan Miller is the same car that Jimmie Wilburn, CSRA champion, drove so brilliantly this season.

In 1934, Harry decided to try the AAA ranks. He spent half a season in that competition without winning a single feature. However, the experience was profitable, because he was a consistent money-winner and took many seconds and thirds.

Going back a little, Harry made his first Indianapolis try in 1934, qualifying his Marine Miller 220 at 111 mph. After less than forty laps of competition, the car blew up. The next year, driving the same car, the Bates Special, he qualified at 114 mph and blew up on the 13th lap.

Indianapolis Heart-Breaker

The gasoline limitation year was 1936 and it was a heart-breaker for Harry. After 199 laps, he had Sampson and Hartz's car in fifth spot. Shed a tear because he ran out of gas before he could cross the finish line.

*Con't…*

# HARRY MCQUINN

Continued…

Last year, he drove Shorty Cantlon's job and turned in the fastest six laps on the 2.5 mile speedway, racing 127.460 mph when he blew another tire while speeding at 126.760 mph! You are only allowed three tries so Harry slowed down and qualified at slightly better than 121 mph. The car was numbered 47 and it conked out with the supercharger trouble on the 47th lap.

This year, he finished in 7th place, turning in the fast lap of 121 mph. The 180-inch Marchese-Miller was put under construction in February and never ran a lap until it reached Indianapolis on the previous Wednesday to the classic race. He ran it two laps on Thursday and ran the 10-lap qualifying distance on Friday. With a virtually untried motor, he entered the 500 and finished 7th. He qualified and raced with the same rubber.

Ralph Morgan bought him a midget in 1935 and he drove a poor race at the Chicago Armory. Throughout the entire season, he won very few features. The following year, he teamed up with Paul Russo and they drove the Bridges' cars. Later he went to work for Lou Schneider driving the No. 4 Tennes Special. He won a lot of mains and set a mess of records in Virginia, Madison Square Garden Bowl, Philadelphia, St. Louis, Fort Wayne, Cincinnati, and Chicago Riverview.

Wins Midget Championship

In the Winter of 1936 he teamed up with Shorty Sorenson and began driving the Marchese cars. Harry won the National Indoor title at the Chicago Armory and took seven out of ten in Texas, bringing home the Lone Star State's trophy.

This year, he again won the indoor title at the Armory and has won 57 features since May 10th. He has had one 2nd, one 3rd, two flat tires and two motor failures this season.

He has had only one serious accident and that was at Roby in 1935 while driving for Lou Schneider. A fine spray of gas filled the cockpit and became ignited. Harry spent two months in a hospital and it took two years for his burns to heal.

Harry is married, is a handsome, fair-haired lad on the burly side, and has a 14-year-old son in high school who doesn't care for auto racing.

Hunting is Harry's favorite pastime and, as we left him, he was scratching an itchy finger."

*Illustrated Speedway News, page 5, September 30, 1938, courtesy of Stan Kalwasinski.*

# HARRY MCQUINN

"1938 Resume of Chicago Area Racing Season

MIDGETS

Mr. Reflow filled Walsh Stadium of St. Louis with 10 and 12 thousand, the Chicago Riverside was Comfortably filled every Sunday night, the Grundy County Fair wins the cup with a total attendance of 27,000 paid in two days, Peoria's opener was a sell out, Blue Island packed every meet, and Milwaukee fans ate it up. It was a splendid season for midgets due to the fact that seasoned veteran promoters knew what they were doing and how to do it.

Harry McQuinn, undisputed midget champion winner of 1937-38 Armory indoor season, added another to his record by taking 60 features and many seconds. McQuinn, possibly the greatest midget driver in the world today, started late in the spring, due to his preparation for the entry into the "500", in which he finished in seventh place and steadily forged to the top by his many successive victories in the famous Marchese Miller, owned by Carl Marchese, himself a fourth place winner in the 1927 "500". McQuinn's greatest 1938 exhibition of stamina and speed was the winning of four features in two days at Mazon and Riverview, 65 miles apart, one running in the afternoon and the other the evening.

Mid-Western fans still claim their drivers the tops, considering the various types of tracks they have run on. Outstanding drivers who have won features over the stiffest competition are Jim Snyder, Duke Nalon, Tony Willman, Paul Russo, Ted Duncan, Ray Richards, Ted Tetterton, Marshall Lewis, Shorty Sorensen, Cowboy O'Rourke, Art Hartsfeld. Mike O'Halloran, Harry Lewis, Howard Dauphin, Bob Muhlke, Myron Fohr, Wally Zale, Johnny Zale, Rex Easton, Jim McClory, Carl Peterson and Doc Shanebrook. All are within one-half second of each other, and everyone a feature winner. Then there's the other group. Jim Caris, Burt Knight, Chuck Neisel, Ted Johnson, Duke Drinka, Martin Wiswald, Dan Hauley, Pete Romcevich, Don Erwin, Bill Klein, Bernie Schecter, Joe and Frank Burray, Dan Kladis, Pip Henson, Al Kotninski and a full dozen others in the Chicago district who would give any invading group a battle for their lives." *National Auto Racing News, December, 1938.*

McQuinn and his famous No. 4 perhaps at Ord (NE), c.1938.

Harry McQuinn in his famous (or infamous) Marchese-Miller No. 4. *McQuinn Family records.*

Harry McQuinn, undisputed midget champion winner of 1937-38 Armory indoor season, added another to his record by taking 60 features and many seconds. McQuinn, possibly the greatest midget driver in the world today, started late in the spring, due to his preparation for the entry into the "500", in which he finished in seventh place and steadly forged to the top by his many successive victories in the famous Marchese Miller, owned by Carl Marchese, himself a fourth place winner in the 1927 "500". McQuinn's greatest 1938 exhibition of stamina and speed was the winning of four features in two days at Mazon and Riverview, 65 miles apart, one running in the afternoon and the other the evening

*Unknown newspaper clipping, McQuinn Family records.*

# The "Mighty" Midgets

"Ace Midgeteers To Clash At Chi Armory

One of the oldest feuds in midget auto racing----the perennial business battle between Harry MacQuinn of Indianapolis and Jimmy Snyder of Chicago, will flare up again here Sunday night at the 124th Field Artillery Armory, Fifty-second street and Cottage Grove avenue, when the 1939 indoor championship season opens.

Since the races were inaugurated at the Washington Park Armory in the Fall of 1934, MacQuinn and Snyder have gone to racing wars with everything but boxing gloves. Their bitter contention has found expression in fisticuffs several times, but of late the two pilots have confined their rivalry to "no quarter asked and no quarter given" driving.

When Harry and Jimmy are driving one-two in any race, woe unto the lad who has the slower car; woe unto the pilot who naps for just an instant; woe unto the weak-hearted racing fan. Both Snyder and MacQuinn apparently feel that the best way to pass each other is to push the leading car out of the way. Only the uncanny skill of both chauffeurs saves them and their cars from serious trouble.

While Snyder and MacQuinn renew their racing feud, other topflight pilots will be out to whittle both of them down. One driver who has never taken a back seat even in the toughest competition is Duke Nalon, who divides his non-racing time between working in the steel mills and tending bar in Snyder's palatial South Side Spa.

A closer study of the entries reveal also the names of such seasoned stars as the ever-consistent Tony Willman of Milwaukee; Pete Nielsen of Beverly Hills, Cal.; Ray Richards, a Chicago workhorse; Ted Tetterton of Waukegan, and Ted Duncan of Chicago. Emil Andres, seriously injured last spring in the

Indianapolis 500 mile classic, is expected also to stage a come back in the midget ovals." *Unknown newspaper clipping, McQuinn Family records.*

## 1939
## 124th Field Artillery Armory, Chicago, January 8, 1939

**M'QUINN TAKES OPENER AT CHICAGO ARMORY**
McQuinn Jumps Over 3 Cars

The first heat was inverted with McQuinn starting last. Lyle Dickey shot into the lead with Jimmy Snyder and McQuinn driving madly through the field. On the second lap, McQuinn jumped over three cars in the south turn to settle into third only briefly. By the fourth lap, McQuinn passed York and Dickey and stretched out his lead. Dickey gave Snyder much difficulties to the pleasure of the crowd but Snyder overtook Dickey when Dickey slid up in one of the turns.

Duke Nalon and Ted Duncan fought for the lead in the second heat. Duncan triumphed on the sixth lap. Tony Willman took third.

McQuinn, the fastest qualifier, started on the pole. McQuinn and Duncan kept in the lead. Drivers in the back got tangled including Hartsfeld and Nalon. McQuinn opened up a lead but Snyder was gaining quickly. The track had suffered much wear and Snyder hit a rut causing him to spin losing all positions. Snyder regained control and managed to pass several drivers racing his way back to the front. McQuinn won the 40-lap feature easily but the thrills for the crowd was the spectacular driving of Snyder who finished third following Ted Duncan [*Chicago Tribune, page 20, January 9, 1939; National Auto Racing News, January 12, 1939*].

## 124th Field Artillery Armory, Chicago, January 15, 1939

Many top drivers were absent for various reasons. "Leadfoot" McQuinn wins the 40-lap feature with Tony Willman finishing second. Cowboy O'Rourke placed third [*Chicago Tribune, page 21, January 16, 1939*].

The first heat was again started in inverted order. Ted Tetterton and Cowboy O'Rourke locked wheels early. Pete Nielsen spun on the slippery track. McQuinn brushed hubs with Lyle Dickey, recovered and started to gain ground. Johnson who took the early lead was not challenged.

In the second heat, Ray Conway and Simmons led from the start, with Simmons grabbing the lead. McQuinn came from last to second in two laps, taking the lead on the third.

McQuinn started in last for the ten-lap handicap race. His advancements were often blocked by O'Rourke until he slid high on the third lap giving McQuinn a path to take the lead followed closely by Nielsen for the finish. O'Rourke and Dickey ended up tangling for third with Dickey prevailing.

McQuinn started on pole. He, Nielsen and Willman drove three abreast around the north turn after the start. The slippery track offered no advantage and it was a case of each driver holding his breath. McQuinn finally gained a three-length lead over Willman. Nielsen experienced two slides setting him back four positions. On the thirtieth lap, McQuinn and Willman had lapped the field. At 35 laps, Nielsen again slipped and let O'Rourke through for third. McQuinn finished with a half-lap lead on Willman [*National Auto Racing News, January 19, 1939*].

> "How that man Harry McQuinn can drive. He can pass cars on the outside, inside, in fact any spot that he sees an opening he just drives through and somebody has to give around and it's not McQuinn." Unknown newspaper clipping, McQuinn Family records.

"THE WINNAH! Harry MacQuinn (above) is shown receiving the checkered flag from Starter Van De Water in the feature race at the Chicago Armory last Sunday night. The Marchese Miller car that Harry has wheeled to two straight wins at this track has been sold. MacQuinn will endeavor to prove to the mid-Western speed bugs that he is "tops" in any gas buggy when he rides a new job that is being built by the Marchese brothers." *Illustrated Speedway News, January 19, 1939.*

Having won 60 (or 61) features from the previous year and started out 1939 with two victories, McQuinn and his No. 4 Marchese-Miller was the car to beat. But… he was beaten off the track by a lady, Mrs. Scheckler, who bought that famous No. 4 car after the January 15th race, sidelining McQuinn while the Marchese brothers began to work on another car. Mrs. Scheckler bought the car for Lou Walker [*National Auto Racing News, page 1, January 26, 1939*].

## 124th Field Artillery Armory, Chicago, January 22, 1939

McQuinn was watching from the stands but because of his first two races of the season, he remained highest in the point standings with 124 with Willman second at only 48 [*Unknown newspaper clipping, McQuinn Family archives*].

## 124th Field Artillery Armory, Chicago, January 29, 1939

*Harry McQuinn, still without a 'ride', did not participate in the armory race.*

## 124th Field Artillery Armory, Chicago, February 5, 1939

*McQuinn still had no car to race but shortly afterwards he bought his own No. 4 Marchese.*

## 124th Field Artillery Armory, Chicago, February 12, 1939

McQuinn and Jimmy Snyder were expected to return along with Tony Bettenhausen. The races of this season were won by McQuinn on Jan. 8 and Jan. 15, and Snyder took the feature on Jan. 22. Ray Richards, title point standing leader, won the main events on Jan. 29 and Feb. 5, setting new track records on successive Sundays [*Chicago Tribune, page 22, February 13, 1939*].

In the first elimination heat (12 laps), McQuinn and Marshall started out front rubbing hubs until McQuinn emerged out front. Pete Nielsen and Bert Knight were third and fourth. Duke Nalon pulled alongside. Nielsen, Knight and Duncan ended in a tangled mess on the 5th lap with Nalon barely escaping and ended third behind McQuinn and Lewis.

The fifth heat was a 15-lap handicap race. O'Rourke led the first three laps but was overtaken by McQuinn who went on to win.

In the main feature, Ted Duncan took the lead at first over Snyder. Nalon was third but his car froze up and he pulled in. McQuinn came up from fourth was side-by-side with Duncan after nine laps eventually taking control three laps later. Duncan retired from the field at lap 19 due to a broken universal. McQuinn lead up through the thirtieth lap until he experienced a broken chain. Snyder then took over the lead and went on to victory [*National Auto Racing News, page 2, February 16, 1939*].

## 124th Field Artillery Armory, Chicago, February 19, 1939

> "Old burn-'em-up MacQuinn just couldn't shake off that old habit of winning Sunday, so after the smoke cleared in the packed 124th Field Artillery Armory, Harry had gone home with everything but the judges' table." -Frank Zuiker, Chicago Tribune

The field was bursting with talent as many drivers returned from the South and Southwest to race. Emotions were riding high.

Ted Duncan flipped his car on the first turn of the first race of the night after running up on Ray Richards who had spun. Duncan was badly shaken and was taken off the field in a stretcher. As the race was getting back underway, Duncan came running out and hopped in his car and began the race again. He didn't fare well in the first elimination race after breaking a spindle and losing a wheel, but he came back to win the fourth qualifying race to start in the main feature. Richards however, recovered from his spin and went on to win the first qualifier.

McQuinn won the handicap race coming from last place but he was not the one to watch. Cowboy O'Rourke and Pete Romcevich where bumping hubs for five laps and eventually locked hubs and slid into the outside retaining wall. Soon thereafter,

O'Rourke and Romcevich started the fisticuffs followed by mechanics and crew on both sides.

McQuinn, who led all the way, won his third feature forty-lap race of the season outrunning Ted Duncan and Bert Knight who trailed him closely in that order. Knight was solidly in second but was overtaken by Duncan on the thirty-fourth lap. After Knight pulled into the pits, he proceeded to confront Pete Nielsen stating if Nielsen, who was a lap behind, had moved over when flagged, he would have remained in second. While the crowd watched intently, no fight broke out to their dismay [*National Auto Racing News, February 23, 1939*].

## 124th Field Artillery Armory, Chicago, February 26, 1939

**MacQUINN SCORES HIS 4TH WIN AT ARMORY**

Lyle Dickey sat on the pole for the first heat with all starters in reverse order. He jumped out into the lead and won setting a new 10-lap record besting the previous record held by McQuinn.

Duke Nalon was the fastest qualifier setting a new one-lap record, again besting McQuinn's. Nalon started on the pole for the feature but McQuinn easily overtook him in a blistering pace winning his fourth straight [*National Auto Racing News, March 2, 1939*].

# MID-WEST WHISPERS
## by Ed (Twenty-Grand) Steinbock

After several weeks of hot and heavy driving in which practically every driver at the Armory was involved in mix-ups, spins, rollovers and leather-tossing, finally came to an end Sunday night when the boys settled down to hard, steady driving.

In the first heat Lyle Dickey set a fast pace to jump into the lead at the end of the first lap and holding it to the finish to set a new 10-lap record of 3:26.08. In the feature he again held his own and placed fifth.

Duke Nalon was easily the shining light of the meet when he out-qualified the field with a fast 13.62 circuit. The Duke started in last position in the first reverse start heat, and although greatly handicapped by having to pump air pressure continually due to the auto pulse having gone haywire, he managed to work his way through the field and finished second about 5 car lengths behind the flying Dickey.

### MacQuinn Sets Fast Pace

In the feature he started on the pole, but was unable to match the blistering speed of MacQuinn's mount, and showed much hoss sense by dropping into a safe second where he eventually finished. When the Tomshe Offy is finally de-bugged, the rotund Chicago flyer will  plenty hard to keep up with, to say nothing of beating.

Not wishing to seem repetitious I'm not going to ask "Who can beat MacQuinn?," as at present that feat seems  be  ond one's wildest dreams, although many drivers do have nightmares. Harry turned in the second fastest time trial, :13.80. Starting in last position in the second reverse heat race he won by a large margin setting a new record for the 10 laps, 2:25.26. In the Handicap he was forced to bow to the hard driving of Richards and Neilsen who finished in that order.

This is the first handicap event that Harry has lost in quite some time. In the feature he again out-drove all opposition to turn in his fourth smashing feature win of the season.

Jimmy Snyder narrowly missed serious injury while qualifying when he blasted into the home straightaway at a tremendous speed and slid into the heavy wall. First the rear hub would hit with a resounding thump, then the front end would connect, gauging out deep ridges in the thick wall. Only by skillful handling and brute strength was Snyder able to keep his wildly careening mount from overturning, a fact that many fans realized, and as he came to a stop they gave him a nice ovation. Later in the evening Jimmy tried to run but had to give up as the rear en housing was cracked.

Warren Erwin and Bill Smith are two drivers who appear every Sunday night and drive their hearts out hoping to attract the notice of a fast car owner who might give them a break. Both of these boys drove heady races to finish third and fourth in the first heat.

Harry Hart, fresh from several nice victories in South America, drove his first race at the Chicago track and turned in a nice performance by annexing third money in the second heat race.

### Richards Consistent Driver

Ray Richards has probably drove more consistently this season than any other driver at the Armory, with one exception, that of course being the present point leader, Harry MacQuinn. In the third heat Ray brought his Offy over the tape in second spot, won the handicap and nosed out Knight for third money in the feature.

Pete Neilsen played safe and picked his spots Sunday night and

*Unknown newspaper clipping, McQuinn Family records.*

The concept of the 'sure' feature winner in the aggressive arena of the Chicago Armory.
*National Auto Racing News, page 1, March 2, 1939.*

"FALK TROPHY—Al Falk (right) presenting Harry McQuinn with beautiful Falk Service Station trophy. Harry won the 1938 outdoor championship at the Milwaukee fifth-mile oval; second place was won by Ted Duncan, who trailed the victorious McQuinn by the narrow margin of ten points."— Milwaukee News Photo. *National Auto Racing News, page 1, March 2, 1939.*

## 124th Field Artillery Armory, Chicago, March 5, 1939

*National Auto Racing News, March 9, 1939.*

McQuinn lead from the beginning pushed on by Duke Nalon. Both lapped the last four cars by the seventh lap and everyone else except Ted Duncan by the 30th lap. They finished in the same running order: McQuinn, Nalon, Duncan [*National Auto Racing News, March 9, 1939*].

## 124th Field Artillery Armory, Chicago, March 12, 1939

McQuinn won his sixth feature and fourth straight of the year winning the midseason midget auto racing championship. Ray Richards placed second and Ted Tetterton was third. McQuinn also won the handicap race setting a new track record [*Chicago Tribune, page 21, March 13, 1939*].

## 124th Field Artillery Armory, Chicago, March 19, 1939

McQuinn set a new record at the Armory winning his fifth consecutive forty lap main event and his seventh overall for the season.

"Harry MacQuinn, who has broken more hearts in the world of speed by his hard driving tactics than Don Juan was ever able to boast about in another heart game, still finds himself at the top of the heap at the end of each speed session every Sunday night at the Armory. In the first heat race Harry met a tarter in one Seidentoph who refused to become flustered at the proximity of the "king" who was riding within an inch of his tail. As both drivers blasted into the north turn, Harry tried to force Seidentoph out of the groove, but the latter also had ideas of his own in regard to sticking on the pole, which resulted in hooked wheels, the usual spin and both drivers out of the money. The second heat race was fast and furious as he tried to close the gap separating him from Nalon who eventually won the race, but it was no go and he had to be content with second money. On the second lap of the handicap he was riding on the tail of Duncan's mount when the latter's car blew up and with no chance to swerve he was forced to drive over the left rear wheel of Duncan's car and almost rolled over. By heady driving he was able to straighten out and continue, but the fracas cost him valuable time, that the best he could do was a third. Holding down the pole position in the feature line-up, Harry wheeled into the lead as the flag dropped and was never headed although he was pressed hard all the distance by Nalon. Next Sunday MacQuinn will have the pleasure of trying out the world's most beautiful and modern midget----the new Marchese-Miller Special. It is an even bet that when this car is unloaded at the track it will be the car to beat throughout the evening, even though it is new and untried" [*Unknown newspaper clipping, McQuinn Family records*].

During the feature, "(Duke) Nalon and McQuinn once again went at it hammer and tong. Harry jumped into the lead with Nalon right on his tail. On two occasions, Duke managed to momentarily move past the ever tough McQuinn only to have the Indianapolis speedster regain the lead to secure a victory. Their evening's combat was described as a 'heated battle'" [*"The Iron Duke", by George Peters*].

# HARRY MCQUINN

"MacQUINN HAS NEW MIDGET SPEEDSTER

Harry MacQuinn of Indianapolis will seek his sixth consecutive feature auto race victory at the 124th Field Artillery Armory Sunday night driving a new Marchese-Miller car, said to be the finest machine ever built for indoor racing.

The car, built by the Marchese brothers of Milwaukee, combines the latest thoughts in scientific race car construction. Every motor part was designed by the Marchese and has been hand-tooled to hair-breath exactness. The Marcheses are confident it will outlast and outrun any car on the midget ovals.

In taking over the new Miller, MacQuinn abandons a car that carried him to the championship in midget circles for the last two years, but he, too, has great confidence in the new car. He is seeking a chauffeur for his No. 4, expecting to get one of the other top flight drivers to take over the machine." *Unknown newspaper clipping, McQuinn Family records.*

"HARRY McQUINN

———

He knows the racing business, he
leads the field today,
Has worked quite hard for years,
which compensated his pay.
He is just a regular fellow, it's
the crowds that know the best,
At the Armory every Sunday,
where he competes with all
the rest.

He doesn't ask for glory, nor a
pat upon his back,
Just goes about his business, just
asks to be called Mac.
He'll shake the hand of anyone,
to him it's all the same,
Be you rich or poor or what
you are, that's how he plays
the game.

He's often thronged by many
after winning a hectic duel,

By men of all professions, and

by children who go to school.

This doesn't make him better,

nor feel that he should not

Take time to talk to all, whether

it's the elder or the tot.


He's just a real businessman

And knows his business best,

You can find this out, my friends,

At the Armory he proves this test.

-George Delismon."


*National Auto Racing News, page 11, March 30, 1939.*

## 124th Field Artillery Armory, Chicago, March 26, 1939

"In the first heat race Nalon and Tony Willman added to the exciting events when the Duke spun on the seventh lap and Tony, who was riding close behind, crashed into him, eliminating both cars from this race. McQuinn, driving the beautiful new Marchese Miller, finished just out of the money in this event.

Harry came back in the second heat and gave the fans quite a thrill when he momentarily lost control of his mount while going thru the south turn. This car, which is the very last word in mechanical achievement, features a new type of independent spring suspension, which was invented by the Marchese brothers. They haven't as yet been able to get the exact adjustment to allow for perfect handling in the turns. This near-accident caused the boys to signal McQuinn into the pits. Harry explained later over the p. a. system that they didn't wish to endanger the life of any driver by remaining in competition until the trouble had been overcome. We feel sure this will be in the very near future. In this same race, Tony Willman, in the famous Marchese Miller formerly driven by McQuinn, ran into trouble when a connecting rod decided to come out for a breath of fresh air and chose the crankcase to use as an exit. This was Tony's first appearance in competition here this season, and evidently he has not forgotten the short way around" [*National Auto Racing News, March 30, 1939*].

Breaking McQuinn's winning streak, Art Hartsfeld won the 40-lap feature followed by Ray Richards and Ted Tetterton. Duke Nalon establishes a new track record of 13.47 besting the prior record of 13.54 held by McQuinn [*Chicago Tribune, page 20, March 27, 1939*].

## 124th Field Artillery Armory, Chicago, April 2, 1939

Duke Nalon set a new track record at 0:13.47 and won the feature, his second in a row. Nalon led all the way in the feature. McQuinn following in second, stalled in the 10th lap, causing Ray Richards to spin. Nalon, Ted Duncan, Art Hartsfeld finished in that order [*National Auto Racing News, April 13, 1939*].

## 124th Field Artillery Armory, Chicago, April 9, 1939

Multiple track records were broken this night. Duke Nalon broke the time trial record for the third time in three weeks, setting the new mark at 13.46 seconds. Pete Nielson set a mark of 2 minutes and 40 seconds for the 12-lap elimination race, and McQuinn, starting to figure out his new Marchese-Miller, lowered the 15-lap mark to 3 minutes and 29 seconds.

Nalon leading most of the way, won the forty-lap main event. McQuinn and Ted Duncan tangled in the third lap and both went out.

McQuinn and Nalon hooked wheels in the second heat and spun knocking both out of contention. In the third heat, McQuinn and Nalon again drove aggressively against one another but McQuinn won with Nalon second.

McQuinn overtook Nalon to take second place on the ninth lap of the handicap. He then pulled ahead of Bert Knight who was in the lead and won by less than a half-car length. McQuinn set a new 15-lap record [*Chicago Tribune, page 21, April 10, 1939*].

## 124th Field Artillery Armory, Chicago, April 16, 1939

Duke Nalon won his third straight main feature leading McQuinn by a quarter of a lap. Nalon overtook McQuinn on the first turn and lead the rest of the way. McQuinn finished second. McQuinn remained the point standings leader [*Chicago Tribune, page 21, April 17, 1939*].

"With the Marchese car just about rounding into top notch form, Harry McQuinn (above), should give Duke Nalon, winner of the last three feature events held at the Chicago Armory, a stiff battle for first place money in this Sunday night's main event at this indoor midget plant." *Unknown newspaper clipping, McQuinn Family archives.*

## 124th Field Artillery Armory, Chicago, April 23, 1939

Duke Nalon rolled over during qualifications. He hit the first turn at great speed then the car flipped. The tail of the car rested on the unconscious body of Nalon.

McQuinn had the fasted qualifying time and started on pole for the feature. Art Hartsfeld moved up the field in what was reported as "one of the outstanding driving exhibitions of the season" finally overtaking McQuinn for the lead on the 13th lap, after McQuinn and Snyder tangled. Willman eventually took over the lead with Hartsfeld second. McQuinn finished "outside the money" [*Unknown newspaper clipping, McQuinn Family records*].

## 124th Field Artillery Armory, Chicago, April 30, 1939

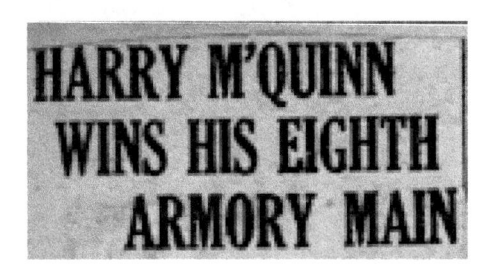

**HARRY M'QUINN WINS HIS EIGHTH ARMORY MAIN**

McQuinn and Duke Nalon continued to dominate at the Armory. McQuinn won the 40-lap feature with Nalon second. McQuinn's win, his eighth of the season, "practically" clinched the 1938-39 indoor championship [*Chicago Tribune, page 20, May 1, 1939*].

In the second heat, Pete Romcevich was really pushing his Model A around in the lead until the ninth lap, when Art Hartsfeld spun while Ray Richards and Ted Tetterton tangled in the north turn. Just after this pile up, McQuinn passed Romcevich, but on hitting the straightaway saw the caution flag displayed and dropped back into second only to again go into the lead as soon as the track was cleared.

"The 40-lap feature was by far the most thrilling race ever seen by your reporter, for as the race started McQuinn took the lead with Nalon and (Jimmy) Snyder right on his heels until the sixth lap, when Snyder spun out in the north turn. (Cowboy) O'Rourke managed to get by, or over, Snyder, but Willman was less fortunate and was forced out as he hit the stalled car. At this time Duncan closed in on Nalon and at no time during the rest of the race was there more than three feet separating the three cars. (Jimmy) Caris went out in the seventh lap and O'Rourke, who was running fourth, was forced out on the 26th lap with a flat tire.—Finish, McQuinn, Nalon, Duncan, Hartsfeld, Richards.—9:21.32" [*National Auto Racing News, May, 1939*].

> "Point standings for the Chi. Armory up to but not including April 27:
>
> McQuinn- 623; Richards- 468; Nalon- 402; Duncan- 350; Snyder- 334; Nielsen- 298; Knight- 250; Tetterton- 197; Hartsfeld- 197; O'Rourke- 145; Willman- 117; Caris- 109; Dickey- 95; Simmons- 71; Romcevich- 66; Willy- 55; Erwin- 52; Walker- 51." National Auto Racing News, May, 1939.

## 124th Field Artillery Armory, Chicago, May 7, 1939

**MACQUINN WINS INDOOR RACING TITLE FOR 1939**

The 50-lap feature saw Duke Nalon, fastest qualifier on the pole. Jimmy Snyder nosed Hartsfeld out of second on the 10th lap. In the scramble to take third place, Duncan and McQuinn pulled alongside of Hartsfeld, and as the three went through the north turn, one of them slid, causing all three to jam up resulting in losing a lap. Nalon hit a hole in the track and upset his car allowing Snyder to overtake him on the 24th lap. Snyder won the feature with Nalon trailing in second. McQuinn, who spun on the north turn, finished in the back of the field.

In the first heat, Cowboy "O'Rourke took the lead from Willman on the first lap, with McQuinn and Duncan on his heels. Nalon, starting from last position, had all eyes turned on him as he fairly flew by Snyder, Hartsfeld, Duncan, McQuinn and Nielsen to take third money. His was a marvelous bit of driving and he received a big hand" [*National Auto Racing News, May 1939*].

McQuinn's point total of 681 was too much to overcome with Ray Richards in second with 486 in the quest for the 1939 Indoor Midget Automobile Race Championship [*Chicago Tribune, page 21, May 8, 1939*].

## Walsh Memorial Stadium, St. Louis, May 9, 1939

Season opener for Walsh Stadium. McQuinn was the defending champion from 1938, having won 12 of the 17 features [*St. Louis Post-Dispatch, page 15, May 7, 1939*]. Duke Nalon won the 35-lap feature. Jimmy Snyder, Tony Bettenhausen, Ted Duncan, and McQuinn were all involved in a pile up on the 28th lap. Duke avoided the pile up and went on to win [*St. Louis Post-Dispatch, page 16, May 10, 1939*].

## Olympic Field, Kansas City MO, May 14, 1939

"Harry McQuinn, the rougher who lost but one race in Kansas City, returns tonight with his Offenhauser after being crowned national midget auto indoor champion at Chicago recently. Harry Hartz, Indianapolis speedway luminary, is another who will make the going tough for Kansas City auto drivers. Ronny Householder, another entry, was injured Friday in a mishap at Indianapolis and will be unable to compete. McQuinn and Hartz are favored tonight."

McQuinn won the feature over Carl Badami, Kansas City indoor champion, and Dee Toran, who finished second and third. Sam Hanks finished fourth.

Sam Hanks ran the track in the first event in record time ahead of McQuinn who finished second [*Unknown newspaper clipping, McQuinn Family records*].

## Walsh Memorial Stadium, St. Louis, May 16, 1939

Jimmy Snyder won the first heat race after Sam Hanks, who was leading, went through the fence. In the second heat, McQuinn and Rex Easton took hard racing on the track to fisticuffs afterwards. Tony Willman won the second heat. Ted Duncan won the 35-lap main feature followed by Willman with Snyder and McQuinn rounding out third and fourth [*St. Louis Post-Dispatch, page 14, May 17, 1939*].

"ACTION AT WALSH STADIUM. Johnny Rogers, No. 4, next to rail; Jimmy Snyder outside; Sam Hanks in No. 3, and Harry McQuinn in No. 4 in the rear. These boys are furnishing plenty of thrills for the fans at St. Louis."
*National Auto Racing News, June 1, 1939.*

## Riverview Speedway, Chicago, June 4, 1939

Harry McQuinn, "claimant to the national midget auto race championship, struck a guard bale during time trials and the car turned over several times. McQuinn escaped with minor injuries and seemed to be more concerned about the condition of his new car than the possibility of broken bones. It was the first race for McQuinn's new car, one of the fastest and most expensive midgets built" [*Unknown newspaper clipping, McQuinn Family records*].

## Walsh Memorial Stadium, St. Louis, June 6, 1939

"Harry McQuinn of Indianapolis scored his first victory of the year here on last night's midget auto racing program at Walsh Stadium, leading home Jimmy Snyder in 9:30.35 in the 35-lap main event. McQuinn drove with three broken ribs he suffered in a race in Kansas City Sunday" [*St. Louis Post-Dispatch, page 16, June 7, 1939*].

# HARRY MCQUINN

"Another Angle- - -

By Parke Carroll

Men Who Flirt With Death

The men who flirt with death in those little mechanical bugs for fun and finances are turning up for another Memorial Day grind in Indianapolis. It is one of our biggest shows each year and the men who are in it love it. It must be all right. In fact, if you're young and your nerves are steady and you've got plenty of paid up life insurance, it's perfect.

We were talking with Harry McQuinn, who came all the way from Indianapolis to win the opening midget race last Sunday at Olympic Field. Now he is back on the brick saucer getting ready to make his seventh bid for fame and fortune May 30, with never a thought of the 25 or 30 old friends who aren't here any more because they made one too many races.

There are those who insist automobile racing isn't the hazardous sport it is made out to be in the papers, but McQuinn knows better.

"When a man is killed the drivers don't mention his name," McQuinn said, "I have been in 25 or 30 races when men were killed. Sometimes you drive to a race with a friend and you come home alone. You just don't think about it. I am not a fatalist, because I believe a man makes his own bad luck. Most of the fatal accidents can be traced to some mistake that was made. Maybe the driver took that long chance.

"Afraid? No, not in a race, but I've had times after a race when I thought about things that I got scared. Now at Indianapolis you go at such a high rate of speed that if you get a foot sideways you're lost. I was lapping Ira Hall one year and he spun." *Unknown newspaper clipping, McQuinn Family records.*

## Horlick Athletic Field, Racine WI, June 8, 1939

Horlick Field was a one-quarter mile dirt track located in Racine, Wisconsin. McQuinn was in the lead in the main feature when, with a sudden burst of speed in the turn, his car bounced off of the car driven by Marshall Lewis and then against Lyle Dickey's racer. The car bounded end over end, crushing him under it. Tony Willman went on to win the 30-lap feature with Ted Duncan, second [*The Rhinelander Daily News, page 1, June 9, 1939*].

McQuinn was taken to St. Mary's, a local hospital. He was considered in poor condition. He received a blood transfusion for internal injuries. He suffered several fractured ribs, broken collar bone, and a lacerated face including a broken cheek bone. He received many visitors during his long recovery but the Marchese brothers were in constant vigil early on and donated blood [*The Franklin Evening Star, page 4, June 10, 1939*].

```
            "Midget Car Drivers To Hold Title Races

CHICAGO—(AP)—Jitterbugs of automobile racing are going to
have a championship meet of their own for the first time.

From the rock-bound coast of Maine to the slopes of the
Pacific, et cetera, the jitterbugs—drivers of those roaring
midget racing cars—are coming here to decide just who's who.

There are champions of Colorado, Kansas City, Toledo and the
townships, but no national champ unless it might be Harry
McQuinn, Indianapolis, claimant to the national indoor title.

The races open Sunday night winding up a week hence with a
100 lap final for the title.

The event, with a prize distribution of $15,000 has attracted
the best of the speed boys in the business. They include Jimmy
Snyder, Chicago, who blistered the bricks at the Indianapolis
speedway to qualify at a record speed of 130.128 miles an
```

hour; Tony Willman, Milwaukee, who drove 450 miles of the Indianapolis "500"; Lyle Dickey, Kansas City; Judd Piccup, Dever; Art Hartsfeld, Toledo, former national motorcycle champion; Paul Swedberg, Los Angeles; Paul Russo, Chicago, national board track auto racing champion, and a flock of others." *Brownsville Herald, page 7, June 14, 1939.*

*Due to the accident Racine, McQuinn could not defend his title of "King of the Midgets".*

*Jimmy Snyder was one of the many visitors of McQuinn while in the hospital. Any racer who died was a tragedy but this felt much more personal to McQuinn as he and Jimmy had a long competitive history and respect for one another, becoming good friends.*

"JIMMY SNYDER KILLED IN MIDGET RACE AT CAHOKIA

East St. Louis, Ill., June 29.—(AP)—Jimmy Snyder of Los Angeles, nationally known automobile racing driver who finished second in this year's Decoration day classic at Indianapolis, was killed tonight in a midget auto race at the Chahokia, Ill., track near here.

Death came to the daring 31 year old speedster as his small white car plowed into an outer guard fence and rolled onto the track, where it was smashed by another car. He died almost instantly. Snyder lost control of his machine as he turned into the home stretch on the twelfth lap of the forty lap feature event. The accident occurred in full view of 4,000 spectators. Paul Armburster of St. Louis, driver of the other car figuring in the smashup, was severely burned." *Chicago Tribune, page 25, June 30, 1939.*

# The "Mighty" Midgets

*Open letter to McQuinn's fans, friends, and family*

"And to Grace Snyder, our deepest sympathy. Jimmy was one of the greatest drivers I have ever competed against and a regular fellow. He came to see me at my worst and stroked my arm saying "Come on Harry, hurry and get well, you know we have to get going around and around again." Remarks like this from Jimmy really gave me courage to fight to live, and now he's gone, but I will always remember Jimmy just as he was when he stood over me." *Unknown newspaper clipping, McQuinn Family records.*

"Reflow always had the best pilots in the mid-West at his oval to entertain the St. Louis fans. Photo above shows Johnny Rogers, the late Jimmy Snyder, Sam Hanks and Harry McQuinn in action at the Walsh Stadium."
*Unknown newspaper clipping, McQuinn Family records.*

*St. Louis Post-Dispatch, page 18, July 25, 1939.*

> "Harry McQuinn was present in the pits for a few minutes, the fans gave him a great ovation where a few months ago he was booed unmercifully. This just goes to prove that the public is fickle. Harry is well on the road to recovery and claims that he'll be just as good as ever." *Unknown newspaper clipping, McQuinn Family records.*

## Horlick Athletic Field, Racine WI, August 25, 1939

McQuinn had recovered enough to participate in a special 3-lap match race with Tony Willman and won. The feature was won by Ray Richards with Willman second [*Racine Journal Times, August 24, 1939*].

## Olympic Field, Kansas City MO, September 1, 1939

McQuinn's first feature appearance since Racine. McQuinn won a match race with Bob Muhlke. Ray Richards won the main event for the second week in a row [*National Auto Racing News, page 2, September 7, 1939*].

## The "Mighty" Midgets

**M'QUINN MAKES A GREAT COMEBACK IN MIDGETS**

"Harry McQuinn, Milwaukee ace, made a grand comeback after an absence of three months, McQuinn has been recuperating from serious injuries sustained from a crackup at Racine, Wis., but the way he took the Marchese Miller around at Olympic Field Sunday, Sept. 17, proved he still packs a leadfoot. He won three victories in that many starts. First the 10-lap heat, the 5-lap match race, staged by the four fastest cars, then stepped into an early lead in the 25-lap feature event and was never headed."
*National Auto Racing News, page 1, September 21, 1939.*

## Grundy County Fairgrounds, Mazon IL, September 3, 1939

Wally Zale won the feature. Shorty Sorenson was racing out East and McQuinn was still recovering from his injuries suffered at Racine [*National Auto Racing News, page 12, August 29, 1940*].

## Olympic Field, Kansas City MO, September 17, 1939

McQuinn won the 35-lap main event in a "near-runaway" victory. This was McQuinn's first endurance test since his injuries at Racine. Johnny Zale placed second and Vito Calis, third. McQuinn won two other events, the first 10-lap heat and a 5-lap match race [*National Auto Racing News, page 2, September 21, 1939*].

"Tests His Endurance in Olympic Field Races Tonight-

Harry McQuinn, Milwaukee ace, who has been on the sidelines with an injury for nearly three months, will make the first test of his endurance since the crackup in the championship feature midget auto race at Olympic Field tonight. He will drive the Marchese Special."
*Kansas City Journal, September 17, 1939.*

> "M'Quinn to Compete at Farmer City Thursday
>
> FARMER CITY—Harry McQuinn, the greatest money winner in the history of midget auto racing, will be on hand Thursday night when leading pilots of the National Midget Auto Racing Association clash for cash and title points.
>
> McQuinn is conceded to be the best all around driver in the racing business as he is equally at home bouncing on the bricks of the Indianapolis Speedway where he has competed in the last six classics. He has also ranked high on the leading A.A.A. dirt track speedways such as Milwaukee, Syracuse, Altoona, Springfield and Roosevelt Raceway. However, his greatest achievements have been on the midget circuits where he has consistently walked off with purses and titular honors regardless of what part of the country he was competing.
>
> A near fatal accident last June put McQuinn on the side lines for many weeks, and last month he drove his first race at Farmer City in a match race. Completely recovered, he is again seeking more cash and laurels.
>
> The feature race Thursday will be 50 laps." *The Decatur Daily Review, page 8, September 19, 1939.*

## 124th Field Artillery Armory, Chicago, October 29, 1939

Opening of the sixth indoor season at the Armory. Forty-two cars attempted qualifying. During the first race, Duke Nalon led followed by McQuinn in a fast pace. Both drivers lost control in different turns at almost the same time and were taken away for evaluations.

Nalon won the first heat. McQuinn took the checkered flag in the second heat but had passed on a caution flag and was penalized two spots placing him in third allowing Bill Smith and Pete Nielsen in first and second. In the third heat, Bob

Muhlke was victorious as was Ted Tetterton in the fourth. The 15-lap handicap had Mike O'Halloran and McQuinn running hard with McQuinn reducing the lead of O'Halloran but was unable to overtake him before the finish.

McQuinn and Nalon were one-two in the lead in the first lap of the feature. They bumped and Nalon went wide. McQuinn opened up a substantial lead. On the 19th lap, he had to pull up to avoid Bill Smith who had faltered in the second turn. This caused McQuinn's motor to stall, losing positions. Ray Richards shot into the lead. McQuinn and Nalon in the middle of the field raced in hot pursuit of the leaders and gained considerable territory but not in enough time to advance their positions. Bob Muhlke finished second; Mike O'Halloran, third; McQuinn, fourth [*National Auto Racing News, page 2, November 2, 1939*].

## 124th Field Artillery Armory, Chicago, November 5, 1939

Duke Nalon took over the piloting duties of the fast Coutre Elto No. 3, previously driven to 11 victories out of 12 starts by Wally Zale. Nalon was able to set two new track records.

In the first heat, "(t)his was the hottest competed race seen in many moons. Gus Klingbeil and Chris Willy led the eight starters into the first turn at a terrific clip. O'Rourke shot into the lead after a battle with Willy on the third lap. At the same time Nalon clipped a hay bale on the south turn, avoiding a direct crash with a spinning car, and was forced out. McQuinn came storming thru from the last row into second position in the seventh with Bob Muhlke following. From there on it was one of the greatest battles the fans ever witnessed. These three speed devils shot down the stretches almost with the Cowboy having a slight edge on the pole time and time again. McQuinn and Muhlke tried to pass only to repeat this nerve-wracking performance. The crowd was wild when Starter Vander Water raised the checker flag as the three whipped into the stretch toward the tape." O'Rourke was first with McQuinn and Muhlke, second and third.

```
            "BLISTERING PACE

     Harry McQuinn set a fast clip to cop last
   Sunday night's feature event at the Chicago Armory,
   defeating Duke Nalon in one of the most heated battles
         staged at this indoor oval this season."
      Unknown newspaper clipping, McQuinn Family records.
```

In the 15-lap handicap, "Hartsfeld and O'Rourke took the lead positions and waxed hot for seven laps, then McQuinn, the handicap specialist, took both on the outside with Nalon following. Tetterton spun on the north turn on the eighth with Duncan crashing, neither car or driver were injured. Hartsfeld and Nalon proceeded to dog-fight to the finish which was almost a repetition." McQuinn was first, then Nalon, Hartsfeld, and O'Rourke.

In the feature, "Nalon, Duncan and McQuinn were abreast when they whipped the first turn. Nalon stretched the gap a few lengths, then proceeded to blister the track on the seventh lap. Duncan went out with ignition trouble. McQuinn set tight in second spot but five lengths behind Willman and Muhlke were running hub-to-hub and a few lengths behind them came O'Rourke, Richards, Hartsfeld and Bettenhausen in blanket formation. This attracted the crowd to the extent that Nalon's terrific riding the turns wasn't noted in general. This continued until the finish. It was a great show and was nearly midnight before the gawking crowd wandered away from the infield." The finished order was McQuinn, Willman, and Muhlke [*National Auto Racing News, November 9, 1939*].

## 124th Field Artillery Armory, Chicago, November 12, 1939

McQuinn started in his new fast Leader Card Special owned by Bob Wilke. "The lead-foot thundered into the first turn wide open, holding an outside position. He pulled the nose into the pole and barely beat Nalon going into the back stretch. These two speed demons then proceeded to blister the track until fire literally flew from the tires. Time and again Nalon made desperate efforts to wedge in, but Harry held stubbornly to the pole for dear life. On two occasions both drivers nearly spun out, due to the scorching pace they were hitting the turns. Starter Van De Water frantically waved the move-over flag at the slower cars so as to enable these leaders to have clear sailing. Owners, mechanics and the frenzied fans had their finger nails bitten to the quick.

The last three laps were perhaps the most exciting ever witnessed here. Nalon at times had the nose of the Coutre poking at McQuinn's elbow. However, Harry had truly found himself and drove a masterful race. Altho many spins and tangle occurred throughout the meet, no one rolled, nor were there any injuries" [*National Auto Racing News, page 2, November 16, 1939*].

## 124th Field Artillery Armory, Chicago, November 19, 1939

All heats were in inverted order. In the first heat, McQuinn and Bob Muhlke mixed it up causing them to fall to the back of the field. Tony Willman won the heat with Cowboy O'Rourke second. The second heat had excitement at the finish line with three abreast as they crossed. Wally Zale was ahead of the threesome but Ted Tetterton and Vito Calia was able to secure second and third, respectively. The third heat saw McQuinn and Nalon barreling through the field from the last row with Nalon leading and McQuinn following. Johnny Ritter continued to challenge McQuinn in a hub-rubbing duel but McQuinn quickly dominated. In the handicap, Zale led all the way to the finish with Zale nosing McQuinn out at the end.

In the feature, Nalon took the lead from pole quickly. Tony Willman followed with McQuinn a very close third. Willman's car sputtered resulting in McQuinn and Zale leaping forward. Nalon won the feature with Ted Duncan second [*National Auto Racing News, November 23, 1939*].

## 124th Field Artillery Armory, Chicago, November 26, 1939

Wally Zale came from the coast with a brand new Offy and ready to race. Ray Richards overtook McQuinn on the first lap taking the lead. Duke Nalon rode a close third but was not able to get pass McQuinn. This duel allowed Richards to increase his lead. They finished in that order with Zale fourth [*National Auto Racing News, page 2, November 30, 1939*].

"STIRRING FINISH

```
Harry McQuinn (No. 4) noses out Wally Zale in a fast moving
   feature event at the Detroit, Mich, indoor coliseum midget
   plant last Saturday night, December 2. The semi-weekly card
   of events at this midget strip furnish plenty of competition
    with the leading mid-West "doodle-bug" pilots competing."
       Unknown newspaper clipping, McQuinn Family records.
```

## Michigan State Fair Grounds Coliseum, December 2, 1939

McQuinn in the No. 4 Leader Card Special started off the night by setting a new one-lap record in qualifying. He then won the first heat. He sat on pole for the 25-lap feature, taking the early lead with Wally Zale right by his side for 12 laps. McQuinn made little ground and Zale finished only a few feet behind in second [*Detroit Free Press, page 22, December 6, 1939*].

## 124th Field Artillery Armory, Chicago, December 3, 1939

Duke Nalon was again the fastest qualifier but so was Wally Zale. Nalon won the pole of the feature on the basis of having qualified first.

The heat races were again inverted. In the first heat, McQuinn and Tony Willman started in the back and on getting through the pack, clipped wheels and nearly spun out. This caused a restart. Duke Nalon shot through the pack on the restart going abreast with the leader, Dan Kladis. Kladis, Nalon, and Willman all collided in a turn. McQuinn, Tony Bettenhausen, and Pete Neilsen were able to swing wide avoiding the mess and winning in that order. Wally Zale screamed from the back to take the second heat. Duke Nalon was able to capture the third heat as did Ted Tetterton in the fourth.

Nalon led off the 40-lap feature. Wally Zale and McQuinn continued to battle for second allowing Nalon to stretch his lead by car lengths. Ted Duncan gained on the pair and overtook McQuinn for third on the 19th lap as McQuinn's mount soured out. Tony Willman challenged Zale and McQuinn, now all battling for second. Willman was able to pass Zale on the 35th lap to hold second place to the finish line after Nalon [*National Auto Racing News, page 2, December 7, 1939*].

## 124th Field Artillery Armory, Chicago, December 10, 1939

In the inverted heats, McQuinn was able to come from the back to win the first heat. The second heat saw Wally Zale, Cowboy O'Rourke and Ray Richards battle it out for the win. Zale had mechanical issues and had to pull off the track. O'Rourke won with Richards second. In the handicap, Wally Zale took over the driving duties in Dauphin's Offy. Zale took the lead with Pete Nielsen following. Nalon was able to pass McQuinn and Zale on a daring move in a turn and he went on to finish first.

Willman and Nalon took the lead in the 40-lap feature. McQuinn went wide in the south turn and was clipped by Duncan that straightened him out. Willman was leading by five car lengths at lap 10 and continued to eight by lap 20. Nalon was second and McQuinn and Richards battled for third. McQuinn was able to get the upper hand and challenge Nalon for second. Richards had won by half a lap with Nalon second and McQuinn third [*National Auto Racing News, page 3, December 14, 1939*].

## Wisconsin State Fair Park Coliseum, Milwaukee, December 15, 1939

Harry "Leadfoot" McQuinn was the fastest qualifier and battled Ray Richards in the 40-lap feature coming out on top. McQuinn won the first heat race as well [*Unknown newspaper clipping, McQuinn Family records*].

## 124th Field Artillery Armory, Chicago, December 17, 1939

In the first heat, Wally Zale and McQuinn again came from the back in neck-breaking speed. Zale took the lead from O'Halloran. McQuinn dove into each turn trying to overtake the leader but was unable to. Zale won with McQuinn following. During the second heat, in the third lap, Duke Nalon came from the back and challenged Ted Duncan for the lead. Nalon took the lead but had to thwart numerous threats by Duncan, holding until the finish. In the 15-lap handicap, Nalon, McQuinn and Duncan were all riding abreast, neither giving an inch with sparks flying from the rubbing hubs. Zale finished first but later said he had broken a stub shaft. McQuinn finished second.

McQuinn sat on pole for the feature after Zale was out for the night. Nalon overtook McQuinn early but McQuinn re-took it in short order and lengthening his lead to five car lengths by the tenth lap and never was challenged from there for the win [*National Auto Racing News, December 21, 1939*].

Harry McQuinn in the No. 4 Leader Card Special
and the Wilke team, 1939.
*Courtesy of the Wilke Family Archives.*

McQuinn in his No. 4 Leader Card Special seen here at the Armory in 1939. *Unknown newspaper clipping, McQuinn Family records.*

**Harry McQuinn in Leader Card Special**
Only 3 time winner National Championship, Chicago, 37-38, 38-39, 39-40. Winner of more features and Championships than any other car in the country.

Midgets on the flat, fifth-mile dirt track at Mazon in 1939.
*Courtesy of Grundy County Hall of Fame Archives.*

Field of midgets at Mazon.
*Courtesy of Grundy County Hall of Fame.*

# HARRY MCQUINN

*Unknown newspaper clipping, McQuinn Family records.*

## 1940

## 124th Field Artillery Armory, Chicago, January 7, 1940

*The Leader Card team surrounds McQuinn during an interview. National Auto Racing News, January 4, 1940.*

"Harry 'Lead Foot' McQuinn dare-devil Hoosier pilot driving the Leader Card No. 4 Miller, copped the 1940 inaugural opening at Chicago Armory 40-lap feature." McQuinn started on pole with Duke Nalon on the outside. Nalon and McQuinn were battling as per usual with Nalon in the lead early after overtaking McQuinn on the second lap. A wide turn on lap five by Nalon allowed McQuinn to sneak through with McQuinn keeping the lead until the finish.

Wally Zale won the first heat with McQuinn second. The 15-lap handicap race saw Wally Zale and McQuinn in a hub-rubbing duel. Zale suddenly shot up toward the wall but held it. He suffered a broken axle and retired for the night. McQuinn went on until the eighth lap when he clipped a hay bale and fell back out of contention [*National Auto Racing News, January 11, 1940*].

## 124th Field Artillery Armory, Chicago, January 14, 1940

The second heat "was the race of the night" packing a dozen thrills. During the race, Pete Romcevich rode over the tail of Tommy Allen's car. A few laps later, Allen spun on the north turn, directly in the path of Paul Russo, who went into a stalling slide hitting the straw bales. McQuinn had taken the lead but was having his hands full trying to keep Ray Richards from passing him. Richards hit McQuinn's car repeatedly, trying every trick in the bag, but Harry refused to give an inch. This worked the fans into their "finest booing style", to make the race a real success [*National Auto Racing News, January 18, 1940*].

Ted Duncan took the lead in the 40-lap main event. McQuinn took the lead in the second lap. Duncan constantly challenged McQuinn but eventually lost ground finishing a quarter of a lap behind. Ray Richards was third and Duke Nalon, fourth. McQuinn set a new track record for the feature. Duke Nalon remained the point leader for the season [*Chicago Tribune, page 19, January 15, 1940*].

## 124th Field Artillery Armory, Chicago, January 21, 1940

McQuinn, driving the Leader Card No. 4, looked like a sure victor at the start of the qualifying heats when he established a new 1-lap record. "Leadfoot" also set a new 12-lap record winning the first heat.

The 15-lap handicap, Ted Duncan and Duke Nalon came from the back to push ahead. Nalon went out on the seventh lap. Duncan, Pete Neilsen, Cowboy O'Rourke and Paul Russo tangled on the eighth lap. Tony Bettenhausen moved by the pile and took first. He warded off McQuinn's advances who spun but recovered to claim fourth. Order: Bettenhausen, Russo, Hartley, McQuinn.

For the 40-lap feature, McQuinn was on the pole with Nalon alongside. McQuinn took the lead in the first turn. Nalon nosed out McQuinn on a turn for the lead. Nalon then stretched his lead to six car lengths by 15 laps. At 25 laps, Ted Johnson spun and got clipped by Duncan. On the 26th lap, McQuinn started to gain on Nalon and at 30 laps these two were whipping the turns hub-to-hub. The crowd was utterly astonished by this terrific speed duel. McQuinn was on Nalon's heels when his motor seized. Nalon continued on to win. Richards moved up to second followed by Duncan, O'Rourke and then McQuinn [*National Auto Racing News, page 2, January 25, 1940*].

## 124th Field Artillery Armory, Chicago, January 28, 1940

The 40-lap feature event winner would receive the Jimmy Snyder Memorial Trophy, a gold car and driver on an ivory pedestal. Duke Nalon, intent upon fastest qualifier to give him an edge in the main feature, rolled his No. 3 Coutre Offy early in the evening. His Offy had to be withdrawn but Nalon took over the Tomshe No. 1 Offy.

In the feature, Nalon pressed McQuinn for 11 laps before spinning out on the 12th. Nalon regained control and continued to rush forward eventually landing third. McQuinn won with Ray Richards second [*Chicago Tribune, page 18, January 29, 1940*].

> "The 124th Field Artillery Armory in Chicago where races are held every Sunday evening, is recognized as the toughest indoor midget track in the entire country. Champions from other sections of the country who drop in for a race, are forced to drive to the limit to make the feature event, and then seldom come in the winning circle. The fans themselves are different from any other fans at different track throughout the country. Generally it is the sinner in any sport who receives the cheers of the crowd. However, when McQuinn wins he generally get a very hearty round of boos. That these same fans were cheering Harry to the gallery in his first few races this when he was attempting a comeback after his near fatal crack-up. Now that they know he can handle himself they have some good natured fun and Harry gets as much enjoyment from it as the fans have in giving it.
>
> Last Sunday, at the Armory, being one of the first to reach Duke Nalon when he flipped during the time trials, we also noticed Harry McQuinn was another of the first to reach him. This just goes to show what kind of a sport Harry really is, and still the crowd boos and boos. All the boys in the racing business are sportsmen and don't let anyone tell you different." Unknown newspaper clipping c.1940, from the Wilke Family Archives.

## 124th Field Artillery Armory, Chicago, February 4, 1940

Ted Duncan and Duke Nalon led from the start. Duncan spun on the 11th lap also stalling Nalon. This allowed McQuinn, then running third, to take the lead and was first across the finish line. McQuinn set record speed to finish first. Nalon was second followed by Ray Richards in third place. McQuinn also finished first in the first heat of the night [*Chicago Tribune, page 22, February 5, 1940*; *National Auto Racing News, page 2, February 8, 1940*].

> "Mr. Everett McQuinn, whose proud son Harry, points out as "That's my Pop", is now associated with Floyd Dreyer at Indianapolis, in grooming out miniature midgets to speedway creations. This combination should prove to be a combined team of mechanical professors of the college of Speed Builders, of which the mid-West may well be proud." National Auto Racing News, page 4, February 8, 1940.

## 124th Field Artillery Armory, Chicago, February 11, 1940

McQuinn and his Leader Card Special developed mechanical issues but was able to overcome this. Duke Nalon, on the other hand, had magneto issues and had to switch to another car.

McQuinn was the fastest qualifier, starting on pole for the main feature and won. Wally Zale was second. Nalon failed to place in the main allowing McQuinn to take over the points standings [*National Auto Racing News, page 2, February 15, 1940*].

# The "Mighty" Midgets

"McQUINN RECEIVES TROPHY—Lieut. Tony Strak (at right), Gen. Mgr. midget auto races at the 124th Field Artillery Armory, Chicago, presenting the Jimmy Snyder Memorial Trophy recently, to the winner, Harry McQuinn, who won the Feb. 11 feature at the Chi. Armory, which puts him in the lead in the point standings with 47 points over Duke Nalon."
*National Auto Racing News, page 1, February 15, 1940.*

*"BIRTHDAY PARTY—Well, here they are, the old Chicago gang down at Jimmy's Tavern. It was McQuinn's birthday party and the festivities lasted well into the wee hours. McQuinn, seated on the floor in checkered shirt, with Chitwood and a beautiful Miami damsel sandwiched between them."*
*National Auto Racing News, page 1, February 8, 1940.*

## 124th Field Artillery Armory, Chicago, February 18, 1940

Ted Duncan and McQuinn started in the first row with McQuinn on pole. At the start, Duncan was able to get out first. McQuinn dogged his tail but never could overcome Duncan who went on to victory in the 40-lap feature [*Chicago Tribune, page 22, February 19, 1940*].

"It was reported that McQuinn came over to congratulate Duncan on the win. Duncan smiled as he shook hands and remarked 'Well Harry will you be back next week?'. The leadfoot grinned and replied 'Well, Ted, I suppose so if remorse and discouragement don't overtake me. The two had a hearty laugh" [*Unknown newspaper clipping from the Wilke family Archives*].

## 124th Field Artillery Armory, Chicago, February 25, 1940

Ted Duncan secured his second straight win at the Armory. Wally Zale and Duke Nalon had mechanical troubles and were not able to make the feature. McQuinn started on pole and Duncan to the outside. The two rubbed hubs continuously but Duncan was able to nose out McQuinn. Duncan expanded his lead with McQuinn several car lengths behind and fighting Ray Richards to maintain second at the end.

McQuinn won the first heat of the evening as did Paul Russo for the second and O'Rourke for the third. The 15-lap handicap was won by McQuinn by taking the lead from Tony Bettenhausen and Cowboy O'Rourke on the 11th lap [*National Auto Racing News, page 3, February 29, 1940*].

## 124th Field Artillery Armory, Chicago, March 3, 1940

Duke Nalon had been deferring some medical care but progressively got worse and could not participate. McQuinn was also not in the feature having had bearing issues during the elimination trials. Emil Andres was driving the new Offy owned by Nalon and captured the third heat but had to retire due to motor issues.

Wally Zale drove Nalon's No. 3 Coutre Offy to victory in the 40-lap main. Ted Duncan was fastest in time trials and started on pole. Ray Richards was on the outside of row 1 and nosed out Duncan on the start. However, Zale was able to overtake both in the backstretch of the first lap. On the sixth lap, Duncan climbed up and sailed over the top of Richards but was able to continue after being disentangled. Richards had to retire due to a broken front axle. This allowed Zale to take a considerable lead with Bob Muhlke and Myron Fohr finishing second and third, respectfully [*National Auto Racing News, page 3, March 7, 1940*].

## 124th Field Artillery Armory, Chicago, March 10, 1940

Wally Zale, Ray Richards, and McQuinn got tangled during the third lap of the 40-lap main event allowing Myron Fohr and Tony Willman, in his brand new Offy, to go forth in the lead. Zale and McQuinn were two laps down while the pit boys had to unlock their cars. Zale and Richards tangled once again on the 18th lap when McQuinn made great speed to cover the lost distance, cut in thereby clipping the wheel of Erwin causing him to wobble and nothing could be avoided. Willman took the lead from Fohr on the 29th lap. Fohr finished second behind Willman and Muhlke was third. McQuinn had made up a great amount of distance (and laps), finishing sixth [*Chicago Tribune, page 21, March 11, 1940; National Auto Racing News, March 14, 1940*].

At the conclusion of the race, "Buzz Saw" Tomshe accused McQuinn of getting his car disqualified but this was done by the technical judge who found that the steering was wired together and deemed unsafe. Buzz Saw, all 5'4" of him let loose on McQuinn and it was said that Ted Duncan joined in while the vast crowd had encircled the drivers in the infield after the race's conclusion. Because of the crowding, two spectators got hurt in the ongoing fisticuffs which drew the ire of Lieutenant Strak, the race promoter [*National Auto Racing News, page 2, March 14, 1940*].

## 124th Field Artillery Armory, Chicago, March 17, 1940

This series of events again saw 46 entrants for the evening. Myron Fohr had the fastest qualifying time and started on pole for the 40-lap main event. Fohr got out to an early lead. Ted Duncan and Myron Fohr piled into each other on the 18th lap when Fohr slipped wide. Wally Zale spun on the 33rd lap and collected McQuinn who could not avoid the midget racer. Ray Richards having avoided the wrecks of the leaders was able to take the lead and hold onto it until the finish. The finishing order was: Richards, Tony Willman, Emil Andres, Paul Russo, and McQuinn.

Zale won the first heat, McQuinn the second, and Willman the third. In the 15-lap handicap, Bob Muhlke and Willman lead the field out. Willman took the early lead and Muhlke went wide in a turn on the sixth lap clipping a bale of hay allowing McQuinn and Zale to push forward but not enough to catch Willman [*National Auto Racing News, page 2, March 21, 1940*].

## 124th Field Artillery Armory, Chicago, March 24, 1940

Wally Zale in Duke Nalon's No. 3
Coutre Offy and McQuinn in the armory.
*National Auto Racing News, March 28, 1940.*

Ray Richards was again the fastest qualifier. Wally Zale won the first heat of the evening. In the third heat, Myron Fohr overturned then got hit by another car. Fohr was not seriously injured but that could not be said for the car. For the 40-lap feature, Richards was on pole. "Leadfoot Mercury" McQuinn took the lead early. Ray Richards got a flat tire but continued to race and even closed the gap between himself and McQuinn. The finish was close with McQuinn, Richards and Duncan in that order [*National Auto Racing News, page 2, March 28, 1940*].

*Several of the midget pilots owned or operated local drinking holes. Many of the drivers were often seen hanging out at these establishments. This definitely help draw the crowds in. Many of the drivers would also tend bar to as part of the local attraction. McQuinn was known to tend at Jimmy's place on 63rd street in Chicago at least for a short while in relief of Cowboy O'Rourke who had to tend to some medical issues [National Auto Racing News, page 7, March 21, 1940].*

**McQUINN 1939-40 CHAMP**

## 124th Field Artillery Armory, Chicago, March 31, 1940

McQuinn in his Leader Card Special captured the feature win and the season championship. Ted Duncan was speediest in time trials. Art Hartsfeld, returning from weeks off after injuries sustained in Detroit, went on to capture the first heat. The second heat found McQuinn crossing the finish line first with Wally Zale inches behind. Bob Muhlke was able to win the third heat without challenge.

The feature saw 14 cars lining up with Duncan on pole. The excitement of fans mirrored the excitement of the drivers. The drivers, constantly jockeying for position before the rolling start were never in order and were not flagged green until 15 laps. McQuinn was able to jump out into the lead followed by Zale and Duncan. Frank Burany, Pete Nielsen and Myron Fohr tangled in the 30th turn. Muhlke pulled into the pits on the 37th lap with a flat. Duncan had to retire for the night after mechanical failure on the 51st lap. Muhlke had resumed racing but by the 56th lap, had engine failure. The first four positions hardly changed the entire race but Zale constantly challenged McQuinn and was said that Zale drove one of his greatest races of his career [*National Auto Racing News, page 2, April 4, 1940*].

The final points standings were: McQuinn-1054; Richards- 671; Nalon- 630; Zale- 444; Russo- 443 [*National Auto Racing News, page 3, April 18, 1940*].

### MacQuinn Wins 3d Midget Auto Title

McQuinn's feature win gained him the season's championship, his third consecutive at the Armory.

## 124th Field Artillery Armory Track champions:

Tony Willman, 1934-35

Jimmy Snyder, 1935-36

Shorty Sorenson, 1936-37

Harry McQuinn, 1937-38

Harry McQuinn, 1938-39

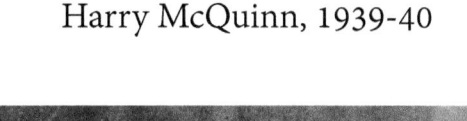

Harry McQuinn, 1939-40

"Keen competition. Above we see Harry McQuinn leading driver Wally Zale into one of the turns at the Chicago Armory indoor plant. With the final and championship card of events slated for this midget strip, Sunday night, Match 31st, mid-West speed fans will see the top ranking stars of this section vieing for the evening's title honors. This indoor plant is offering $1,000.00 purse money for their championship meet." *Unknown newspaper clipping, courtesy of the Wilke family.*

# HARRY MCQUINN

**"LEADER" GROUP RECORDS WINS WITH CHAMPIONS**

Pictured below is a live wire racing team that has recorded a lot of victories in midget racing circles around Milwaukee and Chicago. Mr. R. C. Wilke, vice-president and secretary of the Leader Card Works, Incorporated of Milwaukee, Wisconsin, owner of the outfit can be seen fourth from the left in the front row. Harry McQuinn is seated in car No. 4, and Pete Neilson can be seen in car No. 5.

Mr. Wilke calls our attention to the Champion decals on the car and we agree that they are in a prominent place.

Harry McQuinn and car No. 4 set a new 40 lap track record in the feature race at the Chicago Armory on December 17th, and has been the national indoor champion for the past three years. Ray Richards and Pete Neilson, other drivers of the team have been setting up records, too. Between them and the speedy racers (using Champions, of course) they have won the high point standing for the season at the outdoor track at Riverview in Chicago and won the national outdoor championship at St. Louis, as well as winning pretty regularly in Milwaukee, their home town.

A real outfit of Champion pluggers and we extend our congratulations.

*Courtesy of the Wilke Family Archives.*

"MID-WEST WHISPERS

By Ed (Twenty-Grand) Steinbock

All hail to Harry MacQuinn, the king of all Midgeteers. According to records, the versatile MacQuinn is the only driver in the midget speed sport history to win a track championship for three consecutive years. Ever since the inception of indoor midget racing at the 124th Field Artillery Armory in 1934, which incidently was the first indoor track in the world, a driver winning an Armory championship, has automatically placed his name in the top bracket of small car speed merchants. Hundreds of drivers from all parts of the country have attempted to lift the indoor crown from the strangle hold of the mid-West drivers, but as yet none have succeeded. Since 1934, only four drivers have been successful in their championship efforts. Tony Willman, the worlds first indoor midget champion, for the 1934-35 season. The late Jimmy Snyder held the title in 1935-36. Shorty Sorenson nosed out his team-mate, Harry MacQuinn, to win top-honors in 1936-37. Since the 1936-37 season, MacQuinn has accounted for the balance of the titles, holding top-honors in 1937-38; 1938-39 and 1939-40. MacQuinn's championship drives for the past three years, places his midget achievements on par with Louie Meyers' three Indianapolis wins.

Much credit for MacQuinn's startling victories, goes to the outstanding midget conditioners, the internationally famous Marchese Brothers of Milwaukee, Wisc. Carl and Tudy are probably the best known of this famous racing family, for they devote their time exclusively to racing. There is not a single thing that these two boys can't do with metal. Tudy's abilities as a machinist are phenomenal. The tedious task of making crankshafts, gears and all other necessary parts, is all in a day's work for his nimble fingers and mechanically trained mind. Carl devotes his time to the mechanical end of the business, assembling motors, timing, carburetion, figuring out gear ratios and the thousand and one things that need attention on race cars, are second nature to this versatile member of the Marchese family.

Last year a new member joined the famous racing team. Bob Wilke, vice-president and secretary of the Leader Card Company of Milwaukee, Wisc., bought the famous No. 4 Marchese Special. He retained Carl and Tudy Marchese as mechanics, Harry MacQuinn and Ray Richards as drivers, and experienced great success in his first year as a race car owner. Wilkes' sportsmanship and easy going, yet businesslike manner, has made a host of new friends for his team wherever they have appeared. This year the Leader Card banner will adorn several spanking new Offenhauser powered cars, which will without a doubt add many championships to the already long string of victories to this team's credit." *National Auto Racing News, April 4, 1940.*

## Harry McQuinn Is Master Driver Of Both Midget and Full-Sized Cars

The King of the Midgets could put any one of the seven dwarfs, and possibly Snow White, in one of his vest pockets—but he's more anxious to pocket the first place money of the "500" today.

Harry McQuinn, who makes this Hoosier speed center his home, finished up the midget auto racing season with his third national indoor championship, and now is concentrating his efforts upon one of the biggest and fastest cars entered in the speed classic on the Indianapolis Motor Speedway.

"Hairbreadth Harry" roared into his third title March 31 at the 124th Field Artillery Armory, Chicago. Among the 27,000 spectators in the stands that night was Big Bill White, the Hollywood (Cal.) racing impresario whose racing stable has contained such hot shots as Rex Mays, the Glendale Ghost; Al Gordon, the Los Angeles strong man, and George Souders, the 1927 winner of the "500."

White was scouting the midget field for a driver to take over his powerful Italian Alfa Romeo car, which has been completely rebuilt for Indianapolis by the veteran mechanician, Roscoe Dunning. When the championship race was over, White approached McQuinn.

"Harry, how'd you like to drive that Alfa in the '500'?" White asked.

"Name your deal, Bill," replied the midget king, and before the session was over McQuinn had a new car, and White another driving "hot shot."

McQuinn's Indianapolis car was finished in fifth place by the veteran Babe Stapp of Los Angeles, in the 1939 "500."

"I'm going to finish it up farther front, or else—" McQuinn promised.

"Or else what?" Bill White asked.

"Or else go back to midget racing," McQuinn replied.

*The Indianapolis Star, page 31, May 30, 1940.*

## Walsh Memorial Stadium, St. Louis, June 5, 1940

McQuinn started in second in the 35-lap main feature but gained first by the end of the first lap. While he was challenged by Myron Fohr at times, he never lost the lead. In order: McQuinn, Fohr, and Ted Duncan [*The St. Louis Star and Times, page 30, June 6, 1940*].

## Wisconsin State Fair Park, Milwaukee, June 8, 1940

AAA race and first of the outdoor season for this track. Rex Mays won the first heat as did McQuinn in the second. Mays started the feature, with Paul Russo on outside first row; McQuinn started fifth. Mays lead the race all the way. The battle in the race took place between McQuinn, Davis, Connors, and Russo. Andres took second from Russo in the 11th lap. McQuinn took third place on the 24th lap after Russo got a flat tire. Russo was able to pit, change tire and resume finishing in sixth. The results were: Mays, Andres, and McQuinn [*National Auto Racing News, page 3, June 13, 1940*].

## Riverview Speedway, Chicago, June 9, 1940

Riverview saw the return of Duke Nalon and McQuinn to midget racing from Indianapolis. The crowd gave the two a big welcome back. Wally Zale, Emil Andres and Duke Nalon each won one of the initial heats. Zale captured the main event with Andres second. McQuinn had spun out on the 5th lap and could not recover in time [*National Auto Racing News, page 2, June 13, 1940*].

## Walsh Memorial Stadium, St. Louis, June 12, 1940

Ted Duncan won the 40-lap feature. He had stiff competition from McQuinn exchanging the lead on several occasions but McQuinn spun on the 10th lap and lost all ground. Ray Richards placed second and Tony Bettenhausen was third. McQuinn and Bob Muhlke won each of the initial heats [*National Auto Racing News, page 2, June 20, 1940*].

## Wisconsin State Fair Park, Milwaukee, June 14, 1940

Ted Duncan won the main event beating out McQuinn [*The St. Louis Star and Times, page 20, June 18, 1940*].

## Unknown track, June 25, 1940

Ray Richards won, McQuinn starting 8th finished second [*Unknown newspaper clipping, McQuinn Family records*].

## Walsh Memorial Stadium, St. Louis, June 28, 1940

Ray Richards takes the main event followed by McQuinn [*The St. Louis Star and Times, page 28, June 26, 1940*].

*During the summer seasons, McQuinn found himself "outside of the money" on many occasions until his motor gave out. A new motor was being built by the Marchese brothers but this caused Harry to sit out of many opportunities in June. Eventually, a new Offenhauser was installed.*

Chicago Tribune, page 26, June 20, 1940

**M'QUINN ENTERS $6,000 MIDGET IN 50 MILE RACE**

The most expensive midget racing car made—Harry McQuinn's especially constructed $6,000 Marchese special—will be watched closely by rival drivers in the 50 mile race at the Cook county fairgrounds, River road and North avenue, Sunday afternoon when midget auto racing on a half mile track is presented for the first time in the Chicago section.

McQuinn, who has won the national indoor midget championship the last two years, will be opposed by Sam Hanks, Mal Hanson, Lou Durant, and Pete Nielson of California; Paul Russo of New York, eastern champion; Duke Nalon of Chicago, national outdoor champion; Tony Willman and Dutch Schneebing of Milwaukee; Joe Callo, Kansas City champion, and Chicagoans Emil Andres, Wally Zale, Ted Duncan, Ray Richards, Tony Bettenhausen, Shorty Sorenson, Mike O'Halloran, and Bob Muhlke.

## Olympic Field, Kansas City, June 30, 1940

Peewee Distrace won the 35-lap feature with McQuinn second [*Unknown newspaper clipping, provided by the Wilke Family Archives*].

## Walsh Memorial Stadium, St. Louis, July 4, 1940

"Harry (Mercury Leadfoot) McQuinn of Indianapolis who was the local Class A midget auto racing champion two years ago, had his No. 4 Offenhauser running smoothly on the annual Independence day speed program last night at Walsh Stadium and when the racing was over for the evening he had bagged the honors in the 25-lap, 15-lap handicap and a 10-lap elimination race.

It was in the handicap in which Myron Fohr of Milwaukee suffered the only serious accident of the evening. He was leading during the eighth lap when he spun into the barricade which is placed in front of the flag pole on the north turn. His car appeared to be badly damaged. It took attendants about five minutes to remove Myron from his car. He will be on the shelf for the next two weeks, according to the stadium physician" [*St Louis Post-Dispatch, page 14, July 5, 1940*].

## Wisconsin State Fair Park, Milwaukee, July 5, 1940

McQuinn, having jumped into the lead on the second lap, held on until the finish to win the main event. Ray Richards finished second followed by Ted Duncan. Myron Fohr was injured in the handicap having his foot entrapped in the wreck [*National Auto Racing News, page 2, July 11, 1940*].

## Wisconsin State Fair Park, Milwaukee, July 7, 1940

McQuinn won the 30-lap feature while Ray Richards and Ted Duncan battled for second, finishing in that order [*Unknown newspaper clipping, from the Wilke Family Archives*].

## Riverview Speedway, Chicago, July 7, 1940

Ted Duncan won the main event followed by Wally Zale and McQuinn [*National Auto Racing News, July 11, 1940*].

## Walsh Memorial Stadium, St. Louis, July 9, 1940

Ted Duncan continued to dominate winning the 35-lap main feature. McQuinn finished second and Ray Richards third. The season's standings were similarly reflected with Duncan in the lead having three feature victories and McQuinn in second with two. Richards, McQuinn and Duncan each won a preliminary. McQuinn also won the handicap [*National Auto Racing News, page 2, July 18, 1940*].

## Cahokia Speedway, Cahokia IL, July 11, 1940

"Leadfoot" McQuinn in the Leader Card Special won the 25-lap main feature. Ted Duncan challenged repeatedly but was never able to overtake McQuinn [*National Auto Racing News, page 3, July 18, 1940*].

## Wisconsin State Fair Park, Milwaukee, July 12, 1940

Wally Zale, the "human cyclone", was the fastest in time trials and took the heat and main feature. Myron Fohr and McQuinn tangled on the sixth lap. Fohr was disentangled and put back on the track but clearly had something more wrong as Fohr rolled his car on the next lap. The finishing order was: Zale, Ray Richards, Gus Klingbeil, Knight, McQuinn [*National Auto Racing News, page 3, July 18, 1940*].

## Crown Point Fair Raceway, Crown Point IN, July 13, 1940

McQuinn placed third in heat 1 and won the 12-lap handicap. He had to retire from the field in the main feature due to radius rod failure [*Unknown newspaper clipping, McQuinn Family archives*].

## Riverview Speedway, Chicago, July 14, 1940

Wally Zale captured the 50-lap main event. Paul Swedberg and Ted Duncan lead the feature. Duncan took the lead on the first turn. Swedberg fell back due to broken axle. At the midpoint, Duncan was still leading with Zale second, and Richards third. Richards pulled off with a flat on the 45th laps. Zale was able to surpass Duncan holding the lead to the finish with Duncan and McQuinn following. Zale, McQuinn, Rice and Bob Muhlke each won a heat race. Zale won the handicap with McQuinn second [*National Auto Racing News, page 2, July 18, 1940*].

## Walsh Memorial Stadium, St. Louis, July 16, 1940

Wally Zale battled McQuinn, Tony Bettenhausen, Ted Duncan, and Ray Richards in the 35-lap feature but came out on top [*The St. Louis Star and Times, page 21, July 17, 1940*].

## Cahokia Speedway, Cahokia IL, July 18, 1940

Wally Zale appeared with a new car and the same winning ways. Zale was reported to "blow in", and capture the heat, handicap and main feature. During the feature, Zale followed McQuinn for the first 14 laps then the two entangled with Zale spinning killing the motor. A restart had Zale in fourth. Zale proceeded to pass Duke Nalon, Ted Duncan and finally McQuinn for the win. Zale, McQuinn, and Peewee Distrace won the heats respectfully and Zale the handicap. McQuinn and Duncan had a five-lap special match race that was said to end in a dead heat [*National Auto Racing News, page 5, July 25, 1940*].

## Riverview Speedway, Chicago, July 21, 1940

Wally Zale won the 30-lap main event leading Ted Duncan by four car lengths. McQuinn was third and Ray Richards, fourth [*Chicago Tribune, page 18, July 22, 1940*].

## Starved Rock Speedway, Utica IL, July 22, 1940

This was the inaugural event at Starved Rock which was a short-lived ½ mile dirt track near Utica. The first heat was captured by Wally Zale. Cowboy O'Rourke captured the second heat and the handicap. Duke Nalon won the third. Zale went on to win the feature. Duke Nalon had been burned when oil spilled on him but he managed to finish the feature. McQuinn was running behind Zale but pulled back when a rock hit him in the eye and he dropped back but still finished fourth [*National Auto Racing News, page 4, August 4, 1940*].

### Walsh Memorial Stadium, St. Louis, July 23, 1940

The 35-lap main event was won by Wally Zale who led from the beginning with McQuinn second and Duncan third. Rex Easton and Johnny Rogan crashed into each other during the feature, both were seriously hurt [*St. Louis Post-Dispatch, page 14, July 24, 1940*].

### Tacoma Motor Speedway, Dayton KY, July 24, 1940

The quarter-mile semi-banked track for midget racing was put in place of a dog track that was deemed illegal. The inaugural, 25-lap main event was won by McQuinn with Cowboy O'Rourke second and Paul Russo, third [*Cincinnati Enquirer, page 13, July 25, 1940*].

### Cahokia Speedway, Cahokia IL, July 25, 1940

Duke Nalon broke the winning streak of Wally Zale and took the main event. But, Zale finished second and McQuinn, third. McQuinn also won the 15-lap handicap [*National Auto Racing News, page 4, August 1, 1940*].

### Wisconsin State Fair Park, Milwaukee, July 27, 1940

This race was postponed from the previous night due to heavy rains. The track was very rough from the weather but McQuinn was still able to take the main feature. McQuinn started on pole as fastest qualifier and never gave back the lead. Tony Bettenhausen and Ray Richards battled for second with Bettenhausen triumphing [*National Auto Racing News, page 3, August 1, 1940*].

### Crown Point Fair Raceway, Crown Point IN, July 28, 1940

Wally Zale was the fastest qualifier but had his share of motor issues. Zale went out of earlier heats and won the fourth. In the handicap, he again had to retire from the field in the first few laps. Zale ended up starting 7th in the main. McQuinn retired from the main event with a busted connecting rod. Paul Russo spun and Tony Bettenhausen could not avoid him and plowed into the car. Zale was able to capitalize on their misfortune and was able to take the lead and the win. McQuinn won the 10-lap handicap [*National Auto Racing News, page 4, August 1, 1940*].

## Walsh Memorial Speedway, St. Louis, July 30, 1940

Wally Zale captured four firsts: qualifying, first elimination, 15-lap handicap, and 40-lap feature. McQuinn placed second in the feature and won his elimination event [*St. Louis Post-Dispatch, page 12, July 31, 1940*].

## Tacoma Motor Speedway, Dayton KY, July 31, 1940

McQuinn won the 25-lap feature followed by Tony Bettenhausen and Vito Calis [*Cincinnati Enquirer, page 15, August 1, 1940*].

## Cahokia Speedway, Cahokia IL, August 1, 1940

The three preliminaries were taken by Ted Duncan, Wally Zale, and McQuinn. The feature was won by Zale with Nalon second and McQuinn, third [*National Auto Racing News, page 6, August 8, 1940*].

## Wisconsin State Fair Park, Milwaukee, August 2, 1940

The track was still wet from the previous day and slick. John Dietz slipped on the track in practice, spun, and went into the fence. After the third heat, the feature was started early due to the sense of more rain coming. Paul Swedberg took the early lead from Pat Warren in the feature. At 10 laps, Swedberg was holding off Duke Nalon, Tony Bettenahusen, Ray Richards, and McQuinn in that order which remained to the 20th lap. Swedberg lost his traction on the slippery track giving ground. Ray Richards found the outside grove with loose dirt to help with traction and proceeded to pass all for the win. The order was: Richards, Nalon, Swedberg, McQuinn.

McQuinn also won the third heat with Myron Fohr and Peewee Distrace taking second and third respectively. Point standings for the season was: McQuinn- 294 points; Richards- 261; Duncan- 158 [*National Auto Racing News, page 3, August 8, 1940*].

## Riverview Speedway, Chicago, August 4, 1940

Wally Zale started on the pole for the feature with Bob Muhlke on the outside first row. Ted Duncan nosed out Zale in the very first turn capturing the lead. At 10 laps, Duncan had stretched his lead followed by Zale. McQuinn had moved up the field to challenge for third with Tony Bettenhausen, Cowboy O'Rourke and Ray Richards. On the 22$^{nd}$ lap, Richards dropped out with a broken gas line and Zale on the 26$^{th}$ with a flat. The battle for third continued but Bettenhausen had the upper hand earlier to get second. McQuinn and O'Rourke continued to battle in a hub-grinding duel with O'Rourke coming out in third and McQuinn fourth [*National Auto Racing News, page 12, August 12, 1940*].

## Walsh Memorial Stadium, St. Louis, August 6, 1940

Wally Zale won his fifth straight feature. Zale took the early lead and held onto it. McQuinn did not race in the feature after having a crack-up in the third elimination race [*St. Louis Dispatch, page 15, August 7, 1940*].

## Cahokia Speedway, Cahokia IL, August 8, 1940

The feature saw several lead changes but Ted Duncan was able to take first with O'Rourke placing second. Wally Zale and McQuinn were absent due to mechanical issues in recent events [*National Auto Racing News, page 5, August 15, 1940*].

## Riverview Speedway, Chicago, August 11, 1940

Wally Zale was again on the pole with Ted Duncan on the outside. Zale got out to the lead and was ahead by five car lengths on the second lap. Richards went out on the 18th lap with a flat. McQuinn and Bob Muhlke continued to battle hub to hub. Zale went on to victory followed by Ted Duncan, Tony Bettenhausen, and McQuinn. McQuinn also won the 12-lap handicap [*National Auto Racing News, page 14, August 15, 1940*].

## Cahokia Speedway, Cahokia IL, August 16, 1940

Cowboy O'Rourke won the 25-lap feature taking the lead at the beginning and never giving it back. McQuinn finished second in the feature and won the first preliminary [*St. Louis Post-Dispatch, page 9, August 17, 1940*].

## Mazon Speedbowl, Grundy County Fairgrounds, Mazon IL, September 1/2, 1940

"In those early years of automobile racing, those daring young men were running at the high speed of 46.75 mph in what were basically home built and modified cars without cages, seat belts or helmets. Safety equipment was non-existent. As automobile racing was proving to be a crowd favorite the (Grundy County) Fair became aware of the need to handle larger crowds. A new grandstand was built in 1927 with a capacity of 3500 people and auto racing became a permanent and vital part of the Grundy County Fair.

The old half-mile dirt produced some of the best "Big Car" racing in the Midwest. Many of the best drivers in the country had thrown dirt all over the great crowds, where it was not uncommon to see a car go out through the fence, over a railroad track and into a cornfield. A whole new series of auto racing had been started on the west coast and was quickly sweeping the entire nation. Thus the "Big Car" style of auto racing ended and the run of the "Mighty Midgets" began. In 1936 three days of racing was scheduled for that first big weekend of Midget auto racing at the Fair. A smaller one-fifth mile dirt track was built in front of the grandstands for this new racing series. The "Big Car" drivers had no trouble adapting to the smaller track and the smaller cars."

http://www.grundycountyspeedwayonline.com/history.html

Wally Zale swept his events winning the first heat, handicap and the feature. Ray Richards placed second, followed by Ted Duncan and Tony Bettenhausen. McQuinn had been replaced by Myron Fohr in the No. 4 Leader Card Special with Ray Richards in the No. 5 Leader Card Special [*National Auto Racing News, page 4, September 12, 1940*].

Wally Zale took the first heat; Tony Bettenhausen, the second. Zale again took the handicap and appeared like he was going to sweep the events once again. In the feature, however, his car developed a frozen piston and he was out of the race. Fohr won the feature with Richards second and Bettenhausen, third [*National Auto Racing News, page 4, September 12, 1940*].

Ted Duncan (#15) and Harry McQuinn battle at Mazon in 1940.
(Bob Sheldon Collection Photo)

http://www.kalracing.com/Autoracing/mazon_speedbowl_photo_scrapbook.htm

## Walsh Memorial Stadium, St. Louis, September 3, 1940

The last race of the season was a 100-lap feature that was won by Cowboy O'Rourke with Fohr second and Ted Duncan third (after a dispute of the finishing order); McQuinn placed 7th after having a tire blowout [*St Louis Post-Dispatch, page 33, September 4, 1940*].

Midwest midget ace Harry McQuinn at Mazon in 1940
*(Wayne Adams Photo)*

http://www.kalracing.com/Autoracing/mazon_speedbowl_photo_scrapbook.htm

## Champaign County Fairgrounds, Urbana IL, September 4, 1940

Wally Zale took the lead in the feature on the 5th lap but dropped out on the 9th with a blown tire. Ray Richards took the feature followed by Tony Bettenhausen and McQuinn [*National Auto Racing News, page 6, September 12, 1940*].

## Monee District Fairgrounds, Monee IL, September 8, 1940

Mike McCann flipped on the 6th lap and the race was halted to allow the ambulance on the field on the 11th lap and the race was called. Ray Richards was in the lead on the 11th and was declared the winner followed by Niesel, Backey and McQuinn. This was apparently the last race at this venue [*National Auto Racing News, page 5, September 12, 1940*].

## Farmer City Midget Oval, Farmer City IL, September 19, 1940

McQuinn won one of the 10-lap heats. He retired from the feature due to mechanical failure [*Unknown newspaper clipping, McQuinn Family records*].

## Champaign County Fairgrounds, Urbana IL, September 22, 1940

McQuinn was the winner of the second heat. He placed second in the 12-lap handicap and the 20-lap feature [*Unknown newspaper clipping, McQuinn Family archives*].

## Champaign County Fairgrounds, Urbana IL, September 28, 1940

The last race of the season. McQuinn in his new Nichols Elto qualified first. He won the first heat and Pete Romcevich, the second. McQuinn won the feature and Ray Richards came in second [*National Auto Racing News, page 3, October 10, 1940*].

## International Amphitheatre, Chicago, November 17, 1940

Ted Duncan qualified the quickest in time trials. Ray Richards in the No. 5 Leader Card Special won the second heat and set a new track record. Richards also broke the 15-lap track record in winning the handicap. The first heat was won by Wally Zale. Zale and McQuinn mixed it up battling for second. McQuinn had to pit but Zale went on to win. In the handicap, Pete Nielsen took the lead. Zale and McQuinn again mixed it up. McQuinn went out of control and hit the south wall. In the feature, Zale took the early lead. Duncan in second got entangled with Emil Andres on the 13th lap and lost his ground. The remaining laps saw constant challenges but no changes in the order: Zale, Ray Richards, Bob Muhlke, Myron Fohr, McQuinn [*National Auto Racing News, page 2, November 21, 1940*].

## International Amphitheatre, Chicago, November 24, 1940

The first 12-lap heat was won by Cowboy O'Rourke. The second heat was a hay bale buster with bales scattered by several drivers including McQuinn, the Hoosier Leadfoot, coming from fifth to place second behind Myron Fohr. Ted "Splinter" Duncan set a new one-lap record and captured the 30-lap main. Ray Richards was second and Cowboy O'Rourke was third [*National Auto Racing News, page 2, November 28, 1940*].

## 124th Field Artillery Armory, Chicago, December 8, 1940

"The Race of Champions." Duke Nalon, driving the No. 4 Leader Card Special, formerly driven by McQuinn, was fastest qualifier with Wally Zale. Both started the feature in the first row with Nalon nosing out Zale for the early lead. He was never challenged and finished by almost a lap over second place of Ted Duncan.

The second heat had the crowd in a frenzy. Mike O'Halloran commanded the early lead but was quickly overcome by Cowboy O'Rourke. McQuinn, driving Nalon's No. 8 Offy, had come from last to second followed by Duke Nalon. O'Rourke, McQuinn, and Nalon were battling out for the lead but McQuinn's brake drums started to smoke and he pulled off into the pits. Nalon dove hard into the last turn to nose out O'Rourke for the win by inches [*National Auto Racing News, page 2, December 12, 1940*].

## International Amphitheatre, Chicago, December 22, 1940

Cowboy O'Rourke outlasted the field with several drivers taking their turns at the hay bales. O'Rourke led all but one of the laps in winning the 30-lap main event. Ray Richards was second and Tony Willman, third. McQuinn did not place [*National Auto Racing News, page 2, December 26, 1940*].

McQuinn in the Leader Card Special.
*Courtesy of the Wilke Family Archives.*

## 1941

## International Amphitheater, Chicago, January 26, 1941

"Harry MacQuinn of Indianapolis, defending champion in the national championships, came into his own in the evening's racing. He won the 30 lap feature event, set a one lap record in the trials, won the first elimination and finished second to Wally Zale of Chicago, the current leader, in the 15 lap handicap."

Half a dozen cars piled up during a spectacular crash with three of the machines having rammed into the wall- fortunately no one was seriously hurt [*Chicago Tribune, page 18, January 27, 1941*].

## International Amphitheater, Chicago, February 2, 1941

Tony Willman won the 40-lap feature beatng Mike O'Halloran by a car length. Ray Richards was third and Myron Fohr was fourth. McQuinn won one of the early preliminaries but spun in the feature and could not make the ground back up [*Chicago Tribune, page 23, February 3, 1941; Indianapolis Star, page 16, February 3, 1941*].

## International Amphitheater, Chicago, February 9, 1941

Ray Richards in the No. 4 Leader Card Special was fastest qualifier of the evening. The main feature of the evening and the last for the season was a 100-lapper. Richards and Wally Zale were lined up in the first row. On the eighth lap, Richards swung out and Zale shot into the lead followed by McQuinn and Ted Duncan. Duncan took over second from McQuinn on the 18th lap. Zale went out in the 24th lap when his car caught fire. Duncan and McQuinn in fighting for the lead entangled on the 65th lap and Duncan was forced out. McQuinn was able to continue in the race but lost ground. Art Hartsfeld won the feature. Muhlke finished second; Pete Neilsen, third; Richards, fourth; Cowboy O'Rourke, fifth; Tony Willman, sixth; McQuinn, seventh.

In the first heat of the night, Bob Muhlke sat on pole with McQuinn to the outside. McQuinn in his Caris Offy led the second lap running side by side with Muhlke.

However, McQuinn's car was losing water and was flagged off the track. Adding to the entertainment for the evening was another fisticuffs with McQuinn and Frank Podriznik [*National Auto Racing News, page 2, February 13, 1941*].

## Cahokia Speedway, Cahokia IL, August 1, 1941

Wally Zale was the feature winner followed by Ted Duncan and McQuinn [*Unknown newspaper clipping, McQuinn Family records*].

## Thompson International Speedway, Thompson CT, October 12, 1941

Tony Willman was thrown from his car in the race just after setting a new world's record for the half-mile. The rear of the car locked up pushing him up into the guardrail. He suffered compound fractures of the skull when another car ran over him [*The St. Louis Star and Times, page 13, October 13, 1941*].

> "The runner-up to Tony Bettenhausen in the 1951 National Driving Championship, Banks had a "fair-play" attitude that also served him well and this kind of thing was easily seen at 1941 Midget race at the old Freeport (N.Y.) Stadium out on Long Island when a pair of hard-driving competitors by the names of Shorty Sorenson and Harry McQuinn showed up to race.
>
> Disheartened at Sorenson and McQuinn's presence, a group of drivers told the promoter that they would load-up their Midgets and leave. Henry Banks stayed and raced."
>
> http://www.empaonline.org/banks%20bio.html

## 1945

"Harry MacQuinn, Franklin-Born Race Driver and 3-Times National Midget Champion, Returns to Action Friday

Announcement by officials of the Indianapolis Speedrome today that Harry MacQuinn, "King of the Midgets" and former Franklin driver in the 500-mile race at the Indianapolis Speedway, will get back in action Friday night has caused no little excitement in racing circles.

MacQuinn hung up the greatest record of any midget racing driver when he captured the national championship at Chicago for three consecutive years, 1938, 1939 and 1940. On top of that, he annexed the top prize in 62 of 73 feature events from New York to California during the 1938 season.

Franklin fans best remember MacQuinn for his eight appearances at the big 500-mile race. He always was a colorful driver and provided fans with plenty of thrills when he was driving one of the big cars, but the best that he could do was to land seventh-place money on three different occasions.

Since the early days of the war, MacQuinn has been employed in the inspection department of the Allison Division of General Motors. He is a flight instructor and a licensed commercial pilot. Until recently he was part owner of the Loy Flying Field near Plainfield.

The receipts of MacQuinn's entry boosted the field which will compete in Friday night's opener at the Speedrome to 17 cars."
*The Franklin Evening Star, page 1, August 22, 1945.*

## Indianapolis Speedrome, Indianapolis, August 24, 1945

Ted Hartley took the main feature of 30-laps with Roy Warner second and Swede Carpenter third. Les Singasar, a one-armed driver of San Antonio, showing superb driving skills, took first place honors in the third elimination race. McQuinn won the fourth elimination race but did not take honors in the feature [*Greenfield Daily Report*, page 1, August 25, 1945].

## Indianapolis Speedrome, Indianapolis, August 26, 1945

In the 30-lap feature, Ted Hartley was first with Leroy Warner and Swede Carpenter following. McQuinn in the No. 5 car, won the third elimination race [*The Daily Reporter*, page 1, August 27, 1945].

## Raceland Motor Speedway, Indianapolis, September 9, 1945

This was the inaugural event for this raceway. Duane Carter won the 30-lap feature as well as one of the elimination races. Ted Duncan who placed second in the feature also won a three-lap dash against Carter, who ended up second, and McQuinn, third [*The Indianapolis Star*, page 18, September 10, 1945].

## Raceland Motor Speedway, Indianapolis, September 16, 1945

Pete Romcevich won the 25-lap main feature followed by Ted Duncan and McQuinn. McQuinn had a new midget racer not previously raced. Several drivers pulled out of competition boycotting the race due to the high powered Offenhausers. A similar strike occurred at the Indianapolis Speedrome the week prior [*The Star Press, page 8, September 17, 1945*].

"HARRY MacQUINN

One of the most popular drivers who will show his wares at the formal opening of the Raceland Speedway, located on Road 67, 12 miles northeast of the city today will be Harry MacQuinn. He first jumped into prominence in the local 500-mile race." *Indianapolis Star, page 18, September 16, 1945.*

## Raceland Motor Speedway, Indianapolis, September 20, 1945

This was the first night event of the speedway. McQuinn won the 30-lap feature leading throughout the distance. He also won an elimination race and qualified fastest. Second and third in the feature was Ted Duncan and Duane Carter. All ten entrants drove Offys [*The Franklin Evening Star, page 8, September 21, 1945*].

## Raceland Motor Speedway, Indianapolis, September 23, 1945

Ted Duncan led off the 25-lap feature but McQuinn grabbed the lead on the 16$^{th}$ lap, winning the feature [*The Franklin Evening Star, page 4, September 24, 1945*].

## Raceland Motor Speedway, Indianapolis, October 7, 1945

Several of the Offenhauser cars that have been unable to run in the previous four races this season at Raceland because of lack of tires, have been able to obtain tires during the last week and were ready to go Sunday. McQuinn won the 250-lap feature. Ted Duncan won the season (track) championship [*Unknown newspaper clipping, McQuinn Family records*].

## Edgar County Fairgrounds, Paris IL, October 14, 1945

This was the final program of the season. Bob Muhlke won the feature, his elimination heat and was fastest qualifier. McQuinn led in the feature on the first lap but on the sixth lap blew a tire and spun 'crazily' but handled it not to involve the other racers which got him a standing ovation from the crowd. Muhlke then took the lead from McQuinn [*Unknown newspaper clipping, McQuinn Family records*].

### 1946

## Raceland Motor Speedway, Indianapolis, April 28, 1946

Mike O'Halloran was fastest qualifier with McQuinn third. The remaining events were rained out [*The Indianapolis Star, page 18, April 29, 1946*].

## Crown Point Fair Raceway, Crown Point IN, May 5, 1946

Pete Neilson, swinging to avoid hitting two cars that were entangled, rolled his car crushing him underneath [*Muncie Evening Press, page 8, May 6, 1946*].

## Gilmore Stadium, Los Angeles, June 13, 1946

The 30-lap main feature was won by Johnny McDowell with Swede Lindskog running a close second. McQuinn placed second in the 15-lap semifinal [*The Los Angeles Times, June 14, 1946*].

## Gilmore Stadium, Los Angeles, July 25, 1946

Several drivers had changed cars. Danny Oakes, the defending Gilmore Grand Prix champion, switched to the No. 12 car which was involved in Swede Lindskog's fatal injury the prior month. McQuinn would drive the No. 10 car owned by Bill Krech. Johnny Mantz will take over McQuinn's former No. 47 [*The Los Angeles Times, July 25, 1946*].

## Gilmore Stadium, Los Angeles, August 1, 1946

Perry Grimm won the feature followed by Joe Garson and Duke Nalon. McQuinn placed second in one of the heat races but did not "place in the money" for the feature [*The Los Angeles Times, page 6, August 2, 1946*].

## Rose Bowl, Pasadena CA, August 20, 1946

Sam Hanks, the race director, also won the 30-lap main race. Hanks ran much of the race uncontested until Duke Nalon pressed him at the end. McQuinn spun out early. Louie Foy spun out on the 11th lap [*The Los Angeles Times, page 11, August 21, 1946*].

## Gilmore Stadium, Los Angeles, October 10, 1946

Eddie Haddad won the 30-lap feature and his fourth of the season. He was followed by McQuinn and Duke Nalon. McQuinn won one of the qualifying events ahead of Haddad earlier in the night [*Los Angeles Times, page 11, October 11, 1946*].

## Rose Bowl, Pasadena CA, October 15, 1946

Duane Carter won the main event after taking the lead from Danny Oakes. Ed Haddad came in third. McQuinn won the 15-lap semi-final [*The Los Angeles Times, page 9, October 16, 1946*].

## Gilmore Stadium, Los Angeles, October 24, 1946

Gordon Cleveland won the feature setting another track record. Perry Grimm was second and Ed Haddad was third. The 15-lap elimination race demonstrated the "best race of the evening" with a hub rubbing duel between McQuinn and Bill Schindler. Schindler held the lead until the 13th lap when he was overcome by McQuinn [*The Los Angeles Times, page 7, October 25, 1946*].

*McQuinn Family records.*

## Rain Makes Spectators of Drivers

"That umbrella is no gag, son, the rain really was pouring down yesterday when this group of racing drivers gathered around Ted Everroad to look over the new midget plant opposite the 500-mile track. Ted pointed out the wide, highly banked turn to (left to right) Tony Bettenhausen, Henry Banks, Harry McQuinn, Spider Webb, Harry Hart, Louis Durant and Lt. (s.g.) Bus Wilbert." This is likely in reference to the Indianapolis Midget Speedway built across from IMS. *Unknown newspaper clipping, c. 1945-6., McQuinn Family records.*

Shorty Sorenson and Harry McQuinn, St. Paul MN
*McQuinn Family records.*

Danny Oakes on the outside and McQuinn hugging the inside in his Marchese Miller at Ord Nebraska.
*"The Mighty Midgets" by Jack Fox.*

"Lou Schneider, Harry McQuinn and Sam Hanks, warm up for some Gilmore publicity shots. Fred Friday trails wearing his fisherman's cap." (Craig-Alvarez photo). *Reproduced from: "The Mighty Midgets" by Jack Fox, 1985.*

Harry McQuinn in the hay bales, St. Paul MN. *McQuinn Family records.*

Harry McQuinn in the No. 4 Leader Card Special, c.1939-40. *McQuinn Family records.*

*McQuinn Family records.*

# HARRY MCQUINN

Harry McQuinn in the No. 4 Leader Card Special, c.1939-40.
*McQuinn Family records.*

*McQuinn Family records.*

*McQuinn Family records.*

Harry McQuinn in the No. 4 Leader Card Special, c.1939-40.
*McQuinn Family records.*

Courtesy of Stan Kalwasinski.

McQuinn Family records.

*McQuinn Family records.*

*McQuinn Family records.*

# Zachary Tinkle

## Super Cup Champion

### Late Model Development Driver

### Proudly Sponsored by

**LEFT PAW Press!**

53

# 5
# RACE OFFICIAL

Having sat out of the 1949 Indianapolis 500, it was time for Harry McQuinn to move on. He had a successful career as a driver and, now with airplanes, as instructor and sales manager. But the track still called to him. He was named a race official for the AAA in 1949. For the 1950 Indianapolis 500, Earl Cooper was named referee, McQuinn steward and Herbie Lewis as assistant starter as selected by Wilbur Shaw. They joined Chief Steward Tom Milton. Milton, Cooper and McQuinn served as a three-man committee having complete charge of the actual running of the race. In the case of any disputes or decision on which they fail to agree unanimously, majority opinion would prevail.

Harry Hartz (far left) presenting Clark Gable with an honorary AAA Championship driver's license in 1950. Mr. Gable was at the Indianapolis Motor Speedway as part of the cast for "To Please A Lady." From left to right: Harry Hartz, Harry McQuinn, Colonel Harrington, Clark Gable, Jim Lamb, and Dr. Roger Smith. *IMS Photo.*

It wasn't long when McQuinn's job took a little twist. The first car on the track for the 1950 season wasn't one that was expected. A 1935 Ford with New York license plates was racing around the oval. Apparently, one of the gates was not locked. The Ford was hurriedly flagged down and stopped. The driver was reported to put his head out of the window and asked "How fast was I doin'?". The apparent honeymooners were ushered off the track headed for Texas [*The Terre Haute Tribune, page 2, May 2, 1950*].

Harry McQuinn, Dr. Roger Smith, Harry Hartz, Jim Lamb, Clark Gable, and Colonel Harrington. Clark Gable was at the speedway during the filming of "To Please A Lady."
*IMS Photo.*

The movie "To Please A Lady" was being filmed at the IMS the month of May. The racers had to share the track with the film crew and stars. While filming a scene of cars on the track, ten cars were used in a tight cluster, often at four abreast. The outside cars were running at the edges of the track and threw up sand. Ross Page, car owner, said his car was full of sand and could no longer compete in the race and felt that this was sabotage [*The Pantagraph*, page 15, May 19, 1950].

In late 1950, with the decline of the popularity of midget racing, McQuinn and "Rags" Mitchell of the 16th Street

Clark Gable, Harry McQuinn and Mr. Brown.
*IMS Photo.*

Speedway, went into a three-day huddle, determined to do something about it rather than "sit around blaming everybody and everything else" for the fall-off. The result was 16th Street's September 15th, 100 Lap Midget Championship Classic with over 8,000 fans, to produce what eventually cropped up as the '1951 N.M.A.R.C. Championship AAA Midget Circuit.' [*"A Pen Sketch" by Gene Powell, National Speed Sport News, April 11, 1951*].

1951 saw McQuinn again appointed as race steward for the Indy 500.
*IMS Photo.*

1951 Indianapolis 500 race steward Harry McQuinn greets pole-sitter Duke Nalon. Nalon and McQuinn were fierce comeptitors as midget racers in the midwest.
*McQuinn Family records.*

Indianapolis 500-mile race official Harry McQuinn seen here with Fred Agabashian, 1951. *IMS Photo*.

## Race Official

May 1, 1952. Indianapolis Motor Speedway opens with the arrival of Steward Harry McQuinn, AAA supervisor. Seventy-plus cars are expected.

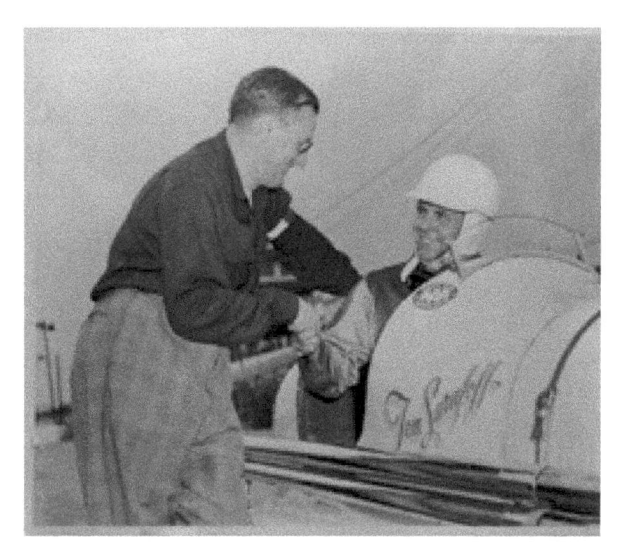

Harry McQuinn as AAA race steward with Cliff Griffith, 1952. *IMS Photo.*

"Admiring the work of Harry Stephens (left) are Harry McQuinn (far right) the race referee, and Ed Walsh, racing car owner." 1952.

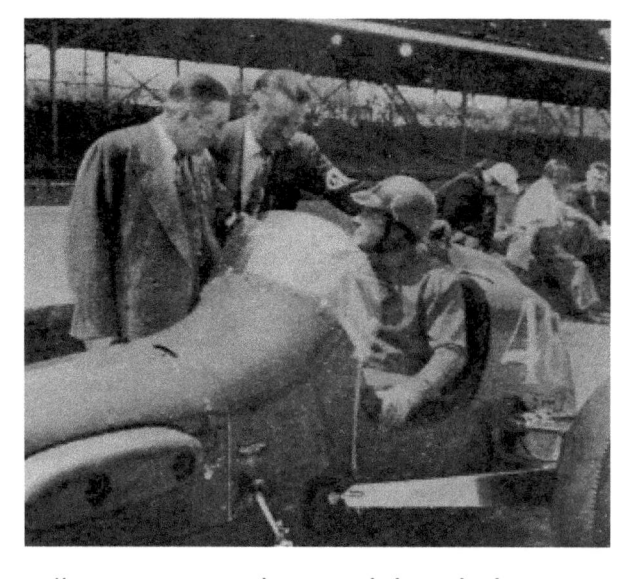

"Roger Ward, rookie driver, gets some timely tips from Hartz and McQuinn prior to driving test." "They Run The Race" by Paul N. Janes, *The Indianapolis Star Magazine, 1952.*

"Plenty of red tape is involved in getting cars and drivers into action. Signing up of entrants is supervised by Harry McQuinn (standing) and William Powell (left), technical committee head. *They Run The Race* by Paul N. Janes, The Indianapolis Star Magazine, 1952.

**HARRY McQUINN**
AAA Track Steward

Once again in charge of the AAA Indiana Zone, is Harry McQuinn, steward at the famed 500-mile classic across the street, and one of the finest names in racing today. Mr. McQuinn will again act as track steward at the West 16th Street plant in addition to his other duties.

Indianapolis 16th Street Speedway 1952 program.

Indy 500 Chief Steward, Tommy Milton, considered one of the great race drivers of all time having won the 1921 and 1923 500-mile Memorial Day race, resigned. Harry McQuinn was announced as Wilbur Shaw's pick to replace Milton. F. R. "Ronney" Householder of Buchanan, Mich., will become referee and Harlan Fengler of Dayton, Ohio, will replace Earl Cooper of Encino, Calif., as steward- all former race drivers. Householder and McQuinn were fierce competitors in many venues while piloting the midgets [*The Terre Haute Tribune, page 23, February 8, 1953*].

**SUCCEEDS MILTON** 1953

## Harry McQuinn Named '500' Chief Steward

Harry McQuinn, of Indianapolis, today was named chief steward of the 500-Mile Race at the Indianapolis Motor Speedway, succeeding Tommy Milton, of Detroit, who resigned.

McQuinn had served as referee and was Milton's personal choice as his successor.

Milton, 1921 and 1923 winner of the Memorial Day classic and chief steward for the last four years, said he was unable to continue directing the race because of his business interests.

Wilbur Shaw, Speedway president, said F. R. (Ronney) Householder, of Buchanan, Mich., will become referee, and Harlan Fengler, of Dayton, O., will replace Earl Cooper, of Encino, Cal., as steward.

Like Milton and Cooper, all three new Speedway officials are former race drivers.

HARRY McQUINN
Promoted at Speedway

The annual 500-mile Memorial Day Classic had its share of celebrity visitors. In 1953, Jane Greer, model, singer, and actress of great fame, was treated with high regard at the track. Seen here is Ms. Greer with Chief Steward Harry McQuinn. *IMS Photo. McQuinn Family records.*

From left to right: Wilbur Shaw, Harlan Fengler, and Harry McQuinn. 1953. *IMS Photo*.

The Hoosier Hundred, a 100-mile 'big car' dirt-track race took place on September 19, 1953 at the Indiana State Fairgrounds. This was another event under the supervision of the AAA Contest Board. Harry McQuinn, would also serve as Chief Steward for this event. "All of the outstanding drivers who have participated in any of the three dirt track championship races held elsewhere this season have indicated that they are looking forward to racing here," said McQuinn, "and the entry list is sure to be the finest assembled any where in the nation since May 30." The winner would receive 200 points toward the AAA National Championship [*The Alexandria Times-Tribune, page 6, July 28, 1953*].

The AAA award banquet was held at the end of the year. Amongst the honors bestowed was Harry McQuinn, in his first year as Chief Steward of the Indianapolis 500, who was cited for his outstanding performance as an AAA 'brass hat' and to the Contest Board in general for their insistence on safety which resulted in a drop of racing accidents (as well as the bonus of decreased insurance premiums for the following year). The "Hoosier Hundred" at Indiana State Fairgrounds last September was voted as the most dramatic race of the last 25 years [*Valley Morning Star, page 8, December 29, 1953; The Billboard, page 39, January 9, 1954*].

James H. Lamb, secretary of the AAA Contest Board, named Harry McQuinn as Chief Steward of the Darlington 200-mile event for 1954. This was his second appointment at Darlington, having performed as Chief Steward in 1950, the inaugural event for this track. Having been voted the press award as the outstanding automobile race official of 1953, McQuinn's rise was considered rapid [*The Anniston Star, page 23, April 29, 1954*].

Probably the most notable (at least widely publicized and contentious for many years to come) was the ousting of Bill France, the founder and president of NASCAR. On Thursday May 13, 1954, an urgent message arrived to the attention of Chief Steward Harry McQuinn at the Indianapolis Motor Speedway. 'Big' Bill France had been spotted in the garage and pit area. Not having a pass of his own, he was escorted out of the garages. There was significant animosity between AAA and Bill France as France

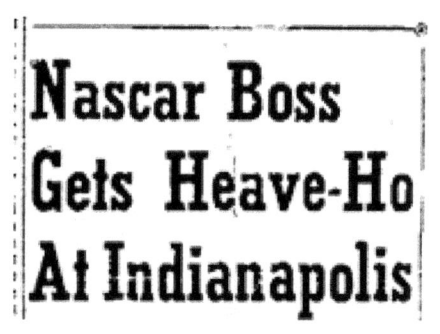

**Nascar Boss Gets Heave-Ho At Indianapolis**

```
The Times Record,
     page 28,
  May 14, 1954.
```

had been thrown out of the AAA for conducting what AAA said was unsanctioned events. "We have a long-standing disagreement with NASCAR on what constitutes good racing," said Harry McQuinn. As part of its feud with NASCAR, AAA officials had suspended some of the organization's licensed drivers for competing in NASCAR-sanctioned races. France was no stranger to the Indy 500 garage area as he had worked there as a mechanic prior to his involvement in stock-car racing. "France said he borrowed a speedway credential from a friend to the garages to shake hands with old friends among the 500 drivers, car owners and mechanics."

France's ejection from the Indy garages received little attention at the time, only briefly been noted in several newspapers including five-paragraph story on page 5 of the May 19 issue of National Speed Sport News. It wasn't until many years later that the true significance of that milestone moment came to light. At that time, France had been working on plans to build a 2.5-mile track in Daytona Beach, Florida, with the intention to rival the Indianapolis Motor Speedway. His dream became a reality in February 1959 with the first Daytona 500 and today the debate continues as to which is this country's premier race, the Indianapolis 500 or the Daytona 500. http://www.nationalspeedsportnews.com/racing-history/torn-from-the-headlines/bill-france-gets-the-boot-from-indianapolis-garage/

"France numbers among his friends today, Tony Hulman, long-time owner of the Indianapolis Motor Speedway." [*Daytona Beach Morning Journal, February 22, 1969*]. However, who knows how he felt about Harry McQuinn, then or later. Unfortunately, France died two years before the NASCAR Winston Cup Series raced at the IMS and the Brickyard 400 instantly became one of the sport's marquee events.

"From that day on, domestic car manufacturers began to devote engineering and marketing efforts to winnings races in France's spectacular "Grand National" series. Ironically, one of the contestants in the Detroit 250 field stood as an example of the immense rift that was beginning to tear the fabric of American automobile racing. For most of the country, competition of all kinds had been controlled by the Contest Board of the American Automobile Association-- an imperious pack of officials known as the "Chicago gang," who held an iron grip on the Indianapolis 500 and its satellite events. Bill France's NASCAR operated outside this empire, thereby being labeled as "outlaw" by the establishment.

Running a Cadillac coupe in the Detroit race was the 1949 Indianapolis 500 winner, Bill Holland, who had been banned by the AAA in 1950. Holland's expulsion came after running in a three-lap charity race in Opa Locks, Florida—an event unsanctioned by the AAA and therefore a mortal sin. Holland would be banished from the Indianapolis 500 by Chief Steward Harry McQuinn, an ex-driver himself. Bill France attempted to run his own open-wheel series with stock-block engines in 1952 and early 1953—both abbreviated seasons. McQuinn tossed France out of the Indianapolis Motor Speedway garage area

> during practice for the big race in 1954. Such overt power plays involving France and Holland only strengthened NASCAR, which was by the mid-1950's being viewed by the American motorsports establishment as a vibrant, potentially lucrative alternative to the rigid dictatorship of the AAA." "NASCAR: Off the Record" by Brock Yates published by Motorbook International, November 12, 2004.

AAA Chief Steward Harry McQuinn sits in the Dodge Official Car outside the AAA Building, 1954. *IMS Photo.*

Chief Steward Harry McQuinn addressing the crowd at the drivers' meeting, 1954. *IMS Photo.*

Later that year, Wilbur Shaw, president and general manager of the Indianapolis Motor Speedway and three-time winner of the Memorial Day classic was killed with two others when their chartered plane plunged into a twisted mass near Decatur IN.

Tony Hulman, owner of IMS said "no possible successor to Shaw was yet being considered. But men who could be in line as new Speedway president include Harry McQuinn, Indianapolis, last year's chief steward; Harlan Fengler, referee of the 1954 race, and (Tommy) Milton and (Pete) DePaolo" [*Logansport Pharos Tribune, page 1, November 2, 1954*].

For the 1955 Indianapolis 500, AAA officials selected jointly by Mr. Hulman and Col. A. W. Herrington, chairman of the AAA Contest Board, were Chief Steward Harry McQuinn and Harlan Fengler. Paul Johnson would serve as assistant steward and his former position as chief observer was filled by Ronney Householder [*The Terre Haute Tribune, page 18, April 22, 1954*].

Duke Nalon recounts his last year at Indy 500. He had taken out Paul Russo's car for a shake down on Carburetion Day. After the session had ended, Nalon completed several more laps and was confronted in the pits by his former racing nemesis and now Chief Steward, Harry McQuinn. McQuinn leveled a $25 fine or one year's suspension. Duke replied "you S.O.B." and reached in his pocket and gave him the $25 [*"The Iron Duke" by George Peters, Bar Jean Enterprises, 2005*].

On the last day of qualifications, Ed Elisian took to the track for qualifications just before the gun went off ending the day. After turning only two of his three laps, Elisian was flagged off the track by Chief Steward, Harry McQuinn. This was met with boos from the crowd. Elisian protested and after rechecking, it was found that someone had counted Elisian's laps incorrectly. Elisian was then allowed to attempt qualification again, which he did, bumping Len Duncan from the field. The event became to be known as "Elisian's Midnight Ride" [*Rick Popley, Indianapolis 500 Chronicle. Publications International, Ltd., 1998*].

Harry McQuinn as AAA Chief Steward at the Indianapolis Motor Speedway with the first row dirvers and Mr. Fengler, 1955. *IMS Photo.*

Harry McQuinn, Harlan Fengler and Paul Johnson with the Borg-Warner trophy, 1955. *IMS Photo.*

On August 3, 1955, it was announced that the AAA is withdrawing from support of auto racing after concerns of raceway tragedies. IMS officials said the AAA's executive committee decided to act after the recent tragedy at Le Mans, where a racing car hurtled into spectators, killing 79 and injuring 91. IMS officials stated that this would not affect the running of the Indianapolis 500. Harry McQuinn, chief steward for the 500-miler for the past few years said, "auto racing doesn't need the AAA." However, all agreed to the necessity of having a regulatory board for racing, setting standards and judging the races [*The Alexandria Times Tribune, page 1, August 4, 1955*].

"Miss Dinah Shore, the television queen, also rode around the track with Chief Steward Harry McQuinn as her chauffeur. Then, accompanied by the Purdue bad, Dinah sang the traditional "Back Home Again in Indiana" and asked the audience to join her in a second chorus." *The Terre Haute Tribune, page 10, May 31, 1955.*

Dinah Shore and Chief Steward, Harry McQuinn, 1955. *IMS Photo. McQuinn Family Records.*

# Race Official

Harry McQuinn, was once again named as chief steward for the Hoosier Hundred to be held on September 17 [*Greensburg Daily News, page 11, August 19, 1955*].

Harry McQuinn continued as Chief Steward for the upcoming 1956 Indianapolis 500 for the fourth straight year. The race would be run under the supervision of the United States Auto Club (USAC) [*Kokomo Tribune, page 13, April 25, 1956*].

Paul Johnson, Harlan Fengler and Harry McQuinn, 1956. *IMS Photo.*

From left to right: Harry McQuinn, Harlan Fengler, and Paul Johnson, 1956. *IMS Photo.*

McQuinn addressing the crowd at the 1956 Victory Dinner. *IMS Photo.*

# HARRY MCQUINN

In 1957, Harry McQuinn was again named Chief Steward of the Indianapolis 500. Leading up the 1957 500, McQuinn's removal was sought by a committee of car owners who said in a petition that he was capable but in effect, they didn't like his attitude accusing him of being dictatorial and high-handed [*The Indianapolis Star, page 25, January 11, 1957*].

```
          "Jep Cadour Jr., Sports Editor

                    Calls 'EM
```

The man in the dark blue suit never is popular on a baseball diamond. Neither is the man in the dark blue coat at the Indianapolis Motor Speedway.

In this instance, the man in the coat we are speaking of is Harry McQuinn, chief steward of the 500-mile race. McQuinn is the auto racing counterpart of the chief umpire in a baseball game. We doubt if any chief umpire ever will win a popularity contest.

During the last hectic month at the Speedway, a loud outcry has arisen from car owners for the replacement of McQuinn before the "500" rolls around again next year.

They have attacked him on the grounds that he is tactless, undiplomatic and arbitrary while admitting his fairness and competence.

In view of the importance of the situation to both the world's greatest auto race and Indianapolis, itself, we are turning over the balance of this column to a letter from the president of the United States Auto Club, Col. Arthur W. Herrington.

Col. Herrignton's strong defense of McQuinn clears up many points in this case:

'Dear Sir:

# Race Official

The 41st running of the 500-mile race has just ended with one of the most successful races we have ever had. In Sam Hanks we have a winner who, but his diligence, has well earned that honor. Thanks to that great sportsman, Tony Hulman, and the improvements completed this year, we have probably the finest automobile race course in the world upon which to hold this event which has accumulated a historical background unequaled by any other similar event in the world.

A combination of the necessity of becoming acquainted with this new physical setup, plus exceedingly unusual weather conditions for this time of year, brought about some incidents about which official comment is necessary. Your sports columns have carried the statements of an attack upon our chief steward, Mr. Harry McQuinn's integrity or efficiency. They appear to seek his removal because they do not like him personally.

As chief steward of the 500-mile race, Mr. McQuinn is the United States Auto Club's official having complete authority to handle the race as far as the rules, the regulations and the control of the track and event are involved. With this authority and responsibility, Mr. McQuinn must answer yes or no to all questions which arise with reference to rule compliance. He is one of the finest and most efficient chief stewards we have ever had for this event. It has been our policy as far as possible to use former experienced race drivers in these positions. They have learned what is necessary in the hard school of experience on the track. To Mr. McQuinn's credit it can be said that he has fully discharged his responsibilities in all respects. Never at any time has he sought to avoid a decision which was his to make and hide behind the skirts of his subordinates or behind the skirts of the competition committee. He has had the authority and responsibility to say no when it was necessary to do so, and we all regret that there are those who should find it necessary to criticize him for this discharge of his duties. The superb and efficient manner in which Mr. McQuinn handled yesterday's race should be fitting answer to his distractors.

The writer would be the first to admit there are those who can say no so diplomatically that one would feel they had done one a favor. But conversely we must recognize that there are also individuals upon which the utmost of diplomacy would be wasted if a decision against their personal interests were involved. In past years we have been unfortunate in having some officials whose attitude toward car owners, drivers or mechanics was not in the best interests of the sport. When such conduct was observed these officials were promptly replaced by those who were in a position to show proper consideration for the rights of others. There are many at the Speedway today who fully realize that the writer has been personally responsible for the removal of such unqualified personnel.

It is interesting that during the past fifty-two years the integrity of automobile racing as a sport has never been challenged. We have a great responsibility to continue that record.

It is perfectly obvious with the above organization which was deliberately set up to give each of the interested segments of those involved in this sport a voice in their own affairs, that the right of appeal from decisions of the Contest Director or our Contest Committee to the Board of Directors of USAC actually exists. All of the incidents which have arisen this year at the Indianapolis Motor Speedway could have been handled in this channel in an orderly manner without involving any personalities. This method, however, is completely devoid of any possibility of making headlines and this more than anything else mitigated against the orderly procedure being used.

```
The game must have an umpire. Being that umpire is not a
good way to make friends and influence people. It is at times
a thankless job. We must recognize that it is necessary, we
must recognize that without it and without the proper support
of the authority and responsibility involved that our event
will soon fade into obscurity. That is a matter in which every
resident of Indianapolis is interested.

Very truly yours,

A.W. Herrington

President—U.S.A.C."

The Indianapolis Star, section 2, page 2, June 2, 1957
```

McQuinn resigns as Chief Steward February 28, 1958. In his resignation letter to Tony Hulman he said: "When I accepted the appointment as chief steward I did so with the knowledge that many of the decisions required of me would be unpopular with some of the individuals affected." Hulman said he accepted McQuinn's resignation with "considerable reluctance" but McQuinn cited increasing duties as vice-president and general manager of Sky Harbor Airport as the main reason to step down. McQuinn then recommended Harlan Fengler as Chief Steward. The speedway president said "Harry's enviable reputation for honestly and fairness is well known by everyone connected with racing. During his five years of service, not a single decision made by him ever was reversed on appeal to the AAA contest board or the USAC contest committee" [*Pottstown Mercury, page 22, February 28, 1958*].

"Much as they all conceded that he was a great guy in most respects, certain other roadster actors like Bob Wilke of Leader Card crabbed that Agajanian was a wily fellow who too often tried using his clout and influence to his own advantage. And usually got away with it. Aggie, for instance, was known to have been the leader of the gang that railroaded out of Indy the 500's stern chief steward, Harry McQuinn, then had McQuinn replaced with Aggie's own friend Harlan Fengler." "Indianapolis Roadsters, 1952-1964" by Joe Scalzo, Motorbooks, 1999.

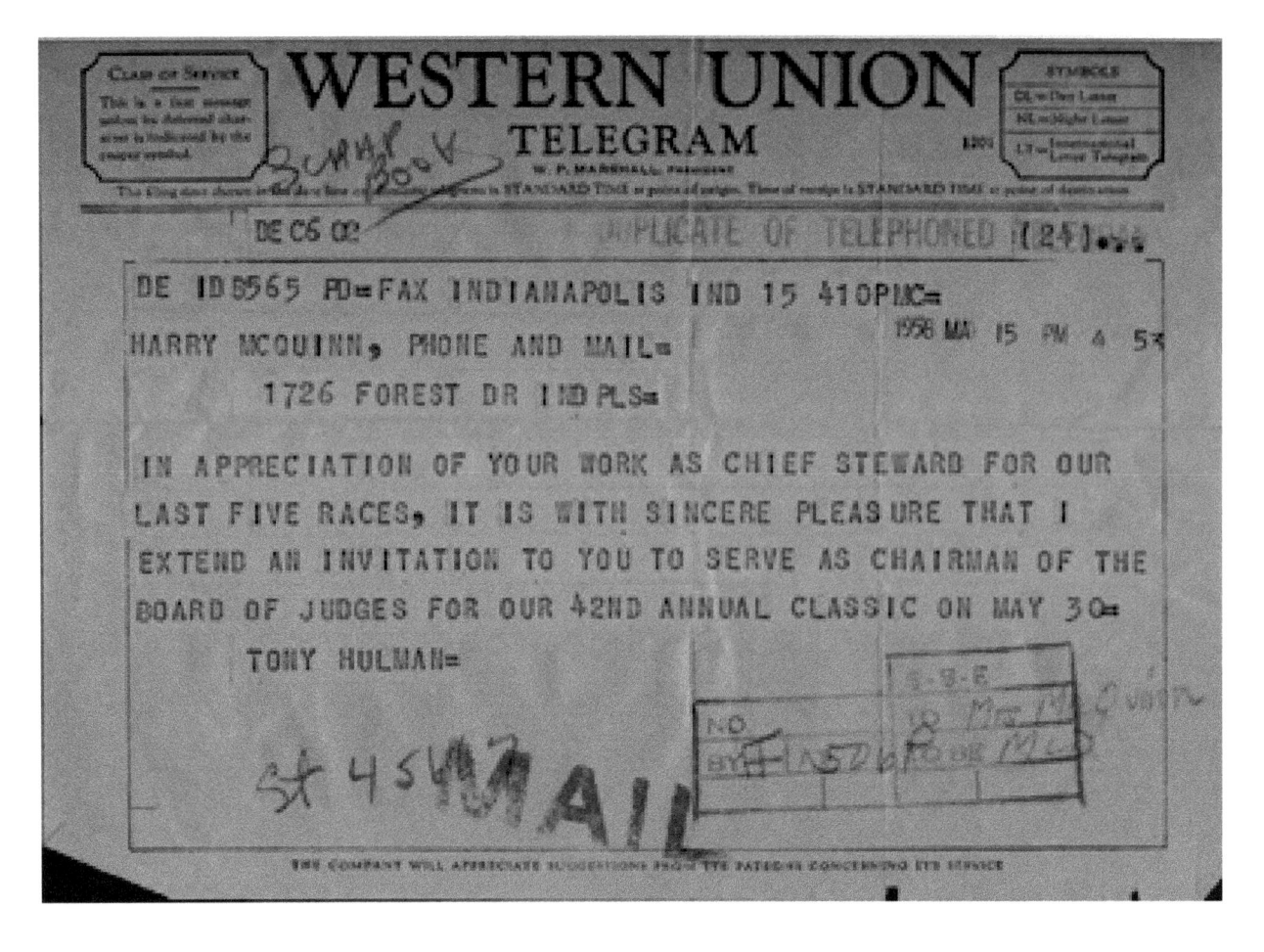

Telegram to Harry McQuinn from Tony Hulman inviting McQuinn to serve as Chairman of the Board of Judges, 1958.

Harry McQuinn, Donald Davidson, and Tony Hulman, 1964. *IMS Photo.*

McQuinn had been the AAA Official for the Indiana zone in the 1950's. With the dissolution of the AAA, he later became an USAC Official eventually being named the USAC National Championship Division Supervisor in 1962 until his resignation in 1969. *[Journal and Courier, page 40, May 26, 1962].*

Future Indianapolis 500 Historian, Donald C. Davidson, had saved his money as a teenager and travelled from England to the Indianapolis Motor Speedway. Davidson spent three weeks at the raceway, impressing those around him with his knowledge and enthusiasm. He met and befriended Harry McQuinn and IMS president and general manager, Tony Hulman. The following year, Davidson was hired to work for USAC.

During the 1966 running of the 300-mile race at Atlanta under USAC, Billy Foster passed under the yellow flag. He was fined and had three laps removed by Chief Steward, Harry McQuinn. The allowed Gordon Johncock to finish ahead of Foster for second place. On appeal, the USAC Board of Directors removed the three-lap penalty citing it was too severe and lowered his fine to $1000 [*The Des Moines Register*, page 19, September 13, 1966].

McQuinn was replaced as supervisor of the USAC Championship Division by Russ Clendenen in the off-season, early in 1969 [*The Indianapolis News*, page 26, February 4, 1969].

Harry McQuinn presenting the winning trophy to Paul Goldsmith for the 100-mile DuQuoin race in 1965.

"I remember when I got my first USAC Championship license. It was a conditional license as well. Harry McQuinn was the competition director at the time, and I recall how he was breathing down my neck like you never saw. Believe me, because of that I behaved like an altar boy." - Mario Andretti [*The Morning Call*, page 63, October 8, 1978].

# 6
# AIRPLANE PILOT

DURING WORLD WAR II, THERE was no auto racing. A thrill-seeker such as McQuinn needed a past-time. He had worked at an Allison Manufacturer Plant as the bearings supervisor of Plant #5 in the manufacturing of airplane parts for the war effort. He, however, ventured into piloting aircraft in the place of race cars.

He made his first solo flight in 1942 at Sky Harbor Airport, previously located on the western fringes of Indianapolis. He became a Lieutenant of the Civil Air Patrol from 1943-1945, being promoted to a squad commander in 1944 [*Greenfield Daily Reporter, page 1, July 10, 1944*], and eventually Captain serving in the Indiana State Guard up to at least 1947.

During the war, IMS was offered to be a staging area for troops or aircraft. As early as 1910, IMS had an aerodome and boasted the largest airfield in America [*The 100th Running of the Indianapolis 500 Mile Race Official Program- Commemorative Edition*]. However, the armed services did not accept the offer and IMS laid fallow during the war. However, IMS hadn't seen it last airplane.

**VIEW NEW PLANES**—Arrival of the new Vultee Navy type planes for the state guard was observed by high guard officials. Left to right are Adjutant General Ben Watt, Lt. Col. John C. Hansen, assistant adjutant general; Maj. Carl F. Meyer, Capt. Harry McQuinn, Lt. Robert Ryan and Lt. Ray E. Davis.

*Unknown newspaper clipping from the McQuinn Family records.*

*McQuinn in the Civilian Air Patrol.*

*McQuinn (second from left) with other officers of the Civilian Air Patrol.*

"History of Civil Air Patrol

In the late 1930s, more than 150,000 volunteers with a love for aviation argued for an organization to put their planes and flying skills to use in defense of their country. As a result, the Civil Air Patrol was born one week prior to the Japanese attack on Pearl Harbor. Thousands of volunteer members answered America's call to national service and sacrifice by accepting and performing critical wartime missions. Assigned to the War Department under the jurisdiction of the Army Air Corps, the contributions of Civil Air Patrol, including logging more than 500,000 flying hours, sinking two enemy submarines, and saving hundreds of crash victims during World War II, are well documented.

After the war, a thankful nation understood that Civil Air Patrol could continue providing valuable services to both local and national agencies. On July 1, 1946, President Harry Truman signed Public Law 476 incorporating Civil Air Patrol as a benevolent, nonprofit organization. On May 26, 1948, Congress passed Public Law 557 permanently establishing Civil Air Patrol as the auxiliary of the new U.S. Air Force. Three primary mission areas were set forth at that time: aerospace education, cadet programs, and emergency services."

http://www.gocivilairpatrol.com/about/

# HARRY MCQUINN

Many former drivers took up piloting as a hobby, for travel, or during the wartime effort. The new Speedway President in 1946, Wilbur Shaw, was also a pilot.

Harry McQuinn, racing out West in early 1946, flew his Aeronca trainer to IMS and landed on the back straightaway. Family folklore states he had little time to hand in his application for the upcoming Indy 500 race. However, since he was third to hand his application in or could have mailed or wired it in time, there is much speculation it was a publicity stunt. With racing having been halted for the war and concerns that auto racing was no longer a thrill-seeking spectacular, interest may have been stirred by such a stunt. McQuinn met Speedway Officials briefly (posing for a few pictures) and then flew off to provide flying lessons at a nearby airport. Nevertheless, this was believed to be the first such landing in Speedway history [*Indianapolis Star, page 21, February 8, 1946*].

*The Indianapolis Star, page 21, February 8, 1946.*

"PILOT, IN THE AIR, ON THE LAND—Harry McQuinn, widely known to Indianapolis fans as a race driver, also is an accomplished airplane pilot. He's shown here delivering his entry for the 1946 Memorial Day race to Wilbur Shaw, Speedway president, after he made the first airplane landing in history on the track Thursday."

"Cliff Bergere and Harry McQuinn own and fly planes. It's not an uncommon sight to see Harry come in for a landing just behind Gasoline Alley on the turf, roll to a stop before the garages and hop out" [*The Indianapolis Star, page 16, April 27, 1946*].

After the 1947 Indianapolis 500, McQuinn went again out West to race midgets. Somewhere along the line, he met and befriended Andy Devine, movie star, who operated the Van Nuys CA airport. Devine had talked McQuinn in testing and flying the latest of Cessna's planes and later suggested that he sell them.

"I may be fortunate enough to win the race," he says, but if I do, the thrill of victory won't be half as great as the thrill of self-satisfaction I received back in 1942 when I made my first solo flight at Sky Harbor Airport. Race driving is tiresome, hazardous work, but flying provides you with real relaxation and pleasure" [*The Indianapolis Star, page 36, December 29, 1946*].

"Here's Harry McQuinn at the controls of the Cessna 140 which brought photographs of the Centralia mine disaster to The Star in 1 hour and 25 minutes."
*The Indianapolis Star, page 19, May 30, 1947.*

## Airplane Pilot

McQuinn and his Cessna would make himself available to the newspapers for "hot stories". For the Centralia IL mine disaster, McQuinn made the journey in less than two hours. The planes put into service had to land in a muddy field. McQuinn's plane was the only one to navigate out of the mud and was able to take off the same day, returning photographs to the Indianapolis Star [*Indianapolis Star, page 19, May 30, 1947*].

A new 1,200-foot runway was put into the IMS by Wilbur Shaw, IMS President. It would be used 11 months of the year but not during May. McQuinn landed and then took off in a Cessna 195, capable of carrying five passengers in less than 500 feet of the strip. Shaw was accused of using all 1,200 feet and then some. In addition to McQuinn, Shaw, Rex Mays, and Cliff Bergere were also both pilots and racers. It was speculated that this move would allow air races at the Speedway [*"Speedway Gets Landing Strip. McQuinn Tests Out Transformed Infield" by Paul N. Janes, Aviation Editor, Indianapolis Star, page 7, November 2, 1947*].

"Wilbur Shaw, Speedway Motor Corporation president, points along with the Speedway's new landing strip, while Harry McQuinn (left), racing veteran, and Orin (Moose) Redhead, regional sales manager of the Cessna Aircraft Company, look on. The plane is the new five-place Cessna 195." The *Indianapolis Star*, page 7, November 2, 1947.

"McQuinn Lands New Plane on Speedway Track"—Harry McQuinn, veteran race driver, flew to the Indianapolis Motor Speedway from Sky Harbor Airport yesterday in a new four-person Cessna 170 airplane. It was the second time in Speedway history for a ship to land on the track, scene of the annual 500-mile race, and it was McQuinn who made the initial landing—two years ago to file his 1946 race entry—in a smaller Cessna. McQuinn is pictured with the Cessna 170 and Maserati car he plans to drive in this year's race." *Indianapolis Star, page 17, May 11, 1948.*

On May 10, 1948, practice was halted and the cars were ushered into the garage area. AAA Officials approved a very radical "stunt". Harry McQuinn, in his Cessna 170 with Indianapolis Star reporter Paul Janes and photographer Maurie Burnett, received permission to land on the back straightaway. As the plane was landing, the story goes that a drowsy guard, who was not informed of the event, began chasing the plane down the back stretch with wildly threatening gestures. Eventually the guard gave up as the plane taxied to the front stretch [*Indianapolis Star, page 17, May 11, 1948; The Journal and Courier, page 32, May 25, 1965*].

*The later recounting of landing on the IMS track often exclaims this as the one and only landing. Both events, that of 1946 and 1948, were known but somehow had gotten confused. Even in the IMS Archives, the photos have one date or the other. McQuinn not only did it once but twice as well as made multiple landings in the infield.*

McQuinn, shown here, was working a bulldozer to clear away land for the Sky Harbor Airport. McQuinn was the General Sales Manager for Sky Harbor. He stated working the dozer was helping him get ready for the 1948 Indianapolis 500. *Indianapolis Star, 1948.*

On August 27, 1948, McQuinn had been playing chauffeur to a staff photographer of the Indianapolis Star newspaper off to cover another news story. However, shortly after take-off, the engine suddenly quit causing the plane to crash into the backyard of an Indianapolis home. Both McQuinn and the photographer, Dale Schofner, survived. McQuinn had facial cuts but Schofner suffered a concussion and cuts to the forehead. McQuinn was lauded for his handling of the 'dead stick' and forcing the landing in the manner to cause the least amount of injuries [*The Indianapolis Star, page 4, August 28, 1948*].

*The Indianapolis Star, page 4, August 28, 1948.*

In 1949, McQuinn again landed an airplane at the Indianapolis Motor Speedway. 'One-Lap' McQuinn was looking for a race entry.

"But he was quick to tell other race drivers, most of whom are pilots, that "I'm not looking for a good airplane—I've got one in the new Cessna 170.'

# Airplane Pilot

Rex Mays (left), veteran race driver, took time out from discussions of 500-mile race prospects last week to size up a new Cessna 170 landed at the Speedway by Harry McQuinn (right), another racing veteran (Star Photo). *"'One-Lap' McQuinn Uses Airplane to Shop for Fast 500-Race Entry", by Paul N. Janes, The Indianapolis Star, page 70, May 1, 1949.*

Harry, who is Cessna sales-manager for Sky Harbor Airport, was trying to sell a few airplanes. He demonstrated that the ship required only a small part of the short landing strip at the Speedway for landings and takeoffs."

"'The 170 has plenty of snap and eager performance,' Harry said, 'and if I find an automobile with the same qualities, I'll be right in there when this year's race gets under way.'" [*The Indianapolis Star, page 70, May 1, 1949*].

"Jim Smith is informative and timely

Jim Smith's Inside Track in The Indianapolis Times is always informative and timely. He tells the story behind the story on sports events interwoven with the human interest of people in sports. He knows the big names in sports and has a personal way of relating the stories he hears from them. His opinion is usually sound and his statistics reliable. He is a good sports editor, and I consider the complete sports coverage of The Times the best during any season. I look forward to reading The Times every day."

Harry McQuinn, Airport General Manager

*The Indianapolis Times, page 20, October 1, 1958*

*McQuinn at Sky Harbor Airport, 1971.*

LEFT PAW Press
PROUDLY PUBLISHES MEDICAL BOOKS BY DR. BRAD T. TINKLE
Best Selling Author
My EDS Journey
(Write Your Name Here)
Developed by Brad. T. Tinkle, MD, PhD.
Joint Hypermobility Handbook
A Guide for the Issues & Management of Ehlers-Danlos Syndrome Hypermobility Type and the Hypermobility Syndrome
Brad T. Tinkle, MD, PhD
www.LeftPawPress.com

# 7
# LATER YEARS

HARRY LIKED MANY ASPECTS OF RACING. He was a fair mechanic, an 'edgy driver', and well-respected (but disliked by some) race official. He also did some promoting during the years as well. He continued to devote himself and was a very active member of the Indianapolis 500 Old-Timers Club serving as in several capacities, including president *[The Indianapolis News, page 42, January 12, 1967]*.

Harry McQuinn at Emil Andres' Party in 1978.
Courtesy of Stan Kalwasinski.

# Ex-Chief Steward at 500 Dies

**STAR STATE REPORT**

MORGANTOWN, Ind. — Harry T. McQuinn, 80, a former Indianapolis 500-Mile Race driver and later the chief steward of the race, died Wednesday in Bloomington Hospital.

One of the pioneer drivers of midget racing cars, he also raced in 10 Indianapolis 500 races 1934-48. His best finish was seventh in 1938 and 1941.

He served as chief steward of the race from 1953 to 1957, resigning following a dispute with car owner J.C. Agajanian in which he told Agajanian, who disputed a McQuinn ruling, "go talk to yourself." He later said he meant that the owner should take the matter up with the car owners' organization.

He cited the pressure of other business when he resigned as chief steward. He was vice president and general manager of the Sky Harbor Airport in Indianapolis.

He continued as chief steward of other U.S. Auto Club races through the 1960s.

Survivors include his wife, Juanita Wagner McQuinn, a sister, five grandchildren and 14 great-grandchildren.

Services will be 2 p.m. Sunday in Meredith-Clark Funeral Home, where calling will be 2-8 p.m. Saturday.

*The Star Press, page 14, January 3, 1986.*

## Later Years

Harry McQuinn died on January 1, 1986, before he could attend his induction in the National Midget Auto Racing Hall of Fame later that year.

*The Midget Hall of Fame located in Sun Prairie WI.*

# HARRY MCQUINN

**National Midget Auto Racing Hall of members as of 1/16/2015, 211 names, including the new inductees:**

Wayne Adams, Fred Agabashian, JC Agajanian, Floyd Alvis, George Amick, Emil Andres, Chuck Arnold, Lloyd Axel, Carl Badami, Johnny Balch, Johnny Baldwin, Bobby Ball, Henry Banks, Bob Barker, Bob Barkhimer, Buzz Barton, George Benson, Gary Bettenhausen, Tony Bettenhausen, Billy Betteridge, Gordon Betz, Tom Bigelow, George Bignotti, George Binnie, Billy Boat, Tony Bonadies, Al Bonnell, Dan Boorse, Johnny Boyd, Don Branson, Ken Brenn Sr, Ken Brenneman, Jimmy Bryan, Frank Burany, Marvin Burke, Hank Butcher, Vito Calia, Don Cameron, Foster Campbell, Billy Cantrell, Duane Carter Sr., Duane Carter Jr., Neal Carter, Mike Caruso, Danny Caruthers, Doug Caruthers, Jimmy Caruthers, Ernie Casale, Gordon Cleveland, Johnny Coy, Art Cross, Charlie Curryer, Jimmy Davies, Dominic Distarce, Pee Wee Distarce, Kevin Doty, Floyd "Pop" Dreyer, Len Duncan, Teddy Duncan, Leigh Earnshaw, Rex Easton, Chris Economaki, Vic Edelbrock, Don Edmunds, Lanny Edwards, Edgar Elder, Ray Elliott, Bill Engelhart, Walt Faulkner, Myron Fohr, Carl Forberg, Nick Fornoro Sr., Jack Fox, Stan Fox, AJ Foyt Jr., Joe Garson, Fred Gerhardt, Ernie Gesell, Joe Giba, Earl Gilmore, Norm Girtz, Jeff Gordon, Andy Granatelli, Cecil Green, Bob Gregg, Mike Gregg, Perry Grimm, Eddie Haddad, Emmett Hahn, Ted Halibrand, Sam Hanks, Mel Hansen, Gene Hartley, Ted Hartley, Allen Heath, Mack Hellings, Ken Hickey, Bob Higman, Bill Hill, Ron Hoettels, Bill Holmes, Pappy Hough, Ron Householder, Dave Humphrey, Eddie Jackson, Page Jones, Parnelli Jones, Dick Jordan, Don Kenyon, Mel Kenyon, Les Kimbrell, Danny Kladis, Ray Knepper, Steve Knepper, Paul Krueger, Frank Kurtis, Jud Larson, Jason Leffler, Roy Leslie, Steve Lewis, Gib Lilly, Swede Lindskog, Howard Linne, Jack London, Steve Lotshaw, Carl Marchese, Chuck Marshall, Johnny McDowell, Mike McGreevy, Harry McQuinn, Don Meacham, Fred Meeker, Eddie

## Later Years

Meyer, Curley Mills, Johnny Moorhouse, Earl Motter, Duke Nalon, Mike Nazaruk, Ray Nichels, Ed Normi, Bob Nowicke, Danny Oakes, Fred Offenhauser, Mike O'Halloran, Kevin Olson, Cowboy O'Rourke, Alex Pabst, Bob Pankratz, Johnnie Parsons, Johnny Parsons, Johnny Pawl, Jerry Piper, Ralph Pratt, Dave Randolph, Norm Rapp, Larry Rice, Georgie Rice, Ray Richards, Dick Ritchie, Johnny Ritter, Chuck Rodee, Lloyd Ruby, Roy Russing, Paul Russo, Troy Ruttman, Dutch Schafer, Bill Schindler, Gordon Schroeder, Joe Shaheen, Bob Shannon, Gene Shannon, Roy Sherman, Ron Shuman, Jigger Sirois, Bob Slater, Jimmy Snyder, Joe Sostilio, Tony Stewart, Dave Strickland Sr, Bob Stroud, Len Sutton, Bob Swanson, Paul Swedburg, Ted Tappett, Bob Tattersall, Shorty Templeman, Johnny Thomson, Johnnie Tolan, Sleepy Tripp, Harry Turner, Jack Turner, Bill Vandewater, Rich Vogler, Bill Vukovich, Bill Vukovich Jr, Rodger Ward, Leroy Warriner, Ed Watson, Bob Wente, Chuck Weyant, Jim Whitman, Bob Wilke, Tony Willman, Billy Wood, Ashley Wright, Crocky Wright, Karl Young, Gordy Youngstrom, Wally Zale, and Bill Zaring.

# ZACHARY TINKLE'S MINICUP DECISION

**#1 HOT NEW SELLER**

A story of making tough decisions and the courage to passionately pursue your dreams!

A book on the uphill battle of competition when you're the underdog that inspires kids of all ages to never give up!

**NEW RELEASE #1**

# ZACHARY TINKLE'S MINICUP DREAM
ROOKIE OF THE YEAR

TAMBIÉN EN ESPAÑOL

**LEFT PAW Press**

www.LeftPawPress.co

# EPILOGUE

## by
## Richard Thomas McQuinn
## (grandson of Harry Thomas McQuinn)

I really began getting to know my grandfather, Harry McQuinn, when I was 10 years of age. He and Grandma Nita (Juanita) invited me to spend the summer of 1954 with them at their home in Indianapolis. I knew Grandpa Harry sold Chrysler automobiles for K. W. Carr and was very successful. I knew that he was the manager of Sky Harbor Airport just south of his home. I knew he was very active man in the church that his dad, Everett, had begun and preached at every Sunday. I knew him as a gentle, loving man who was giving and disciplined.

What I did not know until I spent that summer with him was his racing background. At home, he was 5'11" tall, but when he stepped foot on the Indianapolis 500 grounds, he was known then as "Mr. McQuinn" and seemed to have grown to 25 feet tall.

My grandfather loved midget racing since he first started racing at the age of 17. He won 3 national championships in a row, winning over 60 races in one season, and is listed in the National Midget Racing Hall of Fame.

After his last 500 race, where he finished dead last, Tony Hulman, the owner of the track, came to him and said, "Since you know how to break all the rules, Harry, I want you to be a Steward of the Indianapolis 500." He took on this endeavor with all of the wisdom and fortitude that he had matured with.

Later, as Chief Steward, he was the law giver of the track! He was the last court of appeals to whom decisions would be decided. It takes someone special to stand in the shoes of the Chief Steward; not everyone can handle the pressure and responsibility. Not a single one of Harry's decisions were ever reversed.

The son of a preacher, he walked tall but gentle. He had love in his heart and wisdom in his brain. He blazed through life like he lived- racing. All in all, Harry Thomas McQuinn, Sr. was a man everyone enjoyed getting to know and call a friend.

I was honored when my nephew, Brad Tinkle, asked me to read and provide the Epilogue for this collection of the wonderful life of racing that my grandfather lived. I know you too will enjoy the history that is on these pages and shown in these pictures.

# ACKNOWLEDGMENTS

Thank you to Richard McQuinn for providing
all of the family's scrapbooks, items, and stories.

A special thanks to Donald Davidson for his time, insights and
historical information for, Harry McQuinn, and most of all,
his ever-lasting friendship and devotion to Harry and his family.

We are also grateful to Stan Kalwasinski for providing many details and
photographs of Harry McQuinn's racing history in the Chicagoland area.

Thank you to Mark Wilke for his sharing of the Wilke Family scrapbooks and
stories regarding Harry McQuinn.

A debt of gratitude is owed to Glen Myers and
the Mazon Speed Bowl & Grundy County Speedway Hall of Fame for their interests
in the history of racing and the encouragement they have given us.

# RELIEVE STRESS BY COLORING

PugDala Coloring Book
CatDala Coloring Book
DogDala Coloring Book
ChickenDala Coloring Book
OwlDala Coloring Book
FarmDala Coloring Book
HorseDala Coloring Book
FishDala Coloring Book
HamsterDala Coloring Book
UnicornDala Coloring Book
FerretDala Coloring Book
MonkeyDala Coloring Book

Keep checking LeftPawPress.com for even more pet-related mandala coloring books.

# APPENDIX A
# MCQUINN CAREER HIGHLIGHTS

- First auto (dirt) race, 1924
- First competition win, 1926
- Walnut Grove Track Champion, 1932
- Thirty-three feature wins, 1933
- Second place, Indiana Dirt Track Championship, 1933
- Tri-State Dirt Track Champion, 1933
- First Indianapolis 500, 1934
- Track Champion, Indiana State Fairgrounds Coliseum (Indianapolis), 1936-1937 season
- Western Indoor Midget Auto Racing Champion, 1937
- National Indoor Champion, 1937
- Track Champion, Walsh Memorial Stadium (St. Louis), 1937
- Track Champion, Riverview Speedway (Chicago), 1937
- Walsh Stadium (St. Louis) Track Champion, 1937
- National Indoor Champion, 1937-38 season
- Track Champion, 124th Field Artillery Armory, 1938
- Walsh Stadium (St. Louis) track champion, 1938
- Southwestern Champion, 1938
- Mid-West Auto Racing Circuit Champion, 1938
- Finished 7th at the Indianapolis 500, 1938

- In 1938, despite a late start to the midget season, McQuinn is credited with a total of 61 feature wins, which ranks him second only to Wally Zale

- Riverview (Chicago) Track Champion in 1938

- Milwaukee State Fair Park Track Champion in 1938

- Outdoor Champion, 1938

- National Indoor Champion of the 124th Field Artillery Armory in Chicago for the 1938-1939 indoor season.

- National Indoor Champion of the 124th Field Artillery Armory in Chicago for the 1939-1940 indoor season.

- Finished 7th at the Indianapolis 500, 1941

- First to land airplane on the Brickyard, 1946

- Second airplane landing on the Brickyard, 1948

- AAA "Midget Steward" 1949

- Assistant race steward, Indianapolis Motor Speedway, 1950

- Chief Steward for the Darlington 200-mile race under the AAA, 1950

- AAA race steward at the Indy 500, 1951

- Chief Steward of Cincinnati Race Bowl (midget), 1951

- Track Steward for the West 16th Street Midget Speedway, 1952

- AAA Official (Indiana Zone), 1952

- Race Referee at Indy 500, 1952

- Chief Steward at the Indianapolis 500 under the AAA, 1953

- Chief Steward at the "Hoosier Hundred" held at the Indiana State Fair Grounds, 1953

- Voted the press award as the outstanding automobile race official, 1953

## McQuinn Career Highlights

- Chief Steward at the Indianapolis 500 under the AAA, 1954
- Chief Steward for the Darlington 200-mile race under the AAA, 1954
- Chief Steward at the Indianapolis 500 under the AAA, 1955
- Chief Steward of the Hoosier 100 under the AAA, 1955
- Chief Steward at the Indianapolis 500 under the USAC, 1956
- Vice-president and general manager of Sky Harbor Airport, 1956
- Chief Steward at the Indianapolis 500 under the USAC, 1957
- Chief Steward, Hoosier Hundred, 1957
- Resigns as Chief Steward of the Indianapolis 500, 1958
- Chairman of the Board of Judges at the Indianapolis Motor Speedway, 1958
- USAC National Championship Division Supervisor, 1962-1968
- Chief Steward, Hoosier Hundred, 1964
- Chief Steward Milwaukee 200-mile race, 1964
- Chief Steward, Atlanta 300, 1966
- Elected to National Midget Hall of Fame, 1986
- Elected to the Grundy County Hall of Fame, 2017

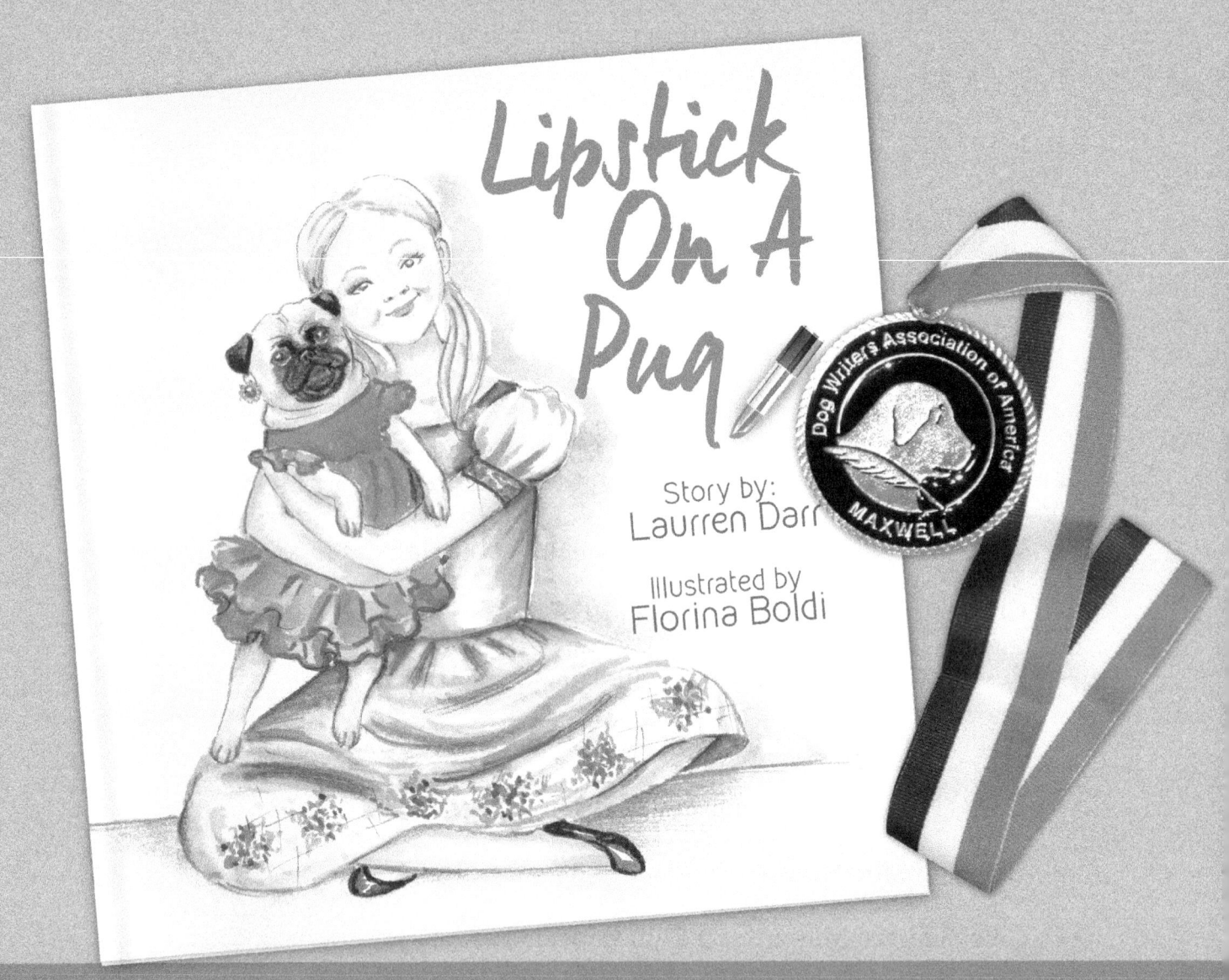

Learn about the roots of Laurren's plumb pug craziness and obsession with pet fashion in this children's book that will teach about the love of dog, pet rescue, and the unbreakable bonds between humans and their pets.

Lipstick On A Pug won the 2015 Children's Book of the Year Maxwell Medallion from the Dog Writers Association of America.

## Also available in coloring book format

### TAMBIÉN EN ESPAÑOL

# APPENDIX B
# PERSONA OF THE ERA

**Andres, Emil**- Racer of the 1930's and 1940's from Chicago running "big cars" in 1932 and midgets in 1933. He was part of the midget car "Chicago Gang" which included Tony Bettenhausen, Cowboy O'Rourke, Paul Russo, Jimmy Snyder, and Wally Zale. He won the American Automobile Association Midwest sprint car title in 1940 and finished 12th at the Indianapolis 500. He became an AAA and United States Auto Club (USAC) official after retiring in 1950. He was inducted in the National Sprint Car Hall of Fame in 1996 and the National Midget Auto Racing Hall of Fame in 2013.

**Bergere, Cliff**- Former stuntman, raced midget cars and at the Indianapolis 500 (16 races) having been the pole-starter in 1946 and several top ten finishes. Inducted into the Indianapolis Motor Speedway Hall of Fame in 1976.

**Bettenhausen, Melvin Eugene "Tony"**- Occasionally known as "Tinley Park Express," he was part of the famous midget racing "Chicago Gang". He was the Riverview midget-car track champion in 1941, 1942, and 1947. He won the track championship at the Milwaukee Mile in 1942, 1946, and 1947. He was the National Champion in 1951 and 1958. Bettenhausen was fatally injured at the Indianapolis Motor Speedway in 1961. He was later inducted into the Indianapolis Motor Speedway Hall of Fame in 1968.

**Brisko, Frank**- Originally a motorcycle racer but he started midget race car driving in the 1930s. Brisko also ran the Indianapolis 500 12 times. He was also a noted engine designer.

**Chitwood, "Joie"**- Occasionally raced under the name "Chief Wahoo," he started racing in Topeka, Kansas in 1934. He drove his own car until Red Campbell got killed at Winchester in 1937 ["Hard Times, Hard Driving", by Richard Sharpless and John Way]. He drove the AAA Championship cars winning the 1939 and 1940 AAA East Coast Sprint car title. He switched to the Central States Racing Association winning its championship in 1942. He competed in the Indianapolis 500 seven different times. Joie operated the "Joie Chitwood Thrill Show", an exhibition of auto stunt driving that became so successful he eventually gave up racing.

**Cummins, Bill**- Nicknamed "Wild Bill". He won the 1934 Indy 500. He was unfortunately killed in his own passenger car after hitting a guardrail and tumbling into the water below in 1939. Inducted into the Indianapolis Motor Speedway Hall of Fame in 1970.

**Duncan, Ted(dy)**- "The Flying Rail" was a midget racing start of the 1930's and 40's. Born of New York, he moved to Chicago when he was young. He was considered one of the "Chicago Gang." Duncan won the Central State Midget championship honors in 1937. He captured track titles in Raceway Park, near Blue Island IL in 1939 and St. Louis (Walsh Stadium) in 1939, 1940, and 1947. He was the track champion at Soldier Field in Chicago in 1946 and 1947.

**Fohr, Myron**- Also known as "The Milwaukee Blitzkrieg". He won the 1946-1947 indoor championship at the Chicago Amphitheater.

**Hanks, Sam**- "Alhambra Assassin" and the "Thin Man". He was the 1949 and 1953 AAA National Midget Champion. He won the Indianapolis 500 in 1957. He was inducted into the Indianapolis Motor Speedway Hall of Fame in 1981.

**Hartsfeld, Art**- Former motorcycle champion who was an early midget driver mostly in the Midwest.

**Hinnershitz, Tommy**- Also known as the "the Flying Dutchman" and the "Flying Farmer". Seven time Eastern AAA sprint car champion. He was inducted in the Pennsylvania Sports Hall of Fame in 1975 and the National Sprint Car Hall of Fame in 1990.

**Householder, Ronney**- Midget car driver of the 1930's, 1940's and 1950's. He won the 1935 Detroit Coliseum championship. He won the 1936 and 1937 Turkey Night Grand Prix at Gilmore Stadium. He also won the 1939 track championship at Soldier Field in Chicago. He was inducted into the National Midget Auto Racing Hall of Fame in 1984.

http://www.autoracinganalysis.com/2010/02/13/midget-racing-legends-ronney-householder/

**Marchese, Carl**- Race car driver of the 1920's and 1930's. He was the rookie of the year for the 1929 Indy 500. Carl was better known as a race car builder and promoter. Carl and his brother Tudy operated an auto repair shop after World War I, by the 1930's, they had become a racing dynasty in the Milwaukee era. In 1938, the brothers built their first "Big Car" as an entrant to the Indianapolis 500. The car was unique housing a Miller engine being cooled by two radiators in side ports in a chassis made of round tubing. It was hoped that positioning the radiators on the sides that the nose could be more narrow giving an aerodynamic advantage. The car was driven by Harry McQuinn who qualified the car in 25th position but having finished in 7th place.

http://www.conceptcarz.com/events/eventVehicle.aspx?carID=14675&eventID=190&catID=1467

**Mays, Rex**- AAA Championship Car driver. He started racing in the Indianapolis 500 in 1934 and won the pole in 1935, 1936, 1940, and 1948. He on the AAA National Championship in 1940 and 1941. He was killed in at the age of 36 in a crash in Del Mar California in November 1949. The race at the Milwaukee Mile was renamed the Rex Mays Classic from 1950 to 1987. He was inducted in the Indianapolis Motor

Speedway Hall of Fame in 1963, the Motorsports Hall of Fame of America in 1995, and the National Sprint Car Hall of Fame in 1990.

**Miller, Henry**- Henry Miller was well known for the master carburetor he invited. From 1924 to 1928, Miller engines won forty-two major races against major competitors such as Duesenberg and Fiat, winning the AAA championship in 1923 and 1929. The Miller company went bankrupt in 1932; however, Offenhauser, Miller's chief engineer, bought most of the equipment and went on to create his own legacy.

**Muhlke, Bob**- Sometimes referred to as "Bombshell", he was a midget race car driver. Owned the Clover Club in Chicago, a hotspot for the racing crowd.

**Nalon, Dennis "Duke"**- Nicknames included the "Iron Duke", "Flying Steel Worker" and the "Chicago Ironman" and one of the "Lakeside twins", he was a midget, sprint, and Indy 500 car driver from Chicago IL being dubbed as part of the "Chicago Gang". He began as a pit crew for Wally Zale. He won midget races on the East Coast in the 1930s. He won the 1938 East Coast AAA Sprint car championship. He started in 10 Indianapolis 500 races having won two poles. He was inducted in the National Midget Auto Racing Hall of Fame in 1987 and the National Sprint Car Hall of Fame in 1991. Inducted into the Indianapolis Motor Speedway Hall of Fame in 1983.

http://alblixtracinghistory.typepad.com/al_blixt_auto_racing_hist/2007/08/duke-nalon---on.html

*For more on Duke Nalon, read "The Iron Duke" by George Peters.*

**Neilson, Pete**- Midget race car driver and master race car builder. He was a Milwaukee native who was fatally injured at Crown Point IN in 1946.

**Offenhauser, Fred**- Chief engineer at Miller who bought most of the equipment from Miller after the business went bankrupt. He developed the famous Offenhauser engine, a longtime favorite amongst racers. Inducted into the Indianapolis Motor Speedway Hall of Fame in 1982.

**O'Rourke, Cletus**- More commonly known as "Cowboy" O'Rourke racing in the 1930's through 1950's. He was part of the famed "Chicago Gang." O'Rourke had the distinction of perhaps being the first driver to win a race upside down when he bested Duke Nalon by about a half of a car length in a match race at the Armory in 1937. "Cowboy" was crowned the indoor midget racing champion at Chicago's International Amphitheatre in 1951. After his racing days, O'Rourke operated a number of gathering places in the Chicago region, each becoming popular stops for the area racing fraternity.

**Richards, Ray**- Known as the "Highland Park Flyer" who started racing in Milwaukee in 1934. IN 1941, he won the national outdoor racing title.

**Romcevich, Pete**- A Serbian-American midget race car driver known as the "Flying Serb". He was killed in a midget race at the Michigan State Fairgrounds in Detroit in 1952.

**Russo, Paul**- Started racing in midgets in 1934. He won the 1938 AAA Eastern Championship. He was known as part of the "Chicago Gang" with the likes of Emil Andres, Tony Bettenhausen, Duke Nalon, Cowboy O'Rourke, Jimmy Snyder, and Wally Zale. He started in 85 races for the AAA and USAC Championship Car series and the Indianapolis 500.

**Shaw, Wilbur**- Race car driver in the pre-World War II era. He won the Indianapolis 500 in 1937, 1939, and 1940 becoming the second three-time winner. Wilbur Shaw saw the deteriorating condition of the brickyard during the war and solicited companies and persons alike to restore the speedway. In 1945, he became president and general manager of the Indianapolis Motor Speedway until 1954 when he died tragically in an airplane crash. He was later inducted into the Indianapolis Motor Speed Hall of Fame in 1963.

**Snyder, Jimmy**- The "South Side Speed King" (also "The Flying Milkman") was a 1930's race car driver. He started racing "big cars" in 1932 and midgets a year later. Part of the "Chicago Gang" which included Emil Andres, Tony Bettenhausen, Cowboy O'Rourke, Paul Russo, and Wally Zale. He won the 1937 track championship at the Chicago Armory and at Riverview. He competed in five Indianapolis 500 races, winning the pole in 1939 and finishing second that year. He was killed later that same year in a midget car race in Cahokia IL. Subsequently, he was inducted into the Indianapolis Motor Speedway Hall of Fame in 1981.

http://www.kalracing.com/autoracing/jimmy_snyder_biography.htm

**Sorenson, Bob**- More often referred to as "Shorty," he drove midget cars in the 1930's and 40's. Bob was a teammate to Harry in the Marchese stable. Their "team driving" and aggressive skills got them barred from a number of tracks in the East and the West.

**Stapp, Elbert "Babe"**- Active racecar driver in the 1920's and 1930's. He competed in 12 Indianapolis 500 races. He was inducted in the Sprint Car Hall of Fame in 1994.

**Swanson, Bob**- Winner of the 1934 Turkey Night Grand Prix midget car race and the Pacific Coast Midget Championship. He was also known as the "West Coast Comet" and the "Blond Bullet". He won 53 features at Gilmore Stadium. He was involved in the 1939 Indy 500 accident that killed the defending champion Floyd Roberts. He was thrown from the car when Roberts had hit him. He died in 1940 while attempting to qualify in a midget car. He was later inducted in the National Midget Auto Racing Hall of Fame.

**Wilke, Robert "Bob"**- At one time owner and president of Leader Cards, Inc., he built many midget cars, including those for drivers Harry McQuinn and Shorty Sorenson who together won over 300 races in the 1940's and 1950's.

http://news.google.com/newspapers?nid=1499&dat=19790812&id=72UaAAAAIBAJ&sjid=6ioEAAAAIBAJ&pg=5268,1622295


**Wiggins, Charlie**- Charlie was a "black" Indianapolis mechanic who owned his own Southside auto shop. He developed a strong interest in open-wheel auto racing and built himself a car from spare parts. Although his connections to white racers enabled him to test his car on local dirt tracks, the American Automobile Association—the chief sanctioning body of the day—used an unwritten whites-only policy to keep Wiggins out of racing. In 1924, the Colored Speedway Association was formed and Wiggins quickly became the series' chief attraction, winning the series championship four times, its premier event—the Gold and Glory Sweepstakes held at the Indianapolis Fairgrounds— three times, and gaining the undisputed title of "Negro Speed King."

"In addition to his prodigious skills as a driver, Wiggins was equally adept at preparing a racecar. His garage became a center for local racers, both black and white, who called themselves "Charlie's Gang." Indeed, Wiggins helped prepare cars for two white members of his "Gang," (American Automobile Association) AAA stars Harry McQuinn and "Wild Bill" Cummings. In 1934 Cummings invited Wiggins to be a part of his pit crew for the Indianapolis 500, but AAA officials would not allow it. In order to circumvent the rules, Wiggins was hired as a janitor, sweeping up when AAA officials were around and working on the car at night when they had gone home. With Wiggins' help, Cummings won the race that year, although he never publicly acknowledged Wiggins' role in his success.

Gould does an excellent job of placing the Wiggins story amidst the racial turmoil of Indianapolis in the 1920's and 1930's. Indeed, Wiggins lived in the very center of Ku Klux Klan activity during the era, in a city that produced perhaps the most powerful Klan leader in the nation—D.C. Stephenson—and in a state where one-third of white Protestant men were members of the Klan. Wiggins once sparked a riot at a Louisville,

Kentucky, speedway and was placed in protective custody when he tried to qualify his "Wiggins Special" for Harry McQuinn. He also became a frequent target for the local White Supremacy League, which was enraged by his dogged determination to enter the Indianapolis 500 and whose members vandalized his shop and even attacked him in his yard. Yet the Wiggins story also highlights the determination of African Americans to demonstrate to the world that they could overcome racism and excel at anything a white person could do.

The Wiggins story ends, as auto racing stories often do, on a sad note. At the 1936 running of the Gold and Glory Sweepstakes, Wiggins became involved in a thirteen-car pileup. As a result of the accident, his badly crushed right leg was amputated, thus ending his racing career. With the loss of its marquee performer and dwindling gate receipts, the Colored Speedway Association folded at the end of the season. In the aftermath of his accident, Wiggins made a wooden leg for himself on a lathe in his shop and continued running his auto shop for forty more years. Unfortunately, poverty because of the medical costs he increasingly incurred and fading memories of the golden age of African-American auto racing led to an old age lived in relative obscurity, death in 1979, and burial in an unmarked grave.

From *"For Gold and Glory"* (2003). Produced and written by Todd Gould.
WFYI, Metropolitan Indianapolis Public Broadcasting, Inc. 60 mins.
http://library.la84.org/SportsLibrary/JSH/JSH2004/JSH3101/jsh3101z.pdf

**Willman, Tony**- Also known as the "Milwaukee Dutchman", he was a native of Milwaukee who raced from 1926 to 1941. Willman won 44 sprint car main events and 85 midget features. He won the 1934-35 indoor midget circuit championship. During the 1935 outdoor season, he was credited with 145 race wins across the Midwest. He also won nearly a dozen season championships. In 1941, he won 33 midget features and was the AAA short track champion. However, his arguably greatest season ended when he died during a midget race on October 12, 1941 when his car flipped ejecting him onto the track where he was ran over by another driver. He was inducted into the National Sprint Car Hall of Fame in 1992.

## Persona of the Era

http://news.google.com/newspapers?nid=1499&dat=19411013&id=FKZQAAAAIBAJ&sjid=zilEAAAAIBAJ&pg=3255,5827696

**Zale, Wally**- Also known as "The Human Cyclone" and part of the "Chicago Gang." He won 238 feature victories in 4 seasons recording two single season records for the most feature wins. Tragically, Zale and fellow racer, Frank Perrone, were killed in a devastating two train, single car wreck in April of 1942.

### MIDGET FEATURE VICTORIES IN A SINGLE SEASON

67 wins Wally Zale .................................................................1940
65 wins Wally Zale .................................................................1936
61 wins Harry McQuinn .........................................................1938
59 wins Wally Zale .................................................................1941
53 wins Mel Hansen ...............................................................1940
53 wins Bill Schindler ............................................................1947
53 wins Bill Schindler ............................................................1948
48 wins Joe Sostillo ................................................................1947
47 wins Wally Zale .................................................................1939
47 wins Johnnie Tolan............................................................1947

http://www.nmdoty.com/lucas.htm

# Pet Fashion Industry Patterns

by Laurren Darr

Written based on many years of observations of the pet fashion industry, is this uniquely stylish business trend book from International Association of Pet Fashion Professionals founder, Laurren Darr. It's broken into four enlightening sections that provide valuable insights to those seeking an understanding of pet fashion industry developments. These sections include Pet Trends, Lifestyle Trends, Market Trends, and Micro Trends.

Readers will find that this book is a lot of information in a concise, informative, and creative package. Each chapter is artfully named to be remarkable. Titles include *Purr-fect Fashion, Chicks Dig It, Furbulous Fashion Meets Function, Tail Wagging Markets, Eco-Fido, Paw-er Shopping,* and *Cosmopawlitan Pets.*

Some of the features that you'll find are:

- ✓ Black and white photos of some of the most fashionable cities in the world with interesting factoids about each
- ✓ Fabulous fashion illustrations demonstrating the topic that is discussed in each chapter.
- ✓ Statistics and facts on pets, business, and the pet industry highlighted throughou

www.PetFashionProfessionals.com

# RESOURCES

Photographs and newspaper articles are from the McQuinn Family's scrapbooks where noted. Citations are made where known. Many of the IMS photos are available through the IMS Museum. Newspaper accounts were found in many places from scrapbooks, local libraries including The History, Philosophy and Newspaper Library at the University of Illinois Urbana-Champaign for their collection of *National Auto Racing News*, historical collections and online resources such as the Chicago Tribune and a paid subscription to Newspapers.com.

"Autocourse Official History of the Indianapolis 500", 2nd ed. by Donald Davidson and Rick Shaffer; Icon Publishing Limited; 2013.

"Dirt Track Auto Racing, 1919-1941. A Pictorial History", by Don Radbruch; McFarland & Company, Ltd.; 2004.

"The Ghosts of Jungle Park. History, Myth, and Legend: The Story of a Place Like No Other", 2nd edition, by Tom W Williams, Woodangett Press, 2008.

"Hard Times, Hard Driving. Dirt Track Racing in the 1930s", by Richard Sharpless and John Way; Xlibris Corporation; 2009.

"The History of America's Speedways. Past & Present", 3rd ed. By Allan E. Brown; 2003.

"Images of America: Blue Island's Raceway Park" by Stan Kalwasinski and Samuel Beck, Arcadia Publishing, 2009.

"The Indianapolis 500 Chronicle" by Rick Popely; Publications International, Ltd.; 1998.

"The Iron Duke: The Illustrious Racing Career of Duke Nalon, 1934-1954" by George Peters; Bar Jean Enterprises; 2005.

"Ludvigsen Library Series: INDY Cars of the 1940s" by Karl Ludvigsen; Iconografix; 2004.

"Ludvigsen Library Series: INDY Cars 1911-1939" by Karl Ludvigsen; Iconografix; 2005.

"The Mighty Midgets" by Jack C. Fox; by Carl Hungness Publishing; 1985.

"Speedway Photos: Early Auto racing in Chicago and the Mid-West" by Bob Sheldon; Witness Publications; 2000.

"United States Auto Racing Biography Introduction" by townsend Bell, Richie Hern, Memo Gidley, Jimmy Kite, Mark Dismore, Alex Barron, Charlie Merz, Jon Herb, Alex Gurney, Fred Agabashian, Buzz Calkins, Swede Savage, H. A. Wheeler, J. R. Hildebrand, Jeret Schroeder, Ronnie Bucknum, Daniel Herrington; Books LLC; 2010.

# About The Author

For his 'day' job, Brad T. Tinkle, M.D., Ph.D., is the Division Head of Advocate Children's Hospital in the Chicago, Illinois area. Dr. Brad, as he's called by many of his patients, specializes in caring for individuals with heritable connective tissue disorders such as Ehlers-Danlos syndromes, Marfan syndrome, osteogenesis imperfecta, and achondroplasia among the many. Dr. Tinkle has authored medical articles, book chapters, and two books on EDS: "Issues and Management of Joint Hypermobility." (2008) and "The Joint Hypermobility Handbook" (2010) and is internationally recognized as an expert in the care and management of those with EDS.

He earned a Bachelor's in Science for Engineering (BSE) in genetic engineering from Purdue University in 1989 and received his Ph.D. in Human Genetics from the George Washington University in the District of Columbia in 1995. Dr. Brad then attended medical school at Indiana University and completed a pediatric/ clinical genetics residency at Cincinnati Children's. He also finished a fellowship in clinical molecular genetics at Cincinnati following residency.

In 2012, Dr. Tinkle left his position at Cincinnati Children's to start his position with Advocate. While living in Indiana and working in Cincinnati, his son, Zachary Tinkle, was always interested in racing, but there weren't cost-effective options to test his drive for sport. Shortly after moving to the Chicagoland area, the family discovered Chicago Indoor Go-Karting where karts could be rented for racing. Zachary proved himself committed and talented by winning his first championship right away. When the facility was sold to K1 Speed, he went on to win three junior championships.

The last karting championship(s) overlapped the family discovering minicup (super cup) cars, which are half scale NASCAR® cars. Even though Zachary was training in an outdoor kart, the switch was made to race stock cars since that was more in alignment with Zachary's dream of racing in NASCAR®. This was the start of Dr. Brad's role (moonlighting job) as crew chief, mechanic, and spotter on the #53 car. While traveling to the different tracks like Grundy County Speedway, he saw photos of his great-grandfather, Harry McQuinn, and started compiling historical information, newspaper clippings, and photos. He interviewed multiple people including track historians at places like Indianapolis Motor Speedway. This process took several years through ups, downs, wins, and championships at various tracks. He is now a racing history buff with archives of information on racing in the Midwest — especially as it pertains to "King of the Midgets," Harry McQuinn.